C0-AOC-478

TALKING IT THROUGH

TALKING IT THROUGH

Puzzles of American Democracy

ROBERT W. BENNETT

CORNELL UNIVERSITY PRESS
ITHACA & LONDON

Copyright © 2003 by Cornell University

All rights reserved. Except for brief quotations in a review, this book, or parts thereof, must not be reproduced in any form without permission in writing from the publisher. For information, address Cornell University Press, Sage House, 512 East State Street, Ithaca, New York 14850.

First published 2003 by Cornell University Press

Printed in the United States of America

Library of Congress Cataloging-in-Publication Data

Bennett, Robert W. (Robert William), 1941–
    Talking it through : puzzles of American democracy / Robert W. Bennett.
        p. cm.
Includes bibliographical references and index.
    ISBN 0-8014-4040-8 (cloth : alk. paper)
    1. Democracy—United States.   I. Title.
JK1726 .B46 2003
320.973—dc21
                                                          2002007266

Cornell University Press strives to use environmentally responsible suppliers and materials to the fullest extent possible in the publishing of its books. Such materials include vegetable-based, low-VOC inks and acid-free papers that are recycled, totally chlorine-free, or partly composed of nonwood fibers.
For further information, visit our website at www.cornellpress.cornell.edu.

Cloth printing   10 9 8 7 6 5 4 3 2 1

For Harriet and Ariana

Contents

Preface   ix
1 The Explanatory Reach of Democratic Conversation   1
2 Majoritarianism and the Vote-Centered Model   9
3 Descriptive Shortcomings of the Vote-Centered Model   18
4 Democracy as Involvement in Conversation   34
5 The United States Senate   49
6 The Electoral Status of Children   66
7 Judicial Review and the Sense of Difficulty   85
8 Rational Choice Theory and the Paradox of Voting   106
9 Evaluating the Power of a Conversational Perspective   116
10 Conversational Explanation and Its Normative Use   139
Appendix   147
Notes   151
Index   215

Preface

I became interested in a conversational account of American democracy in a roundabout way. I have long taught law for a living, and my scholarly efforts have concentrated on constitutional theory. There has been one overarching subject that constitutional scholars like myself have been unable to avoid—the so-called *countermajoritarian difficulty*. Alexander Bickel coined this phrase in his classic 1962 work, *The Least Dangerous Branch*, to capture the problem he perceived with decisions of the U.S. Supreme Court (or of other courts) that legislation or some act of executive officials is forbidden by virtue of judicial policy choices made in the name of the Constitution.[1]

The notion of this difficulty has become the central preoccupation of American constitutional scholars since Bickel first coined the phrase. As I puzzled about that difficulty, I became increasingly convinced that, at a minimum, Bickel had chosen an inapt name, since the rest of the American governmental system is not sensibly described as majoritarian. If the Supreme Court presents a difficulty for American democracy for no reason other than that it is countermajoritarian, then we must wonder why much of the rest of the system is not difficult as well.

After a ten-year stint as dean of Northwestern's law school ended in 1995, I was entitled to a year's leave, which my family and I spent living in the countryside just outside of Florence, Italy. During that year, I set out initially to write about this badly named difficulty. I began with the awkwardness of the majoritarian characterization and found myself thinking increasingly about a conversational alternative that could explain many of the prominent—and some not so prominent—characteristics of the American system. During that delightful year in Italy, this conversational theory of American democracy began to take shape.

At first, I was not sure that there were any lessons about the subject of Bickel's difficulty (that is, judicial review), but I kept bumping up against what seemed to be fresh insights about American democracy more generally. One of those, about which I wrote a separate article, concerns the way children are treated in American politics. Although they are understandably not allowed to vote, usually children are simultaneously included in the population that is used to draw up legislative districts. They are excluded from one important count but included in another that is so closely associated with the first that the dissonance is striking. This seeming anomaly would be resolved, however, if parents were given extra votes in public elections on account of their children. Most people have not even considered this possibility, and it was its very obscurity that I found so intriguing. Whatever one might conclude about the "extra votes possibility," it fits rather nicely into much of the talk of majoritarianism and the accompanying rhetoric that one finds in discussion of American democracy. I came to see the extra votes possibility—or rather the absence of any serious discussion of it—as illuminating simultaneously the impoverishment of the majoritarian frame of reference and the power of a conversational alternative.

I saw still other problems in a fresh light. In many countries, for instance, a good portion of the legislature is elected by a system of proportional representation, in which voters choose among political party lists. The eventual composition of the legislature is made roughly proportional to the total party votes. This approach is in sharp contrast to the American system of geographical districts and votes for individual candidates. Here, too, a conversational perspective seemed better than a majoritarian one in accounting for the actual functioning of the American system. And so it went, as I considered a succession of characteristics of American democracy. Eventually, I returned to the problem of judicial review that had started me on this intellectual journey, and found that the conversational perspective brought new insights for this problem as well.

One problem that the project repeatedly drove home was the difficult relationship between normative and positive accounts of social phenomena such as American democracy. It was often unclear in the work of others whether they considered their work as normative or positive, or perhaps as both at once. I initially conceived of my project as basically positive (and still do), but I came to see that the line between the descriptive and the prescriptive is a difficult one to hold. I also came to appreciate different levels of ambition for positive theories of social phenomena. Theories can describe in relatively flat ways, or conversely provide genuine explanations, drawing connections among aspects of what is studied. My ambitions for the conversational perspective are to provide a rich explanatory framework, rather than mere description on the one hand or a normative approach on the other. In completing this work, however, I came to appreciate the difficulty in respecting the boundaries of these categories.

I have published five pieces that deal with aspects of the problems addressed here; portions of what I say here are taken from those works.[2] I have, however, adjusted a good deal of my terminology and some of my thinking as I have proceeded. I have, for instance, abandoned calling my approach "democracy as meaningful conversation," because I concluded that the word *meaningful* carries stronger normative (and perhaps even descriptive) connotations than seems appropriate. And I no longer refer to the conversational perspective as a "model" or a "theory" because of concern that those words might suggest more encompassing explanatory power than is appropriate.[3] I discuss these issues of terminology and rigor in more detail in chapter nine.

Many colleagues at Northwestern and elsewhere have provided helpful commentary on the work as it has proceeded. I cannot possibly recall and recite all of that help, but I would be remiss if I did not acknowledge special gratitude to Bob Burns, Gary Lawson, Jane

Rutherford, Henry Smith, Mel Durschlag, Daphne Barak-Erez, Barry Friedman, Dan Polsby, Jim Lindgren, David Haddock, Jack Heinz, Paula Wolff, Matt Spitzer, Fred MacChesney, Melissa Williams, Lee Epstein, Al Harris, Beryl Radin, Steve Calabresi, Jack Heinz, Tom Merrill, Marty Redish, Andy Koppelman, Gerry Rosenberg, Susan Herbst, and Ron Allen. I have also benefited along the way from splendid research assistance from a succession of Northwestern law students, most importantly Mark Dowd, Scott England, Maureen Gest, Mary Tait, Ricardo Delfin, Jennifer Carney, Roman Hoyos, Judy Han, Jason Silverman, David Winters, Jeff Glaser, Josh Rittenberg, Simon Banyai, Chris Jones, and Joo Hui Kim. The work on judicial review, in particular, was aided enormously by a research leave during the spring semester of the 1999–2000 school year. And I took pleasure in holding the Stanford and Zylpha Kilbride Clinton Sr. Research Professorship during that year, because of the support it provided, to be sure, but especially because both Stan (now deceased) and Zylpha Clinton have been dear friends since my early days as Northwestern Law School's dean.

TALKING IT THROUGH

The Explanatory Reach
of Democratic Conversation

In 1995, the often playful journal *Constitutional Commentary* asked twenty distinguished constitutional scholars to write short essays explaining their choices for the "stupidest provision of the United States Constitution." The outright choice of two, also receiving (dis)honorable mention from two others, was the assignment of equal voting power in the U.S. Senate to each state regardless of population. According to Bill Eskridge, senatorial apportionment is "antidemocratic," violating the "bedrock constitutional value" of "majority rule." Suzanna Sherry made essentially the same case: senatorial apportionment "is in conflict with the most basic principles of democracy. . . . [allowing] slightly over 17% of the population [to] elect . . . a majority of the members." Dan Farber, in contrast, while mentioning senatorial apportionment as seeming "most vulnerable to criticism," argued that "the imperfections of the original text matter much less than what we have made of the Constitution over two centuries." Of the Senate in particular, Farber noted that he could not "recall any instance of popular outcry against the 'malapportionment' of the Senate."[1]

Senatorial apportionment—or rather the absence noted by Farber of any "popular outcry" about that apportionment—is one of four puzzles of American democracy that I treat at length in this book. My thesis—which serves as the basis for solution of the four puzzles—can be stated simply: American democracy is an extraordinary engine for producing conversation about public affairs. This conversation plays an important role in holding that democracy together and in inducing fidelity on the part of citizens to the decisions taken in its name. The conversation is also an important determinant of the content of public policy decisions, and the pattern of those decisions surely plays a substantial role in citizen contentment with the enterprise as a whole. But there will often be widespread dissent from particular public decisions, and the conversational perspective posits that much private disapproval of public policy outcomes is accepted because of the feeling of involvement generated by the democratic conversation. The democratic conversation, in other words, has a cohesive force that is largely independent of the patterns of popular approval and disapproval of public policy outcomes.

I use the word *conversation* even though there is some danger of being misunderstood. The lion's share of the communication I have in mind flows only one way rather than both to and from conversants, as in most ordinary conversations. It consists mostly of communication *to* varied segments of the citizenry from candidates for public office, government officials, and media of communication. Because of this mostly one-way flow of communication, I considered other terms, but in the end I decided to stick with calling the phenomenon "conversation," for a couple of reasons. First, there is a degree of active participation by the citizenry, often by organized interest groups to be sure, but even on occasion by individual members of the public. Citizens do sometimes write to members of congress and their local newspapers, call legislative staff assistants or bureaucrats, or speak their minds at meetings convened or attended by public officials. Second, and more importantly, even when citizens are cast solely as listeners and readers, what is said is very much crafted in light of what officials and the media can discern about the preexisting and inchoate interests of those citizens. This is a very important difference between "official" communication in nondemocratic settings (which tends to be overwhelmingly didactic) and in democratic ones. Precisely because of the incentive structure set up by democratic elections, the public discourse of politicians is quite attentive to what might be on the public mind. So are the messages of private media of communications, often for reasons that are derivative of the democratic electoral incentives. A word that emphasized the one-sidedness of the communication would fail to capture the important role that citizens play in shaping the public discourse of democracies, even when those citizens are largely passive participants.

Quite apart from its puzzle-solving power, if the democratic conversation is taken to have this cohesive effect, many of the most fundamental elements of American democracy fit together in ways not usually noticed. Near-universal adult suffrage, bicameralism, federalism, a separately elected executive, single-member legislative districts, loose political party discipline, and the central role played by First Amendment protections of speech and press take on meaning as stimulants to and facilitators of wide-ranging conversational involvement.

Over the years, these traditional elements of American democracy have received a variety of explanations, and they may well continue to serve important purposes other than conversational facilitation and enhancement. First Amendment protections are often praised, for instance, as helping to keep governmental officials honest. Bicameralism at the national level has been championed as providing representation for states and the people, and as assuring a degree of deliberation before legislation is adopted. The separately elected executive has been depicted at times as necessary for injecting energy into governmental processes and at times as a check on a powerful legislature, necessary to forestall legislative tyranny. The movement to universal suffrage is often seen as an important indication of our devotion to a normative ideal of political equality. The conversational account does not deny (or, for that matter, affirm) any of these explanations either as reasons inspiring the move or as explaining or justifying its persistence. Conversationalism, rather, reaches out to tell a more comprehensive and unifying story about American democracy. To assess the conversational account of American democracy, we must take up the question of what it means for explanations of complex social phenomena—such as American democracy—to be better and worse. An important part of my case for a conversational approach is that it draws together in a spare and coherent way a variety of the most visible and fundamental features of the system.

If conversationalism simply accounted for fundamental elements of the system in a simple and spare framework, that would make a good case for its inclusion in successful positive theories of American democracy. But there is an important additional feature of conversationalism that demonstrates its power: it helps us "see" things about American democracy that have to date been blurry, if visible at all. It is this power of the conversational approach that I hope to demonstrate with my discussion and solution of four puzzles in the body of this book. The puzzles are interesting in their own right, and I hope that my solutions of them are instructive. But my discussion of the puzzles is presented also to fortify the conversational perspective that I advance more generally for American democracy. If conversationalism can repeatedly bring blurry features of American democracy into focus, that will very substantially bolster the case for it.

Only one of the puzzles I treat has clearly been identified as a puzzle in earlier writing of others. Much of what is puzzling about the two others is that they have been the subject of very little commentary. I have already mentioned the absence of controversy about apportionment of the Senate. Even more puzzling in a way is the dearth of attention to the political role of children. Are children part of the population base, a majority of which is supposed to decide things in a democracy characterized by political equality? Presumably not, but if not, are children nonetheless part of the constituency that is entitled to equal consideration in the politics of such a well-functioning democracy? If so, then how is the required—equal—consideration to be achieved once children are excluded from the mechanisms of decision? The relative inattention paid to these questions makes our professors who worry about senatorial apportionment seem like a crowd. In these two cases, it is the majoritarian perspective from which Eskridge and Sherry seem to operate that makes the scarcity of commentary so strange.

After discussing these two puzzles, I turn my discussion to attention that is lavished rather than withheld. As mentioned in the preface, the central preoccupation of constitutional scholarship in the latter half of the twentieth century has been similarly grounded in a majoritarian perspective. The great legal scholar Alexander Bickel coined the phrase *countermajoritarian difficulty* to capture the concern that courts' interpretations of the Constitution are undemocratic. The puzzle here is that there is so much attention paid to this bit of "countermajoritarianism" while the "countermajoritarian" senatorial apportionment, for instance, receives scant attention.

Finally, I turn to the so-called "paradox of voting": the fact that so many people go to the polls on election day when they have no obvious reason in their self-interest to do so. In contrast to the other three puzzles, large-scale voter turnout has been discussed widely as puzzling or "paradoxical," but not from a majoritarian perspective. The majoritarian perspective is more likely to identify abstention from voting as puzzling than it is voting participation. One of my reasons for including the paradox of voting as a democratic puzzle is that it allows me to introduce the different theoretical literature from the perspective of which voting turnout has been seen as paradoxical. This is so-called rational choice theory, probably the ascendant way of thinking about American democracy today among political science scholars. Discussion of the paradox of voting allows me to show why conversationalism is a useful way of thinking about American democracy, even in the face of competition that might be thought more worthy as a positive account than majoritarianism. With that discussion under our belts, we can proceed to a three-way comparison among conversationalism, rational choice, and majoritarianism.

There are many more than four puzzling phenomena in American democracy that might be made less puzzling under examination with a conversational lens. I treat some of these in more summary fashion, but the four I have chosen for extensive treatment help expose the power of the conversational perspective in many ways. I have already mentioned the differences in the extent to which the four puzzles have previously been identified as puzzling, indeed even the extent to which they have been noticed at all. I have also adverted to the different baseline assumptions that seem to make the phenomena puzzling. In addition, two of the puzzles—those dealing with the Senate and with judicial review—concern the formal decisionmaking structure of American government once public officials have been chosen, while the other two deal with the electoral system. Although the puz-

zle of the Senate is one of popular attitude, the one that concerns judicial review by the Supreme Court is of "elite" attitude, mostly of
the law professoriate. Of the two that concern the electoral process,
the paradox of voting is about behavioral phenomena, whereas the political status of children is a part of the formalities of popular election. If the conversational approach succeeds along these various and
cross-cutting dimensions, it seems safe to say that it has tapped into
something quite fundamental about the system as a whole.

Both the elaboration and the assessment of the conversational approach require taking account of the notoriously uneasy relationship
between "normative" (prescriptive) and "positive" (descriptive and
explanatory) projects. I offer the conversational perspective not as
prescription for American democracy, but as description and explanation, an account of what is rather than a blueprint—or even a suggestive framework—for how it might be made better. But there is a
danger of seduction of positive accounts by normative visions to
which I remain alert as I elaborate and discuss the conversational perspective. I am, for instance, a decided fan of American democracy, and
it is certainly possible that an approving normative stance has crept
into my positive effort. In truth, the description and explanation of
complex social phenomena such as American democracy probably
cannot be stowed in separate compartments where they will not in-
fect one another. But that fact does not prevent our distinguishing the
positive and the normative. They have different purposes, and the
tendency to mingle the two can be resisted, even if not fully overcome.

In any event, the positive account I offer should not be mistaken for
an encomium to American democracy. There are, in fact, many unattractive aspects in the totality of the American democratic conversation, ranging from the insipid to the irrelevant to the demagogic.
The substantive results that the system produces—about which the
conversational account has little or nothing to say—are most surely
relevant in any evaluation of whether the cohesiveness of the whole
is laudable or lamentable. Any such large-scale evaluation of American democracy is beyond my present ambitions. But I do suggest in
the concluding chapter ways in which the conversational account of
American democracy brings into focus considerations that bear on
the assessment of smaller-scale proposals for reform.

The distinction between positive and normative accounts helps distinguish the conversational perspective from Robert Putnam's effort in his much-heralded book, *Bowling Alone*. Since the 1960s, Putnam recounts, there has been an increasing loss in the United States of what he calls "social capital," consisting of "networks of social interaction." These networks are associated with "norms of reciprocity" that facilitate our dealings with one another across a broad range of activities. The book's arresting title is taken from Putnam's observation that Americans now bowl alone when they used to form bowling leagues. He traces a similar decline in vehicles of connectedness across a broad range of social, civic, religious, and political activities. Americans continue to belong to groups, but he insists that they now do so in more passive ways. They send in money, rather than go to meetings. At first blush, it might then seem that Putnam and I are describing much the same thing—that I see a glass of connectedness partly full, and that he sees the same glass rapidly emptying. If mine is a snapshot and his a motion picture of the same thing, then his time series might seem the more instructive.[2]

I think that the more apt figure of speech for descriptive purposes, however, draws on a forest and its trees. Putnam recounts declines in rates of participation in all manner of organizations, from bowling leagues to PTAs to political parties. Others have raised questions about the nature and extent of decline in organizational activity in the United States,[3] but for present purposes I leave those factual questions to the side. Nowhere does Putnam suggest that there is any flagging in the popular sense of identification with the whole. The reason, I think, is that Putnam's real concern *is* with the trees, and moreover that he knows the kinds of trees that are good ones.

Putnam is often ambiguous about why it is that active participation in organizational effort matters. He says he is concerned with a loss of trust, but it often seems that it is really the loss of the reliable information that trustworthiness helps provide.[4] When we bowled in leagues, we discussed lots of other things with the other bowlers on bowling night, and those discussions paid dividends far beyond bowling prowess. Employment might be arranged, marital problems discussed, recommendations of doctors exchanged.

One problem in valuing organizational activity for such informational purposes is that information can often be obtained quite easily without organizational activity. The age of the Internet puts doubt on that score largely to rest. And the evidence is quite mixed about the expected consequences of a decline in trust such as Putnam depicts. Among other indicators, for instance, crime rates are down dramatically in the United States, and at least until recently, the employment market was extremely robust.[5] In the final analysis, Putnam's more important reason for valuing organizational activity is simply that such activity is an end in itself. For Putnam, active social involvement is to be preferred to passive involvement, and greater social connectedness through active engagement is to be preferred to less. This conclusion is most clear when Putnam turns to the political realm. He tells us that it is a "truism" that "democratic self-government requires an actively engaged citizenry," and that "[n]ot to vote is to withdraw from the political community." For Putnam, it matters little that we are "reasonably well-informed spectators of public affairs." What matters is that "fewer of us actually partake in the game."[6]

For this reason, no matter how much sense of involvement the democratic conversation generated, Putnam would lament the passivity that characterizes so much of it. His vision of a publicly engaged life for a worthy democratic citizenry has roots deep in American political thought. Many of our constitutional founders placed great emphasis on an actively engaged citizenry, and there is a lively contemporary literature calling for a "civic republican" revival of such active engagement. Whether the decline that Putnam (and others) depict in active engagement is accurate, the picture he paints of an actively engaged citizenry is an attractive one. But that normative vision does not necessarily tell us anything about whether or why the enterprise as a whole coheres.

Once Putnam's project is seen as basically normative and mine as basically positive, the tension between the two largely dissolves. I am concerned with what makes the forest endure, and he with whether many individual trees in it are worthy ones. Even assuming the decline that Putnam recounts, American democracy is among the most durable forms of government in the world. Quite apart from ways in which the system might be made better, I seek to understand at least some of the forces that so effectively seem to hold it together.

Majoritarianism and the Vote-Centered Model

The association of American democracy with majoritarianism that seems to underlie Eskridge's and Sherry's criticisms of the Senate has become almost routine. In publications by legal scholars, the characterization has become especially prevalent since 1962, when Alexander Bickel published *The Least Dangerous Branch*. That book was devoted to a perceived problem with the democratic *bona fides* of "judicial review," the practice of reviewing legislation or administrative action for its consistency with the United States Constitution. Bickel was by no means the first to perceive a tension between democracy and judicial review, but he used the phrase *countermajoritarian difficulty* to capture the problem, and the terminology has stuck. This ongoing sense of difficulty and its association with an assumed majoritarianism of American democracy poses one of our puzzles, which I return to in chapter seven.[1]

For present purposes, what is of interest to me is the almost routine incantation of the majoritarian nature of American democracy, extending well beyond the world of legal scholars. The shorthand description is made by commentators associated with the political right, left, and center in the United States, and usually approvingly.[2] It is most often used without much elaboration on what is meant, but

in this chapter and the next I try to lay bare its most plausible meaning—first clarifying (in this chapter) what the term might be taken to
mean in operation, and then in chapter three exposing the deficiencies of that meaning as a description of the reality of American
democracy.

Majoritarianism and Its Most Fundamental Ambiguities

In simple cases, an institution is typically described as majoritarian if it regularly makes its important decisions by a vote of all its
members in which a necessary and sufficient condition for approval
of a position is that it receive at least one vote more than half the total membership, or at least such a majority of those voting. An important component of this definition is the equality of members in
the decisive tally; each member's vote counts for one.

All kinds of contemporary institutions operate more or less in this
way. I occasionally invoke the example of a modern condominium association as a majoritarian institution, assuming that each apartment
owner has the same one vote. In the political realm, this is the way
the "direct democracy" of ancient Athens apparently functioned.
"All citizens met to debate, decide and enact the law," and in the decisive votes they were treated equally, so that a majority governed.
Aristotle explained (not particularly approvingly) that "the democratic idea of justice is . . . numerical equality."[3]

Whether the context be political or nonpolitical, a number of con-
ceptual questions must be confronted by majoritarian institutions,
even on the intimate scale of a condominium association or the
democracy of ancient Athens. A fundamental issue is the identification of the class of "members" entitled to vote. This process is fairly
straightforward for a condominium association that has a certain economic integrity and an established legal structure. But membership
determination often is not obvious or somehow predetermined by
natural grouping or the law. Thus the eligible "citizens" of Athens
were a small subset of the total population, and some mechanism or
standard of voter qualification was required. Obviously, the outcomes
of votes may be determined by prior decisions about who gets to cast
them.[4]

Second, there is the problem of defining issues that are to be put to a vote. Again, there may be some governing direction, but aside from that possibility, there is no natural definition of an "issue." If a condominium association for a three-story building were voting on cleaning hallway carpets, for instance, would the carpets for each floor define a separate issue, or would all three need to be taken up as a package?[5] Would the method of financing (e.g., use of regular assessment, special assessment, or borrowing) be included as part of the issue, or could it form a separate issue? And what of repairs to the mailboxes and doorbells that some owners think should foreclose carpet cleaning unless there is room in the budget to do all of them at the same time? Again, the definition of what is an issue may well have an effect on outcomes.

Focusing on issue definition suggests additional ambiguities. One reason that majority voting may yield different results depending on how issues are framed is that voters may care about matters differentially. The way in which differential concern might affect voting outcomes is perhaps easiest to appreciate with issues that seem quite disparate, such as carpet cleaning and whether to build a garage for the condominium: one voter might be passionately in favor of the garage and mildly opposed to carpet cleaning, whereas another might hold the opposite sentiments, including the intensities with which they are held. If the two voters are allowed to trade their votes on both matters, and if the other voters are evenly divided, then each of the two could prevail on the issue about which he or she feels most strongly. This trading possibility then raises the question of whether the "equal" treatment that is taken as axiomatic for democratic voting is to be accorded one matter at a time, without trading, or with trading across the entire agenda of the majoritarian body. These two notions of what equally weighted votes might mean I call a pure model and an intensity-weighted model.

When vote trading occurs, disparate matters are in a real sense packaged together as a single issue, at least for voters who have traded. At the extreme, with freewheeling trading allowed (and even facilitated), the entire agenda of the voting body could be treated as a single issue, fine-tuned through trading to obtain the required assent. But that brings us back to the most fundamental matter of all, for the intensity-weighted model forces us to question the point of decision by majority vote. In theory at least, trading provides a mechanism through which each and every voter can be accommodated "equally," with unanimity obtained. Anything less than unanimity would leave the possibility that because of intense feeling on certain issues, one or more voters in the minority would have lost "more" than the combined gains of a majority. If the equal treatment of each voter is taken to be fundamental—rather than an equal vote—then unanimity rather than majority vote might be the appropriate way to decide.[6]

Another problem of issue definition arises where there are more than two possibilities among which the body is to choose, as often occurs in real-world decisions. A decision could be made by a plurality of those voting, but that opens the possibility that a prevailing plurality choice is one that would have lost in a head-to-head confrontation with one (or conceivably even all) of the losers.[7] It would seem that the only way to ensure that no choice is made where a majority would have preferred another is to conduct a series of head-to-head votes among all possibilities. This process in turn gives rise to the problem of cyclical voting that was apparently first noticed by Condorcet in 1785 but given its modern and rigorous formulation in Kenneth Arrow's 1951 book, *Social Choice and Individual Values*. The circular voting possibility is additionally illustrative of the importance of issue definition: posing the initial issue as A versus B with the winner to then pose a further "issue" in a vote against C might lead to a different outcome than that reached with posing the issues as A versus C with the winner to go up against B. Issue definition thus takes a variety of forms and indeed can be seen as only one aspect of the larger problem of controlling the agenda of a "majoritarian" proceeding, a problem to which I return in chapter three.

Majoritarianism in the United States

If the problems of membership, issue definition, agenda control, and the fundamental appeal of majoritarianism are set aside for the time being, there is an immediate source of puzzlement in characterizing the United States' form of democracy as majoritarian. Its scale is, of course, enormous in comparison with the condominium association or the direct democracy of Athens. But this fact need not prevent at least some things from being decided by majority vote of the entire membership. Some individual states among our united fifty conduct votes of the electorate to decide certain matters of policy. These are the processes known as "initiative" and "referendum," adopted by a number of states as a part of the progressive movement in the early part of the twentieth century. Although popular lawmaking through initiative and referendum is often hedged in by substantive and procedural constraints, approximately half the states now make available some version of such direct democratic lawmaking. However, no mechanisms of direct democracy are deployed for the United States as a whole. On a national level, not a single decision—not even the choice of the president of the entire nation—is committed to an integrated nationwide vote.[8]

Still, majority vote *is* the decisional rule for the most salient political decisions in the United States, including those decisions made at a national level. It is the rule by which we typically choose legislators in geographically based candidate elections—although a plurality often suffices in a contest among three or more candidates. Majority rule is also the standard basis for final action by the legislative chambers that are voted into office during the first-stage elections (after an issue has been defined). Popular elections and legislative decisions are two separate stages of the process by which we make laws, however, not the one that we find in direct democratic settings. But perhaps the majoritarian characterization is a shorthand way of characterizing decisionmaking through such a series of separate majoritarian steps.[9]

Such usage would introduce awkwardness on various levels. We shall see that the move from one stage to two will likely have a substantial effect on the outcomes of the process such that a majoritarianism oblivious to the number of separate voting stages would confound any systematic connection between inputs and outputs that the term might be thought to imply. In particular, staging majoritarianism in this way introduces confusion about the total population of which a majority is supposed to decide. In addition, final decisions of the U.S. Supreme Court might well qualify as majoritarian. The Court makes its decisions by majority vote, and its membership is chosen only with the "consent" of a majority of the Senate, the membership of which is in turn chosen by what are basically majoritarian elections in the individual states. As we have seen, however, the Court is quite commonly said to be countermajoritarian.

The *majoritarian* label is, no doubt, often used loosely, without close attention being given to what it really imports for a large-scale representative political system. But the characterization is so pervasive and persistent in the United States that there is probably more to it than just loose talk. A large-scale system might be considered majoritarian if the results that it produces could be seen as an extrapolation of what might have been expected if only direct democracy had been possible—and if questions of entitlement to vote, issue definition, agenda control, vote trading, and the like are taken to be under control. The use of the term *majoritarian* in the American context is, I believe, traceable to an assumption—albeit one most typically unstated—that this is the way American democracy in fact functions. American democracy is majoritarian in this view because it is the closest we can come to a direct democratic meeting of the whole. The mechanism that produces this approximate replication of direct democratic results is what I call the vote-centered model of American democracy.

The Vote-Centered Model

In the vote-centered model, the interests of the electorate are "represented" in the second stage by the representatives voted into office during the first. Two important features of American democracy that might be thought to shore up faithful re-presentation are a competitive electoral system and open communication, particularly between the electorate and their would-be re-presenters. The information flow from candidates to the electorate might, in combination with competitive politics, be taken to ensure the election of reasonably faithful re-presenters. And the reverse flow, from the voters to the vying re-presenters, provides the latter with information about the interests they are to re-present.

I describe this model as vote-centered because it depicts the citizen vote as the engine of final majoritarian results, just as it is in the intimacy of direct democracy. To be sure, communication between voter and representative continues between elections, and so does the competitive pressure for faithful representation exerted by the prospect of future electoral contests. Between elections, however, the process is haphazard and imperfect, because most people remain silent during this time. It is only in the vote that virtually all adult citizens have (on the surface at least) an equal opportunity to have their say. To speak of the process as majoritarian is thus to emphasize the vote to the exclusion of other possible determinants of the outputs of this process.[10]

The belief that representative democracy in the United States produces results that would be expected if the country could be made into one gigantic projection of direct democracy has deep roots. Many of those who took part in the debates over the U.S. Constitution apparently believed just that. One prominent federalist, writing in the *Hartford American Mercury* in support of the proposed Constitution, said, "are not the Congress and Senate servants of the people, chosen and instructed by them, because the whole body of the people cannot assemble at one place, to make and execute laws?" Another, writing in the *New York Daily Advertiser*, extolled the contemplated representative government because "[b]y this simple expedient can the sense of the people of an extensive Empire be collected with ease and certainty." The historian Jack Rakove quotes John Adams, one of the most prominent federalists of all, in concluding that "[i]f one maxim reflected [early] Americans' ideas of representation . . . it was the belief that a representative assembly 'should be in miniature an exact portrait of the people at large. It should think, feel, reason and act like them.'"[11]

Normative embrace of something like this vote-centered model can be seen in the work of many contemporary political theorists. Almost all such theories start with the premise that political equality is the central desideratum of an attractive political system, and that political equality means an equal ability to contribute to the outcomes of the system. Joseph Bessette is probably the most explicit of all, and in his formulation the vote-centered model comes clearly into view:

> The electoral connection is the chief mechanism for ensuring . . . a linkage between the values and goals of representatives and represented. If that linkage is sufficiently strong, then the policies fash-

ioned by political leaders will effectively be those that the people themselves would have chosen had they possessed the same knowledge and experience as their representatives and devoted the same amount of time considering the information and arguments presented in the national councils.[12]

It is also possible to sense the vote-centered model as a normative ideal in the 1964 U.S. Supreme Court decision requiring that both houses of state legislatures be apportioned by population—a fateful decision to which I return in chapter six. According to the Court, this "one man one vote" requirement is necessary to give each citizen an "equally effective voice in the election of members of his state legislature," as part of an "*inalienable* right to full and effective participation in the political processes of his State's legislative bodies."[13]

Although these recent invocations of something like a vote-centered model have normative inspiration, they also assume a connection to the actual operation of American democracy. I have suggested that the vote-centered model lies behind the repeated description of American democracy as majoritarian. The association may not, of course, always be appreciated by those who use the characterization. And there is likely another unappreciated association that may be at work. A normative embrace of vote-centeredness may migrate to the depictions of the system as it operates in practice.

In the case of the Supreme Court, the relationship between the normative and the descriptive is fairly straightforward. The Court was not only rationalizing changes that it was insisting on in the name of the Constitution, but it was also describing the way the world would be once changed. More generally, political theorists are likely to construct their normative ideals within shooting distance of real-world systems, even if, unlike the Court, they do not imagine that they can simply order that the gap be closed. Genuine reform is usually a part of what motivates normative thinkers, and if the distance is too great between what is and what they believe should be, the task of bridging that distance will likely seem—to them and to others they may seek to influence—too substantial to justify the effort.

There is another reason that commentators move from the normative attractiveness of the vote-centered model to the description of

American democracy as majoritarian. Positive accounts of complex social phenomena such as American democracy need not describe or account for each and every feature of the system of interest. The central concern of the vote-centered model is the relationship of popular inputs to policy outputs. But an especially intriguing feature of democracies that one might seek to explain further is the level of popular satisfaction with democratic government and the consequent stability of democratic regimes. The American version has had periods of instability, but it is probably the most long-lived of existing democracies. That "popular" government is popular may not at first seem to require explanation, but in action democracies produce a multitude of decisions with which many citizens can be expected to disagree. After all, only a majority is said to be required, and in populous democracies such as that of the United States, that leaves a very large number of people potentially disaffected. If the vote-centered model were realized in practice, it might help explain the appeal of democracy. For if all citizens are treated equally, reconciliation to outcomes with which one disagrees might nonetheless seem fair.

The possibility of a mingling between the normative and the descriptive aside, the problems with a vote-centered depiction of American democracy are legion. That is the subject of the next chapter.

CHAPTER THREE

Descriptive Shortcomings
of the Vote-Centered Model

In this chapter, I explain in some detail how far-fetched the suggestion is that American representative democracy replicates—or
even remotely approximates—what would be expected in large-scale
direct democracy, whether through the vote-centered model or some
other mechanism. We saw in chapter two the fundamental importance of defining who it is that is entitled to vote in a democracy. For
the United States, that problem has been far from trivial. For present
purposes, however, I am going to assume that questions of suffrage
have somehow been answered. Not only has no meeting of the
"whole" ever been held in the United States, it would be literally impossible to do so. Indeed, such a meeting would have been impossible
even at the time of debates about ratification of the Constitution,
when various federalists touted the constitutionally crafted legislature as providing the vaunted imitation of a meeting of the whole. As
a result, we must supply numerous features of that gathering from our
imagination, recognizing that there neither is, nor could be, any fact
of the matter. Actual direct democratic gatherings can vary in ways
that have powerful effects on outcomes. The imagined outcomes of
our imagined gatherings would then presumably also vary, depending
on the features we ascribe to those meetings.[1]

Initially I deal with three of these determinants that are of special interest, two of which we encountered in chapter two. The novel element is the attitude toward voting that voters adopt in a political setting. The two that were mentioned previously are the degree of vote trading encouraged or tolerated at the meeting, and the devices employed for control of the meeting's agenda.

Voting Mindset: Republican and Liberal Approaches to the Vote

There are voting bodies in which the voters have little or no personal stake in the decisions they make. In such contexts, voters function essentially as pure "trustees," concerned with the interests not of themselves but of others. In political settings, in contrast, voters are often affected personally by the decisions they make. Indeed, it is a source of pride in America's democracy that laws apply to lawmakers and constituents alike.[2] That fact of political life brings into relief a distinction between republican and liberal approaches to decisionmaking—ideal types that have played important roles in American political thought.[3]

In a republican setting, the voter conceives of his or her vote as that of a trustee for the community.[4] The republican must surely be concerned with the interests of actual people, for there is no apparent meaning to the interest of the community that is not in some sense a function of the interests of its members. Initially, however, at least the republican decisionmaker has no basis for preferring the interests of some community members over those of others. He or she takes the community as a whole as the unit of account, resisting quantification of the regard due any particular community members.[5] In a liberal approach, in contrast, there is only private interest, and the individual is the unit of account. Each voter votes to further his or her own interest insofar as it is implicated in questions on the public agenda.

In both the liberal and the republican conceptions, it is an article of faith that each person's vote counts equally.[6] Despite this common theme, however, the republican and liberal approaches are so fundamentally different that replication as we move from a hypothetical direct democratic gathering to an actual representative one would seem to require that an approach taken to predominate in the former would do so in the latter. The great American constitutional theorist and statesman (and fourth President) James Madison was no seeker of replication. In the *Federalist Papers,* Madison wrote that the two gatherings would be rather different; a nationwide legislature would provide "a chosen body of citizens, whose wisdom" would produce decisions with a good chance of being "more consonant to the public good than if pronounced by the people themselves, convened for the purpose."[7] Madison was probably extrapolating from large real gatherings, which he viewed with suspicion.[8] Even larger gatherings, he presumably supposed, would be worse still, and that importantly fed his preference for a representative democracy. But even assuming with Madison that a representative democracy would be characterized by republican self-denial, there is no fact of the matter of the republican or liberal mindset of voters at a meeting of the gigantic whole that never could be held. There is, then, no fact of the matter of replication in liberal or republican terms, only what we might imagine or stipulate.

Vote Trading

In initially characterizing a majoritarian system in chapter two, I assumed that each issue was addressed in complete isolation from other issues. As the discussion proceeded, however, it became clear that such a characterization might badly distort what happens in many real voting bodies. Voters often care about issues differentially, and as a result have available mutually beneficial trades of votes on separate issues. Indeed, as we also saw in chapter two, there is no natural definition of an "issue," so that trading could take place implicitly through expansion, contraction, or other reworking of the matter to be subjected to a vote. At the extreme, the entire agenda of the voting body could be treated as a single issue, with a whole host of accommodations of more and less intensely held concerns having preceded a single, final vote.

This is not to say that wholesale trading will in fact take place. Because votes will not all take place simultaneously, a system of trading requires some method of keeping track of accounts, which might be done by emulating the private market, making promises of trades enforceable, and providing some currency with which voters could buy and sell votes. But those devices are suggestive of an individuation of interests that meshes more easily with liberal assumptions than with republican ones. To be sure, the republican might not shun trading altogether. It is possible to feel more strongly, or be more certain, about some questions of the community's interest than about others. In such circumstances, republicans might be willing to trade votes. But because no republican voter is in personal touch with the "public interest" that is to inform his or her decisionmaking in the way that the liberal voter is in touch with his or her own interests, the republican basis for quantification of the "worth" of votes is fragile. The republican might then be wary of a free-wheeling trading environment, perhaps even suspicious of insidious liberalism on the part of his or her colleagues. In any event, we do not observe devices that facilitate vote trading in most real-world voting bodies, even as a great deal of trading surely occurs.[9]

What, then, are we to take as the level of trading in our hypothetical gathering of the "people of an extensive Empire"? Madison, as we saw, favored the move to representative government because it would facilitate republican decisionmaking. But a liberal theorist drawn to an intensity-weighted conception of equality might urge that the move to representative government is advisable in part because trading is not feasible in large gatherings but should be encouraged as a means for taking intensities into account.[10] Each approach assumes different levels of trading in representative government, on the one hand, and in a meeting of the whole, on the other. In truth, however, neither approach describes some knowable reality. The level of vote trading is surely a major determinant of outcomes in voting bodies, but we can hypothesize freely about the meeting of a whole such that the comparison is again no more than what we choose to make it.

Agenda Control

Finally, control of the agenda of a voting body can have a decisive effect on outcomes in a variety of situations. As we saw in chapter two, the "size" of issues can be manipulated by separating or combining seemingly disparate matters. And the prospect of a voting cycle is entirely common in which even for quite pure "issues" no single choice can be said unequivocally to represent that of the majority. The order in which the possibilities are taken up in pairwise voting may then prove decisive.[11] Even beyond these questions of issue definition and circular voting, agenda control can influence the timing of votes, which can influence outcomes. Those in control of the agenda may be able to keep a matter from coming to a vote at all; or they can affect outcomes by manipulating the phrasing of issues.[12] There is no real "majoritarian" solution to the problem of agenda control, no obvious answer to how the agenda would be controlled for our hypothetical gathering of the entire nation state; and hence there is no answer in this realm either—other than one we choose—to whether replication would be expected.[13]

Simple Representative Setting

Even if we somehow circumvent the unanswerable questions of the republican or liberal mindset of the voters, of the level of trading, and of agenda control,[14] a series of additional problems confounds any attempt to find the vaunted replication. Some of these problems are produced by complexity that is intentionally built into the American version of representative government, and I turn to those shortly. But some problems show up even in the simplest of representative settings. For ease of presentation, I assume for this simple setting the presence of American-style, single-member, geographically defined districts.[15]

Perhaps the most straightforward reason that majority voting in a representative assembly could not be expected consistently to replicate the results of the expected majority voting of a gathering of the entire electorate is that the assembly need not be chosen by such an electoral majority. Elections in individual districts can be close or not so close. As a result, even if the districts are equally populous or equally populated with voters, a minority of the electorate can select a majority in the legislature.[16]

A second reason not to expect such replication is the unreality of the vote-centered assumption that legislators seek to act as faithful representatives of their constituents' interests, using their best judgment to replicate what the constituents would have done had they been present. This assumption ignores the incentive and the leeway that agents almost inevitably have to disdain their principals' aims, a disdain that is said to be an "agency cost" when measured against an ideal of entirely faithful re-presentation. Republican theorists might count the freedom of representatives not as a "cost" but as a good thing, because the job of a republican "representative" is the search for a larger community interest. A republican search would still not produce republican *replication*, unless it is assumed that each and every sincere republican body would reach the same answer when confronted with any particular question. In any event, for the liberal, this freedom is a cost—and indeed one that is likely to be more serious than agency costs in private settings. Most members of the great body of "principals" in an electorate have little incentive to see that their interests are truly being served, and that fact constantly presses home the possibility that they will not be.[17]

Third, the representative system does not ensure that legislators will have the necessary information to represent the sentiments of their constituents, except perhaps on the most salient of issues and in the grossest of fashions. The popular vote that is the pivot of vote-centeredness tells republican representatives next to nothing about any differences in constituent visions of the public interest they might seek to represent.[18] Nor for the liberal legislator does the popular vote disaggregate positions on the variety of issues that the representative assembly will have to decide. As one commentator puts it, voting "exerts diffuse pressure on public decisionmakers . . . without informing them of specific citizen preferences . . . [and is therefore] a rather blunt instrument for citizen control over government."[19] The flow of information that accompanies elections, or that proceeds between them, might be thought to put some content into the void. For liberal and republican alike, however, that flow of information is bedeviled by the variety of sentiments in any large-scale constituency (again, except perhaps for the republican, if the republican "answer" is obvious to all who seriously consider it). For the liberal, it is additionally complicated by the problem of intensities of preferences that we have already glimpsed, one manifestation of which in the representative setting is the problem of "interest group" politics.

To have an effect in the representative setting, intensely interested voters form groups and hire professional lobbyists or publicists through which they can make their sentiments known, while the less intensely interested—if they are paying attention at all—must rely almost exclusively on their individual votes. The observable role of interest groups has given rise to an "interest group" theory of legislation, a notion to which I return in the discussion of rational choice theorizing in chapter eight. For present purposes, interest groups simply raise an additional set of questions about the accuracy of the descriptive account of the vote-centered model.[20]

At first blush, interest group politics might be thought to provide intensity-weighted inputs into the representative decisionmaking process. But even assuming that intensity-weighted inputs are what representation is supposed to replicate, the interest group mechanism can provide only the crudest reflection of intensity. It basically lumps together all interests held with less intensity than that required to sustain organization. And even successfully organized groups, whose representatives might accurately convey the nature and extent of the members' interests if known, have their own agency cost and information flow problems in doing so.

Even the simplest of representative settings, then, with a majority necessary for decisive action, is likely to produce decisions on discrete issues that reflect a variable, uncertain, and interactive mix of interests and sentiments: egalitarian but unweighted interests of members of the electorate; weighted egalitarian interests of the electorate; republican sentiments of members of the electorate, sometimes (somewhat) weighted, sometimes not; disproportionately weighted interests and republican sentiments of the members of particularly well-organized groups formed from members of the electorate; further disproportionately weighted interests and sentiments of individuals who lead such organized groups or who lobby for them (sometimes engaged by a genuine search for the group's "real" interest or sentiment, and sometimes not); and still more disproportionately weighted interests and republican sentiments of that subset of legislators who exercise agenda control. In addition, it seems likely that a greatly disproportionate weight will be felt of the interests and sentiments of those with a disproportionate influence in the dissemination of information and opinion, such as the owners and managers of communications media. It is fanciful to think that the system replicates what would be expected from a hypothetical gathering of the whole, or to call that system "majoritarian" with anything terribly coherent in mind.[21]

American Complexity

The American form of representative democracy introduces substantial additional complications for any claim that in the name of majoritarianism it replicates what would be expected from a direct democratic gathering of the whole. This is no accident. Despite the claims of some federalists that our constitutional system would approximate what could be expected from direct democracy (see chapter two), Madison and others particularly influential in crafting the system were, as we have also seen, wary of direct democracy and had no desire to produce a system that would somehow emulate the results that direct democracy might be expected to produce.

A transcendent fear of the constitutional framers was that governmental power would be exercised in an oppressive manner; however, several different forms of oppression were in view. When the Constitution was formulated and ratified in 1787 and in 1788, the possibility of the oppressive monarchy depicted in the Declaration of Independence was fresh in mind. But the principal architects of the constitutional system were also concerned that government officials might pursue their own agendas and engage in self-dealing and accumulation of power for its own sake, even when they were installed in office by popular election. As James Madison put it in the 62nd *Federalist*, "[i]t is a misfortune incident to republican government, though in a less degree than to other governments, that those who administer it may forget their obligations to their constituents and prove unfaithful to their important trust."[22] That government officials may behave in this way, even in an honest electoral system, is an example of the type of agency "cost" mentioned earlier, the leeway that agents almost inevitably have to pursue goals other than those of their principals. If the goals of the representative were republican, Madison had no problem. What concerned him was that they would be selfish instead.

Beyond these forms of misbehavior, however, the government oppression that seems to have been of most concern at least to Madison, generally conceded to have been the chief constitutional architect, was control of representatives by a stable majority *of the citizenry* that would ignore the interests of those not in that majority—agents that were too faithful representatives, rather than not faithful enough. To put the matter a different way, it was a government *responsive* to a self-regarding electorate that was often more to be feared than an unresponsive one. For Madison, direct democracy was in this sense more the problem than the solution.[23]

This concern was addressed most directly and forcefully by the design of the national government, certainly by the use of representative rather than direct democracy, but also by making a virtue of the necessity of federalism and by dividing and sculpting a government into three parts—four, if each "branch" of the legislature is counted separately.[24] Thus, unlike many modern democracies, in the United States the executive is elected independently rather than being chosen by the legislature, and the judiciary has substantial independence from each of the other branches. The branch that embodied both the hopes and fears of a realized majoritarianism, moreover, was the legislature, and the design of the national legislature leaves it far distant from anything that might be supposed to effectuate a vote-centered translation of a direct democracy.

The U.S. Congress has two houses, and each must concur for the passage of ordinary legislation. It matters a great deal how these houses are chosen, but the simple decision to employ two of them significantly complicates the political calculus and causes an incremental divergence from what might be expected in a direct democracy. This complication would exist even if apportionment for each house were governed strictly by population, the houses were of equal size and terms of office, and the voters were both diligent about voting and entirely constant in their sentiments as they voted for representatives in one house and then the other. In a reasonably competitive environment, all that would typically be required to compound the obstacles to legislation is that the borders of the electoral districts be drawn differently for the two houses. In the simplest of cases, with only two sentiments about in the land, for instance—call them Libertarian and Egalitarian—it is quite conceivable that one house could have a Libertarian majority and the other with differently constructed districts an Egalitarian one. Even short of different party control, a varying mix of represented interests could be expected in the two houses.[25]

Because a unicameral legislature need not accurately replicate direct democratic "majoritarian" sentiment, even on a single overriding issue, the addition of a second house might on occasion stifle some minority that dominates a single house and in that way move the process back toward a vote-centered majoritarian ideal. However, movement in the other direction seems just as likely, for the addition of a second house adds a second hurdle that the most majoritarian of sentiments must overcome. Madison clearly perceived this extra bicameral hurdle for majoritarianism and he embraced it, even though the second obstacle would stand as an impediment to "good" legislation as well as bad. In representative systems like that of the United States, he explained that "the legislative authority necessarily predominates," and "the facility and excess of lawmaking" are "diseases" to which the government is "most liable." For this "inconveniency," Madison had a number of antidotes, the first of which was "to divide the legislature into different branches."[26]

Of course, the two houses of the United States Congress are not simply two iterations of a simple representative model, differing only in how the districts are constructed. Neither of the two houses is crafted individually in the Supreme Court's "one person one vote" image. This fact is most obvious with regard to the Senate, the apportionment of which by states leaves it worlds removed from the best that geographic districts might do in effectuating that ideal.[27] Less noticed is that the House of Representatives is not all that close to apportionment by population either. The constitutional requirement that each state have at least one representative—and that congressional districts not cross state lines—means that the number of constituents varies significantly from one House member to an-other.[28] Thus Montana's delegation to the House was reduced from two to one by virtue of the 1990 census. The Supreme Court upheld the action despite the fact that Montana's single district would have a census population of 803,655 whereas the average district popula-tion in the country as a whole would be 572,466—a divergence of over 40 percent, far higher than the Supreme Court has tolerated as a mat-ter of fair (*i.e.,* "one person, one vote") legislative apportionment in the intrastate congressional context.[29] More generally, with House districts confined within state borders, districts in less populous states often diverge quite substantially from the norm.[30]

There are other differences between the two houses that draw the combination even further from the call of majoritarianism. Since pas-sage of the Seventeenth Amendment, the Senate has been popularly elected. Even with that change, however, the two houses differ in their sizes, in the duration for which members serve, and—impor-tantly—in the fact that the entire House of Representatives is up for election every two years, while senators are divided into three groups with staggered elections every two years. Madison clearly appreciated that these differences were important above and beyond the fact of bi-cameralism: "as the improbability of sinister combinations will be in proportion to the dissimilarity in the genius of the two bodies, it must be politic to distinguish them from each other by every circumstance which will consist with a due harmony in all proper measures, and with the genuine principles of republican government."[31]

The other branches of the national government do not fare partic-ularly better in majoritarian terms. It is by now commonplace among lawyers and law professors that the federal courts are a "counterma-joritarian" branch of government. Insofar as that characterization is meant to set the courts apart, it misfires. Insistence on the charac-terization poses yet another of our puzzles of American democracy, which I explore in chapter seven. For present purposes, we need only note that while the courts may hark more to popular sentiment than they acknowledge when they exercise constitutional review, it would be a long stretch to call them majoritarian.

More pervasively important than the courts in shaping American public policy is the executive branch. In this day and age, the executive is a many-layered thing, exercising a large measure of discretionary—and not always internally consistent—authority over policy, once legislation has been passed.[32] But even focusing narrowly on the president, the acknowledged head of (most of) the executive branch, and on the formality of legislation, executive input is achieved through the leverage of the executive veto. And as noted in chapter two, the president is not elected by a national majority.

As the country better appreciates since the 2000 presidential election, the president and vice president are chosen by what has come to be called the "electoral college," a body apportioned among the states according to the total state representation in the Senate and the House of Representatives.[33] Under the Constitution, the designation of electors need not be by popular election. A common original assumption seems to have been that they would be chosen by the state legislatures, and that once chosen they would engage in genuine deliberation about the choice of president (and vice president), albeit in separate state meetings.[34] Indeed, the electoral college vote was to be determinative only if a single person obtained a majority, and it also seems originally to have been assumed that an electoral college majority for a single candidate would be the exception rather than the rule. When no candidate commanded a majority, the selection was (and is) to be made in the House of Representatives, where each state delegation was to have one vote. The point of this convoluted procedure seems to have been to ensure a distinguished selection, in major part by insulating the process substantially from majority sentiment in the electorate.[35]

The selection of the president is one of several respects in which the constitutional framers failed quite badly to foresee how matters would play out over time. Since at least 1876, all states have provided for popular election of members of the electoral college; and by custom or (state) law, all electoral college members declare their presidential preferences beforehand.[36] Voters then effectively vote not for the electors but for the candidates to whom the electors are pledged. However, even with the role that popular election has in practice come to play in the selection of members of the electoral college, it is quite possible that a president will be chosen with less than a majority of the popular votes in the country, or even with less than the popular vote total of a rival. The former has happened sixteen times in our history. Lincoln was elected the first time with 39.8 percent of the popular vote, and Clinton had 43 percent of the popular vote in 1992. Election as president with a smaller popular vote total than a rival is more unusual but has happened on as many as four occasions since popular election became the norm. The election of 1960 is an arguable instance, and the elections of 1876, 1888, and, of course, 2000 are clear ones. Two presidential elections (1800 and 1824) have been decided in the House of Representatives.[37]

These possibilities are produced by several features of the electoral college balloting. Because apportionment of the House, and especially the Senate, diverges substantially from population proportionality, so does the electoral college apportionment. In addition, while all states now choose their electors by some form of popular vote, with the exceptions of Maine and Nebraska they employ a presidential-candidate-winner-take-all system, with the result that a candidate who manages to eke out a narrow victory over his rival in a state typically takes all of a state's electors.

As a result of these various features of the electoral college system, one prominent analysis of the electoral college after the 1990 census concluded that a member of the California electorate had 2.663 times the presidential "voting power" of a Montana voter—despite the fact that the less populous states have a nominally greater per capita say in the electoral college.[38] Even when (as is usually the case) a president does come to office with at least a plurality of the popular vote, the contortions in the design of the selection system for electors undoubtedly have a substantial impact on the process—on the places candidates campaign and on the substantive positions they take.

Perhaps even more important than these complications at the national level is the vertical dispersion of power. The ongoing political importance of the states was an unassailable assumption in the constitutional design. Even since the popular election of senators required by the Seventeenth Amendment, the power of the states—and of local units of government subordinate to the states—doubtless acts as an important counterweight to federal power (or, better, counterweights, since the various states and localities within them often have varying agendas). That power has waxed and waned over the years as a matter of court-made constitutional jurisprudence—with the most recent phase one of waxing—but with or without those formal developments, state and local power further complicates any claim of some coherent phenomenon called "majoritarianism."[39]

All these decisional cross-currents expose the vote-centered model as dismally inadequate to the task of describing American democracy.[40] The continuing talk of American "majoritarianism" is particularly surprising, since so many of the structural limitations on majoritarianism that are peculiar to the American context are a product of the Constitution itself, an object of almost reverential treatment in this country.[41] Bicameralism, the separate selection and independent authority of the executive, the apportionment of the Senate by states, and the continued importance of the states are all put beyond the reach of ordinary political processes by constitutional design.

The Pluralist Move

In the book in which he first introduced the phrase *countermajoritarian difficulty*, Alexander Bickel stuck to a majoritarian characterization of American democracy despite recognizing that many of the separate decisionmaking elements were obviously not majoritarian. He mentioned specifically the separation of powers built into our governmental structure, as well as "the more important complicating factor" of the disproportionate political power of interest groups. In the end, he saw these factors as relatively minor impediments to a realization of the majoritarian norm. That the legislature and the executive represent different constituencies, he assured us, "tends to cure inequities of over- and underrepresentation." And groups, he said, can in the final analysis be effective politically only by "combining in some fashion, and . . . constituting . . . a majority."[42]

This belief—that imperfections in one part of the system will be offset by imperfections elsewhere, and that the final result will come out alright, by the light of majoritarianism—was, and perhaps still is, a fairly widespread belief among American political theorists. The belief is associated with the "pluralist" strain in American political science. The word *pluralism* is often used to characterize a system in which organized interest groups are dominant and legislative outcomes are simply "'[t]he balance of . . . group pressure,'"[43] a notion to which I return in chapter eight. But there is a more optimistic note sounded by some who would style themselves "pluralists": in the complexity of interest group battles, each person is likely sometimes to win and sometimes to lose, with the pattern of results more or less conforming to the ideal of equal representation of interests. The final accounting, then, supposedly justifies the characterization as majoritarian. This idea is voiced by the "Pluralist" in one of the dialogues in Robert Dahl's 1989 book, *Democracy and Its Critics:*

> in a democratic order on the large scale of a country, associational pluralism, combined with a good deal of decentralization of decisions to local governments, would help to ensure that the interests of citizens in the different publics would be given more or less equal consideration. In that sense, the public good would be achieved in a pluralist democracy.[44]

Although there does not seem to be any decisive basis on which to defeat the optimistic pluralist conclusion, neither is there much reason for accepting it after the vote-centered mechanism is discredited. It is always possible that the "more or less" is doing all the work, and that nothing much is meant by the conclusion of "equal consideration." But if some genuine approximation is meant, it is hard to fathom the mechanism by which a bottom line of approximately equal consideration is reached. There is not even any apparent accounting mechanism for knowing equal consideration when we do have it.

To be sure, it seems plausible to expect instability in an open democratic society such as the United States if there is widespread and deeply held dissatisfaction with governmental decisions extending over a substantial period; the stability we do observe suggests that there is no such extent or level of dissatisfaction. The stability may also suggest some rough compromise of satisfactions, even if there is also a good measure of inequality and legislator discretion along the way.[45] But even if stability implies some compromise of satisfactions, that is a far cry from implying any real approximation of equal consideration. It seems at least as likely, as E. E. Schattschneider famously put it, that "[t]he flaw in the pluralist heaven is that the heavenly chorus sings with a strong upper-class accent."[46] Most likely, optimistic pluralists, like majoritarian theorists more generally, succumbed to a temptation to allow normative predispositions to color descriptive accounts of a system of which they know they approve.[47]

Majoritarianism and the vote-centered model do not have much to offer as depictions of American democracy. I now turn to an alternative that is decidedly superior in integrating and understanding the functioning reality of democracy in the contemporary United States.

Democracy as Involvement in Conversation

While *majoritarianism* is at least a serviceable word to describe a normative ideal frequently embraced by American political theorists, it is not, as we saw in chapter three, very apt as description, or as explanation, of the functioning reality of American democracy. Viewed in isolation, the Presidency and the House of Representatives might each be called majoritarian if the term were understood quite loosely. But there is scant justification for extending the encomium to the larger system of which those institutions are a part. In this chapter I advance a decidedly superior descriptive and explanatory framework for understanding American democracy, which I call "democracy as involvement in conversation."

The Conversational Approach

American democracy in all its complexity can be understood as an engine for producing a diverse menu of conversation about public affairs, largely carried on in public. Competitive politics and popular elections with a broadly distributed franchise are the signature of modern democracies, and they provide the root incentive for what might be called "primary" democratic conversation between candidates and eligible voters. Conversation is probably the single most important technique that candidates for office employ to win elections. At a minimum, a candidate deploys a conversational armamentarium fashioned to appeal to a majority (or plurality) of those likely to vote. The candidate communication often invites return communication, and on occasion voters take up that invitation, directing conversation back toward candidates. This primary democratic conversation becomes particularly intense as elections draw near, of course, but it continues on an ongoing basis, as those in office contemplate the possibility of reelection, and others test the waters for possible challenges.[1] Building on the base of this primary conversation, an even more extensive "secondary" conversation takes place among varying and overlapping segments of the citizenry, the bureaucracy, and media of communication. This secondary conversation would proceed to some degree regardless of the primary conversation, but a robust primary conversational environment provides a context that is highly influential in encouraging and shaping the secondary conversation.

The natural tendency of this democratic conversation is to produce a sense on the part of American citizens of involvement in the processes of government. As one commentator puts it, "ordinary common sense . . . shows that if people are part of a communications area in which politics is carried on, they are likely to experience identification."[2] The conversational approach posits that the identification produced by the democratic conversation has a cohesive effect on American democracy, inducing citizen satisfaction with—or at least reconciliation to—the substance of public decisions that might not otherwise be forthcoming. This conversational effect is felt despite—or perhaps in some ways because of—the geographic expanse of the United States and its extraordinarily heterogeneous population, which might otherwise have been expected to produce instability. To be sure, at the extreme the democratic conversation can take the form of unrelieved negativity about democracy itself, or about the tolerance without which the cohesiveness would not work. No doubt there are nonconversational features of American democracy—such as American prosperity and the absence of a single predominant societal cleavage—that keep such negativity under control. There may also be events, such as the attacks of September 11, 2001, on the World Trade Center towers and on the Pentagon, which help generate a feeling among the citizenry of involvement in a common enterprise. But the conversational account claims that the democratic conversation that is naturally produced by the American system of competitive politics is an important component of the centripetal forces that hold the larger enterprise together.

Because the conversation is rooted in competitive politics, all genuine democracies are "conversational" to a substantial degree. But the American version of democracy has a large number of distinctive, or at least unusual, features that seem likely to be especially congenial to a diversified and robust democratic conversation. Thus, the federal structure of American democracy multiplies the offices subject to election and thereby carves up issues appropriate for conversation in a variety of ways. The same can be said of the separate election of the U.S. president (and vice president), the variety of executive officials who must stand for election on the state and local levels, the rich mix of authority reposed in local elected bodies in the United States, and the American tradition of bicameralism at the national and state levels.[3]

The combined effect of federalism, localism, bicameralism, and the variety of elected executive officials is to produce an extraordinarily diverse menu of primary conversational possibilities. In addition, the routine use of single-member legislative districts in American democracy establishes easily identifiable constituency relationships that serve to direct and focus primary conversational interactions.[4] Relatively loose party discipline affords those relationships the room to adapt to the felt needs of the participants. Near-universal extension of voting eligibility to the adult population broadly extends the conversational reach. All these stimulants of primary conversation are, of course, projected into the secondary democratic conversation as well. In addition, the secondary conversation is greatly encouraged by the strong legal tradition of free and open communication in the United States and by the wide rein encouraged for media of communication by the play of market forces.[5] The resultant web of democratic conversation is observable all about us.

There is constant feedback between the primary and secondary conversation. Politicians do not simply tap into some preexisting pattern of conversational yearning. Maldistribution of healthcare resources and violence in the schools grab our attention one day, the problems of hunger and of urban sprawl the next—but why these subjects and not others, and why at one time rather than another? There is no simple answer to what makes a subject ripe for conversation, but it is surely a mistake to imagine that there is any one-way street from a pattern of voter interests to conversational subjects to which candidates, officials, and media pay attention. As the parent of a fifteen-year-old, for instance, I have learned that fashion designers, department stores, and their publicists can generate talk about quite evanescent things—and that the talk once started can call forth more of it. Even for longer lasting phenomena, a large role is played by what might be called "conversational entrepreneurs" in defining the subjects and constructing the contours of the conversation. Mass media have a great deal of influence over conversational agendas, as do private individuals. And so do politicians, albeit with a fragile base of information. Even appearances before membership organizations, mailings by zip code, telemarketing by area code, and chatroom chat reach audiences that are to some extent unknown and unpredictable. Although there is no easy route to answers about what will excite conversational attention, candidates are both anticipating what will work in conversational terms and helping determine what works at the same time.[6]

An important part of this conversational picture is the large number of conversational possibilities available to each and every member of the electorate. Although genuine democracy requires real political competition in the country as a whole, there are often legislative districts or jurisdictions in which competition is stifled. The point is important, because it is only in genuinely competitive electoral contexts that candidates have strong incentives to reach out conversationally to marginal voters. The result is that in competitive contexts, the political conversation as a whole is likely to hold something of interest for much of the population eligible to vote. In uncompetitive contexts, however, the issues that are joined and the sentiments expressed may have little to attract significant portions of the voting population. This is why the rich American electoral mix is important for the explanatory power of conversationalism. The variety available from the system as a whole produces an amalgam of sentiments expressed and topics joined, from matters of economic theory to recess policy for the local public school, from the peccadilloes of public officials to the advisability of a constitutional amendment. The large number of possibilities importantly extends the involving effect of the democratic conversation.

This is not to say that one bit of this public conversation will be fungible with any other bit in its capacity to involve. There surely are differences—in topics discussed and in the officials and candidates involved—that bear importantly on the sense of involvement that democratic conversation generates. The unwillingness of the state's governor to confront an abortion question may not be so easily forgotten just because of a state legislator's willingness to discuss the matter—to say nothing of a school board member's readiness to engage questions of recess policy. Nor will the availability of what is perceived as a sensible discussion in the local newspaper necessarily dissipate frustration with a felt sense of stupidity in what one's congressman has to say. At the extreme, it may be that all the possibilities ring hollow for some members of the citizenry. But the conversational account posits that the availability of alternatives contributes importantly to the system's involving capacity. Almost any opinion or sentiment in the citizenry that is not utterly idiosyncratic may well seem important to candidates in one electoral setting or another.

Nor is the picture otherwise one of unmixed conversational plenty. Many Americans have a limited interest in absorbing conversation about public affairs, which surely feeds back to limit the amount of conversation that is forthcoming. In addition, the political dynamics push strongly toward uncompetitive legislative districts, because legislative incumbents exercise substantial authority over the configuration of legislative districts, and they have incentives to protect their turf—and that of their political allies—by keeping competition down. When districts are uncompetitive, as we have seen, the incentive of candidates to reach out broadly to the entire legislative constituency is limited. To be sure, uncompetitive districts may allow a candidate to project a consistent message with less electoral peril. This strategy may foster a deeper sense of conversational involvement for the dominant faction in the district population as a whole, as opposed to the broader conversational reach and consequent involvement in competitive contexts. And as noted, the variety of electoral contexts in the United States softens the conversational dampening that uncompetitive districts can produce. However, the power of incumbency surely acts in a significant way to narrow the overall conversational reach of American democracy.[7]

The full picture is also not necessarily normatively attractive. While the content of the democratic conversation may be uplifting, it need not be. Much of the candidate's or elected politician's incentive is simply to direct conversation that will garner more votes at the next election than it will repel. At least on occasion, the unelected bureaucrat will then mimic the conversational program of elected officials. The incentive of the media involved in secondary conversation about public affairs, although no doubt at times to convince for the joy of bringing people around to a position thought right, is also often predominantly to sell a product. These incentives can easily lead to conversation that is simplistic or petty, or worse. They can produce conversation that many would consider appropriately left outside the public realm. The conversational perspective is offered as description and explanation, and there is nothing in the account it offers requiring that the democratic conversation be enlightened or high-minded, except insofar as those things provide payoffs to those involved in conversational interchange.[8]

In addition, most popular participation in primary and secondary conversation about public affairs is passive. Reinforcing constitutional protections, the United States has developed traditions of uncensored mail and telephone communication, and its media of communication provide a large variety of outlets for popular protest and the expression of opinion. These outlets provide the potential for active participation by individual voters. Modern communication media and devices have multiplied the outlets for active voter participation in conversational interactions. But given the size of the American population and the role of mass media, most popular participation in primary and secondary conversation about public affairs must be as readers and listeners rather than as writers and speakers. Indeed, greatly unequal citizen contributions to any ongoing dialogue about public matters seems an irreducible fact of our public life. Political theorists who import an equal treatment ideal into the ongoing process of American government run up against the brute fact that most citizens most of the time are uninterested in *active* contribution to public affairs and could not be accommodated if they were interested.

I do not suggest that pervasive and broad-ranging conversationalism was wrought into the American system at its inception. There is little indication that the involving effect of public conversation was appreciated by our constitutional framers. They sought wisdom, not conversationalism, in public officials, and hence seem to have valued a world in which "gentlemen simply stood by and waited to be called" to public office.[9] Perhaps ordinary citizens in those earliest times felt as much, or even more, involved in public affairs than citizens do now, but some of the most prominent contemporary conversational mechanisms of involvement have emerged or gelled gradually over the years. These include the use of popular elections in the choice of the president and of the members of the U.S. Senate; the extension of the franchise to its present availability to almost the entire adult citizenry; loose political party discipline; and the central role that is played by First Amendment protections of speech and press.[10] Instead of original design, I posit that the contemporary explanatory power of the conversational approach is a result of a kind of natural selection. Conversation-inducing features have emerged for a variety of reasons, but they survive because they aid the system in weathering its storms. As with Darwinian theory, a conversational approach can account not only for American stability in general, but for many of the details of the system.

I am certainly not the first to notice the sense of belongingness that can come from participation in even large-scale democracy. Learned Hand depicted both the mystery and the power of democratic participation:

> If [a bevy of Platonic Guardians] . . . were in charge, I should miss the stimulus of living in a society where I have, at least theoretically, some part in the direction of public affairs. Of course I know how illusory would be the belief that my vote determined anything;

but nevertheless when I go to the polls I have a satisfaction in the sense that we are all engaged in a common venture. If you retort that a sheep in the flock may feel something like it; I reply, following Saint Francis, 'My brother, the Sheep.'[11]

Hand's emphasis on the vote is traditional.[12] Voting might be seen as a part of the conversational interactions, but the communicative content of voting is limited. The vote may well help instill a sense of democratic involvement, but I put the stress on conversation sent and received outside the voting booth to allow us to see the important cohesive force exerted by those extra-voting conversational interactions. This viewpoint also serves to highlight the difference between a conversational perspective and the vote-centered model. In the vote-centered model, the popular vote is the engine of governance, the singular democratic mechanism of "self-government." Equality of inputs is an important component of this vote-centered depiction of the way things work. In contrast, the conversational incentives of candidates, officials, media, and citizens vary from one to another, and conversational interactions differ in myriad ways. With few exceptions, each individual has the capacity for conversational involvement, but there is little else about that involvement that is helpfully thought of as "equal."

Others have also previously stressed the role of "ongoing talk" in fostering a sense of democratic belongingness.[13] Contemporary civic republican theorists extol the virtues of public "deliberation."[14] Robert Post insists on the central role of "public discourse" in what he calls "responsive democracy." Post quotes John Dewey as saying that "'democracy begins in conversation.'"[15] But the root concern of these and similar theorists has been with a normative vision of democracy.[16] Post certainly believes that American democracy is characterized by a large measure of "public discourse," and indeed he seems to give the Supreme Court a good deal of the credit for making it so.[17] Even Post, however, devotes little attention to showing that a sense of common venture produced by the ongoing conversation is important to understanding the functioning reality of American democracy.

My priorities are just the reverse. The inspiration for my project is to increase our understanding of that functioning reality. To that end, I try to see if the real-world characteristics of American democracy can be tied together in a persuasive way by a conversational account. If that account is persuasive as description and explanation, normative implications may be found. But the involving conversation that I notice has many unattractive features. I would certainly not be minded to ground any wholesale normative theory in the totality of contemporary American democratic conversation. If normative implications flow from a conversational account, all well and good, but my eye is on its descriptive power instead.

The contrast with the majoritarian characterization is telling. "Majoritarianism" purports to tell us about outcomes. They are said to be a reflection of majority sentiments. As noted in chapter three, intractable ambiguities lurk in the majoritarian characterization. But regardless of the way those elements are wrestled down, the basis for a claim of descriptive accuracy is hard to fathom. For a small selection of issues, public opinion polls might allow some judgment of whether a "majority"—in an issue-by-issue sense—has prevailed (and often tells us that it has not);[18] but more generally, there is neither before-the-fact process nor after-the-fact information that could ground a claim for the descriptive accuracy of majoritarianism via the vote-centered model. In the case of the conversational account, there is both.

A Preliminary Look at the Justification

In chapters five through eight, I discuss four puzzles of American democracy that can be illuminated by a conversational account. After we have wrestled with the puzzles, chapter nine turns to the justification of the conversational approach: why it should be thought superior to the vote-centered model, and more generally why it might be thought to further understanding of American democracy. Part of the answer is found in the fact that there are conversational solutions to the four puzzles. But the discussion thus far allows us to take a preliminary look at the justification for a conversational account of American democracy.

There are two very different elements to the account I have provided. One is bare conversational phenomena, like the claim that districts that are relatively homogenous along politically salient dimensions are likely to see less concern by district politicians with fashioning political messages for the minority interests in the district than are politically heterogeneous districts. I doubt that there are many who will quarrel with such claims, but they are largely the product of my casual—though quite longstanding—observation of the way American politics and American society generally function. I have not tried to measure or substantiate those phenomena in any systematic way. More likely to be controversial are causal connections I posit—in particular, the claims that the democratic conversation produces a sense of involvement, that it contributes to the stability of the system, and that because of this contribution conversationalism can help account for a variety of features of the American democratic system.

None of those causal claims can be observed directly, even in theory. There are, nonetheless, bits and pieces of empirical evidence that suggest a cohesive effect of democratic conversation. Nonvoters in the United States, for instance, evidence a sense of belongingness in American democracy that is roughly comparable to that of voters.[19] And a good deal of work suggests that reconciliation may come from a sense of having been treated fairly in the resolution of disputes, regardless of the substantive outcome.[20] Such reconciliation also seems to extend to the political arena. As two major figures involved in this work put it, "[p]rocedural justice may be the key force that binds members of a political group together."[21]

The sum total of hard if suggestive empirical results, however, is quite meager. I can point to no work testing the possibility that involvement in democratic conversation is correlated with a sense of having been involved fairly in the process of democratic decision-making. Indeed, empirical evidence of what is perceived as "fair" involvement in the political process is almost nonexistent.[22] I make no particular claims about the "fairness," or about the perception of fairness, that may derive from conversational involvement. But systematic empirical research is not necessary to establish a solid foothold for descriptive theories. Thoreau quipped that "[s]ome circumstantial evidence is very strong, as when you find a trout in the milk."[23] As we see in more detail in chapter nine, even if grounded in "circumstantial" evidence, there is great power to a theory that draws together disparate features of a system into a simple and coherent account.

Substantiation of the conversational perspective is provided by such a capacity to make sense of disparate features of American democracy for which majoritarianism and the vote-centered model come up empty. As we have seen, these phenomena include the use of single-member, geographically defined districts, weak party discipline, and the large variety of offices filled by popular election. Other aspects of American democracy, while not necessarily awkward by the lights of majoritarianism, are assimilated readily to a conversational account. These include the broad extension of the franchise, and the central importance attached by the legal system to the protection of expression. To my knowledge, no prior commentator has been able to integrate such diverse phenomena into a simple but coherent understanding of the way American democracy works in practice.

This is precisely the approach to justification that is used more generally for social theory. In chapter three, for instance, I discussed a standard account of the reconciliation of the inevitably large number of losers in the variety of American battles about public affairs. Reconciliation is often said to be produced by a loose version of the vote-centered account that optimistic "pluralists" such as Alexander Bickel embraced.[24] Losers one day accept defeat in the reasonable expectation that later victories will come. In a diverse society like that of the United States, the optimistic pluralist insists that cross-cutting concerns in the citizenry mean that many people will find something to their liking in the results achieved. Over the not-so-long run, virtually everyone perceives that things will even out, perhaps with everybody gaining at least a bit. This optimistic pluralism is no more subject to measurement than are the causal connections I posit. Its deficiencies, however, lie not in this absence of measurement, but in the fact that its proponents provide no convincing reason why for large groups of voters victories and defeats will in some meaningful sense even out, let alone provide net gain for the society as a whole. There is no apparent process that would produce such results, nor even any way for someone bent on spotting them to recognize them if they showed up. Conversationalism is more plausible simply because it does a better job of coherent and plausible explanation.

We have seen that the public conversation in the United States is not a unitary phenomenon that might be understood along a single dimension. An individual voter's involvement in the conversation can be active or passive, episodic or sustained, concentrated in primary or secondary conversation, more or less intense. The individual can be engaged by democratic conversation directed to the entire nation or to some small subset of it. Involving conversation can be followed by satisfaction or by frustration of substantive interests. Frustration once experienced may linger, or it may be dissipated by new conversation. These many faces of conversation may even allow it to explain apparently inconsistent phenomena. As we have also seen, for instance, closely competitive electoral districts may stimulate more conversation directed to marginal voters, whereas politically lopsided districts allow candidates to ignore marginal voters while maintaining a more coherent message. The one may produce a broad but shallow sense of conversational engagement, while the other creates a narrower but deeper sense. The involving effect of "conversation" could then "explain" the existence of either type of district.

This problem is, however, more apparent than real. Ordinary private conversation is similarly multifaceted. It can also be casual or intense, held closely or shared broadly. It can calm or anger. But its complexity does not prevent our appreciating that in its totality private conversation plays an important role in holding social beings together. Its very complexity may be part of the secret of its cohesive powers. When our closest private conversant has aroused anger, talking to a more casual acquaintance can help restore the calm; and so it is with public conversation. In competitive districts, district-level conversation draws in large segments of the population. But in politically lopsided districts, a persistent minority need not sign off from the system, because there are other loci of conversation vying for attention.[25]

Still, I do not want to oversell the explanatory power of the conversational perspective. There is no such thing as a comprehensive account of a complex social phenomenon such as American democracy. To provide an explanatory theory of such a complex thing is to cut through much of its detail. If a theory succeeds, the elements that it highlights and the causal connections that it posits tie important aspects of the subject together in a relatively simple fashion. The result is a construct that can be manipulated and applied in other contexts to open up new insights.

The focus of the conversational approach, for instance, is on the communication within American democracy rather than the system's responsiveness to substantive interests. Conversationalism posits that conversational attention—and conversely, neglect—can have important centripetal or centrifugal effects, quite apart from whether substantive interests are served by eventual public policy decisions. The two are separate phenomena in important ways, for they proceed at different points in the larger system. Substantive authority resides mainly in entire legislative bodies, whereas conversation is carried on largely between individual legislators and their constituents.[26] Before the Supreme Court's apportionment revolution of the early 1960s, for instance, many state legislatures in the grips of a "rural strangle hold" neglected the interests of city dwellers.[27] Still, those city dwellers may well have constituted majorities or important constituencies in their own districts, in which case conversational attention would likely have been lavished upon them.

Drawing a stark line between substantive and conversational responsiveness, however, also oversimplifies a complex reality. In the real world, concern with public policy outcomes is no doubt an important determinant of satisfaction with American democracy. The conversational approach draws on that fact, assigning citizen concern with outcomes an important place in structuring the incentive of candidates to reach out conversationally. But for purposes of drawing out the power of the conversational perspective, the pattern of outcomes is put aside as an explanation of citizen satisfaction. In addition, there surely are complex interactive effects, which I also ignore. If substantive inattention becomes chronic, for instance, and is perceived as such, it may well feed a cynicism about democratic politics that could drain even seemingly robust district-level conversation of its capacity to instill a sense of involvement, or to defuse the next substantive disappointment. Indeed, chronic substantive inattention could itself become the subject of democratic conversation, generating a measure of disenchantment alongside a sense of involvement.[28] Despite the complexity, and the very real effects of substantive attention and neglect, I ignore them, the better to see the role of conversational phenomena.

Although conversationalism enjoys a good measure of success in these terms—and certainly more than majoritarianism and the vote-centered model—I also want to avoid imperial claims to which political theorists too easily fall victim. Precisely because an explanatory account need not be comprehensive, it is entirely possible that two (or more) successful accounts of complex phenomena can comfortably coexist. In chapters eight and nine I discuss a perspective—commonly called "rational choice theory"—that is a more worthy competitor for the conversational approach than is majoritarianism. The relative assessment of the "success" of conversationalism and rational choice is considerably more difficult and need not be resolved. But rational choice theorists have occasionally made imperial claims, or at least have been understood as making them, thereby diverting attention from the content to the pretentiousness of the theory. To emphasize the limited nature of the claim I make for conversationalism, I have intentionally avoided attaching the words *theory* or *model* to the conversational approach, using *account, perspective,* or *approach* instead.[29]

The claim for the success of a conversational account is therefore a limited one. Conversationalism provides no account of certain important features of American democracy. It avoids, for instance, all claims about the pattern of democratic outcomes. And even when conversationalism offers a causal account of phenomena, it does not claim to be the only force at work. Conversation helps explain the broad extension of the vote, for instance, but not necessarily the pattern of remaining exceptions to the universality of the franchise.[30] Given this disclaimer, however, the power of a conversational perspective is substantial. The conversation itself is readily observable all about us, not only as elections near but on an ongoing basis. That conversation can plausibly account for many of the most salient phenomena of American democracy. Perhaps most telling, however, is the way in which conversationalism can aid in understanding aspects of American democracy that are otherwise puzzling. The next four chapters are devoted to the light that conversationalism can shed on some puzzles of American democracy about which preexisting explanatory accounts have had little to offer.

The United States Senate

The United States Senate is an unusual body among democratic legislatures. There are bicameral legislatures in other democracies of the world, but in the versions outside the United States, only the house more closely tied to popular election typically has the full range of legislative powers. In the U.S. Congress, this would be the House of Representatives, which is chosen by "the people" and apportioned among the states by population.[1] In the original constitutional design, senators were to be chosen by state legislatures rather than through popular election. That process has now been changed by the Seventeenth Amendment, but the Senate is still composed of two senators from each state, with the result that by the standards of population proportionality, the Senate is far less representative than the House. Yet the only respect in which the Senate and the House are assigned different functions for ordinary legislation is that "[a]ll Bills for raising Revenue shall originate in the House of Representatives." Senate concurrence in revenue measures is still required, and indeed, in revenue matters the Constitution explicitly cautions that "the Senate may propose or concur with Amendments as on other Bills." In any event, this House prerogative has not proved to be of much practical significance. In far more momentous respects, it is the Senate rather than the House that has the more sweeping powers. Most importantly, the "consent" of the Senate, but not of the House, is necessary for the appointment of major executive officials and federal judges.[2]

The Senate's distinctiveness is particularly striking in light of the dominance of majoritarianism and the vote-centered model in American political discourse. Against a standard of population proportionality, it appears that the Senate is the most malapportioned elected legislative body in the world.[3] The anomaly is brought into sharp relief by the Supreme Court's 1964 decision in *Reynolds v. Sims*. In holding that both houses of state legislatures must be apportioned by population, the Court said that what it called this "one person one vote" requirement is necessary to give each citizen an "equally effective voice in the election of members of his state legislature," as part of an "*inalienable* right to full and effective participation in the political processes of his State's legislative bodies." Given this portentous language, the Court naturally felt compelled to explain how it was that the national legislature—most importantly the Senate— is not only allowed but required to deviate from the inalienably rightful pattern.[4]

The Court's explanation is reasonably persuasive on its own terms:

> The system of representation in the two Houses of the Federal Congress is one ingrained in our Constitution . . . . conceived out of compromise and concession indispensable to the establishment of our federal republic.

> Political subdivisions of States—counties, cities [on each of which legislative districts were often based], or whatever—never were and never have been considered as sovereign entities. . . . [T]hese governmental units are "created as convenient agencies for exercising such of the governmental powers of the State as may be entrusted to them," and the "number, nature and duration of the powers conferred upon [them] . . . and the territory over which they shall be exercised rests in the absolute discretion of the State." The relationship of the States to the Federal Government could hardly be less analogous.[5]

Still, this is lawyers' language. Persuasive as the distinction might seem as a matter of law, it cannot explain the absence of popular concern about the apportionment of the Senate. This absence of popular concern is the first puzzle I discuss. If "full and effective participation" requires population-based apportionment in the state context, no reason appears from what the Court had to say in *Reynolds* why the Senate apportionment would not be defective as well. Even if the Constitution requires us to live with a "defective" Senate, that is no barrier to the expression of dissatisfaction about senatorial apportionment. Not only has there been an absence of controversy about Senate apportionment, but the Supreme Court's requirement of population-based apportionment for state legislatures has also become rather uncontroversial, coexisting in apparent ease with the Senate apportionment it seems with its talk of "inalienable right" to brand as *in principle* foreign to the central tenets of American democracy.[6]

There is, I think, a comfortable conversational explanation of the apparent satisfaction with the U.S. Senate, but this explanation will be given added force if we first canvass two conventional justifications for the Senate: the representation it provides for the states, and a "calm" second look that it has been said to provide before legislation is passed.

The Senate as Representing States

The Senate is often said to represent the states, whereas the House of Representatives represents the people. James Madison, for instance, saw the House as ensuring the approval of legislation by "a majority of the people" and the Senate by "a majority of the States."[7] But this distinction is more than a little misleading. Senate membership is apportioned equally among the states, but apportionment and representation are not the same thing, nor does either one require equality. The "Virginia plan," which became something of an initial agenda for the constitutional convention that was to craft the scheme for the Senate, would have apportioned the Senate by states but instead made that apportionment proportional to "quotas of contribution or to the number of free inhabitants, or to both."[8] Even with each state entitled to two and only two senators, moreover, the Senate is far from a simple representative of state interests to be contrasted with the House, in which the people at large are represented.

First, the House—like the Senate—is *apportioned* by states. By rather clear constitutional design, no member of the House has a constituency that overlaps state borders.[9] The Supreme Court has suggested, moreover, that despite the use of geographical districts, this design is for representation of the entire state by each state's delegation. "It has never been doubted," according to the Court, "that representatives in Congress . . . chosen [by districts] represented the entire people of the State acting in their sovereign capacity."[10] In any event, it is not uncommon for most or all of a state's delegation in the House of Representatives to cooperate on some matter thought to be of interest to the state as a whole.[11]

In addition, a state's two senators vote as individuals rather than as a delegation. The senators often belong to different political parties, and in such cases their votes frequently align more closely with those of senators of their respective parties from other states than with that of the other senator from the same state. This was so even before passage of the Seventeenth Amendment, when state legislatures occasionally attempted to use their power of senatorial appointment to control votes of their senators on some issues.[12] Since passage of the amendment, popular election of senators now further confuses any attempt sharply to delineate the representational relationships of the House and Senate. Because they are statewide officers, senators may deal more readily with state officials than do members of the House, and it seems likely that they are asked to carry the burden of state interests in the Congress more often than are House members. But this distinction is decidedly a matter of degree. In truth, both House and Senate delegations represent the interests of states as a whole on some matters, and interests of more complex alignments of concerns among "the People" on others.[13]

State equality in the apportionment of the Senate was actually more a concession to the less populous states than it was a concession to states as such. Aside from their common interest in not becoming subservient to the voting power of their more populous neighbors, however, it is not clear how much the less populous colonies had in common with each other. In the contemporary United States, more and less populous states are mingled geographically, and while some of their concerns—decay of housing stock, or problems of racial minorities, for instance—may be correlated with population size, state interests are just as likely to be defined regionally, or by economic or political fortuity, and hence cut across state population size.[14]

The contemporary Senate *is* nonetheless protective to some degree of the interests of states, if only because the Senate is a sufficiently small body that *any* state's two votes can be important. The House delegations from the smallest states have only one vote apiece—out of a grand total of 435—and hence are relatively powerless there. But in the smaller Senate, each state's two votes can be marshaled more effectively in defense of prerogatives thought to be in jeopardy. This arrangement is due in part to differences between the political systems of the United States and of many other democracies. The independent election of the president, and the substantial assumption of power by the executive, means that governments do not stand or fall on the outcome of any congressional vote. For these and probably other reasons, members of Congress more than occasionally break party ranks. Close votes are then uncertain in a way that they are not where the stakes are high and party discipline strong. Two votes out of one hundred (the size of the Senate since the admission of Hawaii as the fiftieth state in 1959) can give any state's senators a good deal of leverage, not only on particular close votes, but also through the use of those votes as bargaining chips across the range of legislative matters. This being said, senatorial representation of states in this way is limited and differs from representation of states in the House only by degree. In the final analysis, the notion that the Senate provides a valued representation of the states seems too fragile to provide any persuasive explanation of the absence of controversy about its (mal)apportionment.

The Senate as Providing an Additional Obstacle and a Calm Second Look

In one of the constitutional framers' boldest moves, they provided for ratification of the Constitution by special conventions in the several states rather than by the state legislatures, which had been responsible for selecting the state representatives in the preconstitutional Congresses and in the constitutional convention itself.[15] The selection and deliberations of these ratification conventions stimulated an extraordinary outpouring of public debate about the Constitution, the most famous portion of which has come down to us as the *Federalist Papers*, produced by Alexander Hamilton, James Madison, and to a minor extent John Jay, as part of the ratification debate in Hamilton's (and Jay's) state of New York.

The *Federalist Papers* represent the United States' most distinctive contribution to eighteenth-century political theory. They are often cited as highly persuasive material in interpreting the Constitution.[16] The papers pay only scant attention to the notion that the Senate represents the states. Lip service is paid to the sovereignty of the states, and to the equal suffrage in the Senate as reflecting that sovereignty. But neither Madison nor Hamilton originally favored equal state representation in the Senate, and the dominant tone adopted in the *Federalist Papers* toward the "Great Compromise" that had produced the senatorial apportionment scheme is apologetic. The Senate is depicted first and foremost as a compromise, necessary for the accomplishment of the Constitution's great purposes.[17] Making a virtue of this necessity, the *Federalist Papers* then offer a justification for bicameralism and for the Senate that is drawn from a different realm, and that for a time dominated conventional American wisdom on those subjects.

An important theme of the *Federalist Papers* is the distrust of popular government. Madison was, as we saw in chapter three, a "republican." He variously described the end of government as "justice" and the "happiness of the people."[18] While it is not entirely clear what he meant by either of these declarations, Madison did believe that there is such a thing as the "public interest" (he would have been more likely to call it the "general good"). At the same time, he was a staunch believer in individual prerogatives, particularly property rights, and likely thought that protection of these was a good part of serving the public interest. For this reason, popular government provided no magic route to the right decisions. The War of Independence had been a response to government without representation, and the authors of the *Federalist Papers* had no illusions about the dangers of unrepresentative government. With those dangers taken as given, however, popular government simultaneously was the solution and the carrier of further problems.

The root problem was that of self-interest—or, as Madison famously put it in the *Tenth Federalist*, of "faction": citizens "actuated by some common impulse of passion" who would employ the mechanism of majority vote to pursue measures "adverse to the rights of other citizens, or to the permanent and aggregate interests of the community." This problem was not seen as contingent, but rather was "sown in the nature of man," produced by "the connection . . . between . . . reason and self-love." The best one could hope for was to contain the operation of faction, and the Constitution was championed as doing so primarily through structural mechanisms, "contriving the interior structure of the government as that its several constituent parts may, by their mutual relations, be the means of keeping each other in their proper places." "Ambition," Madison counseled in a different number of the *Federalist Papers*, "must be made to counteract ambition."[19]

Beyond federalism, which was taken essentially as given for the new nation, the Constitution followed Montesquieu in providing for separation of powers among three branches of government—the executive, legislative, and judicial. But still more was required lest the legislature overwhelm the other two branches. "In republican government," as Madison put it, "the legislative authority necessarily predominates." The remedy "for this inconveniency" was bicameralism. "[B]y requiring the concurrence [in legislation] of two distinct bodies," Madison argued, bicameralism would double "the security to the people . . . [against] schemes of usurpation or perfidy . . . ." He acknowledged that the extra check "may in some instances be injurious as well as beneficial," but he insisted that the net effect would be salutary, since "facility and excess of law-making seem to be the diseases to which our governments are most liable."[20]

The real danger, moreover, was in the House. According to Hamilton, "the most *popular* branch of every government partaking of the republican genius, by being generally the favorite of the people, will be as generally a full match, if not an overmatch, for every other member of the government."[21] The second chamber—the Senate—then was designed to provide a specific antidote to the dangers posed by the first. Its large powers were no doubt a part of this plan. But the Senate was not just a coequal legislative partner. The Senate was to be special; it was to provide a calm and reflective second look before proposed legislation became law.

The *Federalist Papers* depict the smaller size of the Senate, the longer terms of office, the greater age and longer period of citizenship required of senators, and the provision for gradual change as a third of the Senate seats become vacant every two years as safeguards against "the propensity of all single and numerous assemblies to yield to the impulse of sudden and violent passions, and to be seduced by factious leaders into intemperate and pernicious resolutions." The Senate was to hold fast against impulsive and "intemperate" legislation that the people themselves might well later be "the most ready to lament and condemn." Independently of this, the longer senatorial terms and the provision for staggered tenure were taken to ensure a greater stability in legislation, which Madison extolled as consistent with "every rule of prudence and every prospect of success." Perhaps even more important was the fact that the Senate was to be chosen not directly by the people but rather by the state legislatures. The Senate would thus bring a measure of "due acquaintance with the objects and principles of legislation," in contrast to the House, to which "men [would be] called for the most part from pursuits of a private nature [and] continued in appointment for a short time. . . ."[22]

Although the rationale that the *Federalist Papers* provides for the Senate also retains some force, it has been undercut severely by developments since that time. The Senate, of course, is no longer appointed by state legislatures, and service in the House has come to be characterized by a high degree of incumbent retention, with the result that in the modern day there is little difference between the two houses in terms of their "acquaintance with the objects and principles of legislation."[23] The smaller size of the Senate and the longer tenure of senators may make that body a more appealing place in which to serve, but members of both houses now face electoral—and attendant fundraising—hurdles. It is sometimes thought that the Senate may attract a more "elite" group than the House. Contemporary career movement between the houses is almost all one way, from the House to the Senate.[24] Still, any difference in "quality" or deliberateness would be hard to quantify or establish with confidence.

In addition, the authors of the *Federalist Papers* had no inkling of the growth and change that the U.S. economy would experience. The growth has been attended by vast expansion of the presumed field for operation of the national government—a development that likely would also come as a surprise to the constitutional framers. Today, there are few limits to what the federal government can regulate in pursuit of its commerce power,[25] and these developments have been accompanied by incredible increases in the speed and effectiveness of communication. The developments have conspired to put vastly more resources in play on the national public agenda, and thus have greatly increased the incentive for the two houses (and the executive) to bargain away their differences over legislation.[26]

The result may be a lower volume of legislation than would be produced by a unicameral House of Representatives, but hardly the modest volume that the *Federalist Papers* seem to have envisaged. And although the Senate's apportionment surely affects the pattern of legislative outcomes, there is just as surely a great deal of attentiveness to legislative constituencies (whether or not thought of as "factions") by the contemporary Senate as well as the House.[27]

Finally, if the Senate were valued as providing a "calm second look," it is not apparent in the present day why apportionment by states facilitates the desired distance. A body the size of the Senate (or smaller) and elected, say in staggered nationwide elections or in multistate districts that more nearly approximated equality of district population, seems as likely as the present Senate to provide the desired coolness and deliberation. Of course, no such thing is politically feasible, but that fact need not hinder our using the possibility as a rhetorical device in public condemnation of a Senate (mal)apportioned in the present way. Like representation of the states, this rationale for the Senate as providing a "calm second look" is thus difficult to feature as accounting for the essential absence of controversy about senatorial apportionment.

The usual rationales for the Senate apportionment are only mildly convincing, singly and in combination. In their 1999 book, *Sizing Up the Senate*, Frances Lee and Bruce Oppenheimer note their amazement "that previous scholars had given so little attention to the effects of Senate apportionment."[28] Their explanation for the "omission" is that "Senate apportionment is typically just taken for granted."[29] Senatorial apportionment is "not one of the burning issues of our time," in part "because most of the people disadvantaged by it are unaware that they are disadvantaged."[30] That may be part of the explanation for both scholarly and popular inattention. There is no one-way street from an abstract pattern of interests to conversational attention. In chapter seven, I go more deeply into some determinants of that attention and conclude that change in the status quo plays an important role in garnering conversational attention. That being said, inattention to the question of Senate apportionment cannot simply be chalked up to obliviousness and to the fact that it has always been so.

The Senate is not only a central institution in American democracy, it is one that regularly takes part in decisions that gore one ox or another. Given the salience of the Senate and the routine importance and controversial nature of so many of its decisions, it is worth searching for deeper causes of the inattention to its (mal)apportionment. Commentators who object to the Senate on normative grounds aside, the lonely few who express surprise at the dearth of discontent with Senate apportionment have, I believe, been misled by the conventional majoritarian characterization of American democracy. It is that characterization, of course, that suggests the anomalous character of the Senate, but majoritarianism is not, as we have seen, important in the actual functioning of the system. Conversationalism has much more to teach about the way American democracy operates, and from a conversational perspective the Senate may contribute more effectively to the smooth working of American democracy than does the House. Before turning to the conversational explanation for the Senate, I digress briefly for some relevant history of the senatorial selection process.

A Bit of History of Senatorial Selection

In several respects, the original provision for the selection of senators by state legislatures was not well thought out. It seems to have been assumed that the two houses of bicameral state legislatures would each have to concur in their selections—an arrangement that may in part have been a product of a "republican" way of thinking about the Senate. Political parties had not coalesced at the time of the original Constitution, and the document contemplates no role for them. Perhaps it was assumed that a state's choice for Senator would be relatively straightforward, since few people would be seen as clearly possessing the requisite wisdom and capacity for self-denial. In any event, the possibility of deadlock between the two houses of a bicameral state legislature was not anticipated or seen as serious. Such a lack of concern with the deadlock possibility might well have proved a modest problem had political parties and attendant partisanship not quickly become a commonplace feature of American politics. But that was not to be, and in those cases in which the two houses of state legislatures were controlled by different parties, state legislative selection of senators frequently courted the possibility of partisan deadlock and senatorial vacancies.

Some states adopted the awkward response of a joint vote by both houses of the state legislature—awkward not only because such a response was not originally envisaged but also because the two houses were not necessarily of equal size. A joint vote would give the larger house more say in the selection. The Constitution provided for congressional alteration of state decisions on the "manner of holding elections for senators," and this possibility was taken up in 1866 with a requirement of joint vote by the state legislatures if separate votes in states that used them failed to provide a definitive choice. The same legislation perversely required a majority vote in that joint gathering—a plurality would not suffice—which served to exacerbate rather than ameliorate the problem of deadlock. By one count, there were forty-five serious deadlocks from 1891 to 1905 alone.[31]

The process occasionally broke out into embarrassing public displays, as illustrated by the following account of a 1905 Missouri senatorial selection in the jointly convened bicameral legislature:

> Lest the hour of adjournment should come before an election was secured, an attempt was made to stop the clock upon the wall of the assembly chamber. Democrats tried to prevent its being tampered with; and when certain Republicans brought forward a ladder, it

was seized and thrown out of the window. A fist-fight followed, in which many were involved. Desks were torn from the floor and a fusillade of books began. The glass of the clock-front was broken, but the pendulum still persisted in swinging until, in the midst of a yelling mob, one member began throwing ink bottles at the clock, and finally succeeded in breaking the pendulum. On a motion to adjourn, arose the wildest disorder. The presiding officers of both houses mounted the speaker's desk, and, by shouting and waving their arms, tried to quiet the mob. Finally, they succeeded in securing some semblance of order.[32]

But even when the process went more smoothly, it remained remote from anything that might seriously be thought to serve the republican ideal. Charges of bribery and corruption in the selection of senators were not uncommon. More generally, the selection process often came to be "dominated by the party caucus, a body unknown to the law, meeting behind closed doors, its proceedings known to the public only through unauthoritative reports which leaked into the newspapers."[33]

Even as the selection process often proceeded in private, however, the pull toward public conversation was evident. The state legislators who were to make the selection were themselves subject to popular election, and that policy provided considerable leverage in drawing out public conversation about senatorial selection and the issues that senators would have to face. The role of public conversation was evident at least as early as the fabled Lincoln-Douglas debates of 1858. The stage had been set for that public clash when the two major parties made their favorites for senator known before the state legislative elections. There were seven public debates in various parts of the state. They were reproduced in Illinois newspapers and commanded great public attention. While "[i]n point of law, the great debate . . . was but an incident in the election of a legislature, with which alone rested the power of electing a senator . . . ," in fact "the whole country knew who was to be senator as soon as the votes for the members of the legislature had been counted."[34]

Those historic debates provided a particularly compelling example of public conversation surrounding senatorial selection, but the movement toward popular involvement proceeded in other, less storied ways well before the adoption of the Seventeenth Amendment in 1913. Starting in the 1870s, agitation for a constitutional amendment to require the popular election of senators gathered force, but resistance in the Senate was understandably fierce. In this environment, various states experimented with measures that would draw the public into the process by attempting to constrain or even dictate the state legislative choice: selection of party "candidates" for senator through party primaries; state "elections" expressing a nonbinding popular preference for senator; official "transmittal" to the legislature of the results of a ballot of popular preferences; official announcement of those results before the legislative senatorial balloting; and a variety of mechanisms for purporting to bind state legislators to a popular choice either through precommitment or even the sanctioning of expulsion from the state legislature.[35] In many ways, the process tracked the earlier movement toward the popular vote as the mechanism of presidential selection, despite the fact that the Constitution required (and still requires) no such thing. In the case of senatorial selection, however, once the movement toward popular election had gathered steam, the Senate relented, and state ratification of the Seventeenth Amendment quickly followed.

The Seventeenth Amendment might be viewed as one step in the direction of majoritarianism and the vote-centered model. It is notable, however, that the cry for popular election does not seem to have been accompanied by expressions of concern about the apportionment of the Senate. The dynamic at work can more comfortably be seen as a movement toward the sort of public conversation exemplified by the Lincoln-Douglas debates than toward a majoritarianism in public decisionmaking. But whether or not some yearning for a conversational outlet fed the movement for popular election of senators, the result has been to provide every state with important additional vehicles for involving conversation about public affairs.

The Conversational Explanation for Comfort with the Senate

Elections for the Senate in the United States are, of course, based on geographically defined districts (i.e., states), just as they are for the House. In the United States, we may think of geographical districting as the "natural" basis for selection, but in fact many democracies choose some or all of the members of the legislature in "at-large" elections from the country as a whole. Variations on that theme have even been tried on occasion in the United States. Multimember state delegations to the House of Representatives, for instance, were often chosen in at-large state elections, particularly until the middle of the nineteenth century. At present, most states choose their "electoral college" delegates in such wholesale fashion. There are no real conversational consequences of this approach to electoral college selection, since it is the presidential candidates with whom conversation takes place, and at-large elections of congressional delegations are now forbidden by federal law.[36] If allowed to proceed, however, at-large elections might have serious effects in dampening the involving democratic conversation, for geographic districting seems particularly congenial to such conversation.

Geographic districts define a special relationship between those elected (and those seeking to be elected) on the one hand, and their constituencies on the other, directing the focused concern of each to the conversational concerns and activity of the other. This relationship is not confined to the few minutes spent every year or so in the polling place, or even to an election campaign that leads up to election day. The relationship is ongoing, and it can easily transcend partisan electoral politics. Thus, we typically find that representatives in the United States speak of "my" constituents and members of the electorate of "my" senator and "my" representative, regardless of what may have taken place in the secrecy of the election booth. Surveys of popular opinion repeatedly show that constituents have a higher opinion of their own representatives (including senators) than they do of the Congress as a whole.[37]

The conversational contrast between at-large elections and geographic districting need not be stark, for a country might be divided into a small number of districts with multimember delegations chosen "at-large" from each. Still, the conversational relationship seems most likely to flourish when each district elects only a single member with whom constituents can most easily identify. In this respect the Senate, with two representatives from each district, may seem less effective a conversational vehicle than the House. Indeed, other differences between the two contexts might lead to a similar conclusion. Because House districts are usually less populous than states, and House elections more frequent than those for the Senate, voters might find it easier to keep up with the identities of their representatives in the House—and of candidates for the position. That assumption surely accompanied the originally divergent mechanisms for selection of members of the two houses.

Lee and Oppenheimer's comparison of senators from more and less populous states lends weight to this conclusion. It surely comes as no surprise that a resident of a less populous state is more likely to have had a personal meeting with one of the state's senators than is a resident of a more populous state.[38] Campaigns in less populous states need rely less on mass media and more on gatherings that allow constituents to catch a real glimpse of the candidates.[39] More populous states are also more likely to have antagonistic constituencies, making it harder for senators to keep the bulk of their constituents happy with particular substantive positions they espouse.[40] In any event, it seems fair to conclude that "senators from . . . [more populous] states are inescapably more distant from their constituents."[41] In all these respects, a typical congressional district is more likely to resemble a less populous state, suggesting that elections for the House of Representatives may elicit more involving democratic conversation.

There are, however, considerations that cut toward the opposite conclusion. Apportionment of the Senate by states means that district lines for the Senate are stable, while district lines in the House of Representatives shift as population shifts. Combined with the fact that senatorial tenure is more sure, if only by virtue of the longer term of office, the stability of senatorial "districts" may actually lead to easier identification of and with senators than representatives, and hence more ease in developing a conversational relationship.[42]

This ability to keep track of officeholders and candidates may also be affected by the geographic reach of the district and state as well as the relationship of that reach to major media markets. In my hometown of Chicago, for instance, the major electronic and mass media markets extend over several congressional districts. Partly as a result, senators and senatorial candidates receive far more major media coverage than do their counterparts in any single congressional district.

The same seems to be true in other populous areas as well.[43] For this reason, the greater size of the typical senatorial "district" need not lead to greater anonymity. Even the fact that each citizen has two senators but only one representative need not interfere seriously with the development of a sense of relationship; two is a quite manageable number, and, with rare exceptions, the citizens of any given state are called on to choose only one Senator at a time.[44]

At least once the major party candidates have been selected, senatorial elections are also more likely to be competitive than are House races. The single most important reason appears to be the attractiveness of the office. Senate seats are rarer and are characterized by longer tenure. In any event, it seems undeniable that "[t]he [contemporary] Senate has more glamour than the House."[45] Senate races thus attract more money per voter, more media exposure, and—for all these reasons—more effective challengers than do House seats.[46] There may be other reasons for the competitiveness as well. The larger population in a typical senatorial district brings a greater likelihood of a diversity of constituencies, providing openings for more effective challenges. Whatever the reasons, it seems clear that "[a] much smaller proportion of House elections than Senate elections . . . [are] hard fought . . . ."[47]

These differences have important conversational implications. The greater media exposure means that the members of the voting public are exposed more frequently to senators and Senate challengers than they are to members of the House and contenders for the position.[48] In chapter four we encountered the distinction between broad and deep conversational interactions, associated respectively with more and less competitive legislative districts. Simply by virtue of the greater size and diversity of constituencies, senatorial elections are more likely to be characterized by broader but shallower conversational interactions.[49] The nature of the subjects discussed may also be affected. Lee and Oppenheimer conclude that "'with their access to the media, [large state Senators] seem to put more emphasis on position taking than House members; probably House members rely more heavily on particularized benefits.'"[50]

These incentives continue once a senator is in office. Lee and Oppenheimer suggest that a constituent in a single district state faced with a choice of talking to a senator or his or her representative in congress may opt for the former simply because the senator is the more influential legislator. They also argue that senators from less populous states can enhance their electoral prospects through public works and similar projects in their states more efficiently than can their more populous state counterparts. Put most crudely, it is cheaper to appeal to voters' economic self-interest when there are fewer of them. This fact should lead to a larger "ideological" component for the appeal by populous state senators (and candidates).[51] This tendency may then be reinforced by the readier media access for senators in more populous areas.

None of this is to deny that the differences in size among Senate constituencies bring conversational differences. Far from it. Other things being equal, the senators and the representative from a state with a single congressional district seem likely to be similar in their conversational proclivities. But most senators serve in states where there are multiple congressional districts, where as a result both district lines and electoral incentives are more complex. The typical senator in those states seems likely to be a democratic conversationalist at least the equal of a member of congress in the same state.

If satisfaction with American politics is in substantial measure a product of conversational involvement, the Senate seems as much entitled to credit for a widespread sense of involvement as is the House of Representatives. Whatever weight that "credit" might be given in some overall normative assessment, the Senate might still be an inferior democratic body—or even a quite mischievous one. Senate apportionment surely has an impact on legislative outcomes, and normative criticism of the pattern of that impact is not difficult to fashion.[52] Whatever the normative case against Senate apportionment, however, that apportionment has not created any popular movement in protest. It is the political invisibility of the issue of Senate apportionment that the conversational perspective quite effectively explains. And that ability to explain what seems so puzzling from the perspective of the standard rhetoric about American democracy bolsters the case for the conversational account.

CHAPTER SIX

The Electoral Status of Children

Approximately one quarter of the American citizens who are resident in the United States—some sixty-two million people—are children under eighteen years of age, the near universal cutoff for eligibility to vote.[1] The rhetoric of American public policy places these children at or near the apex of public concern,[2] and yet without the vote they are deprived of the vote-centered mechanism for asserting their interests. While there is no way to know with any precision what changes we might observe in public policy outcomes if children were more effectively "counted" in the political calculus, it is not at all far-fetched to imagine that those changes would be quite substantial. Even given my criticisms of the vote-centered model (see chapter four), when the numbers are as large as they are with children, it is entirely plausible to imagine, for instance, that public expenditures on schools and playgrounds, on early intervention public health measures, or on the preservation of endangered species or of virgin forests would be higher—and those on benefits for the elderly, or on research on prevention of diseases that typically strike later in life, would be lower.[3]

There is, of course, plenty of room for argument about the right cutoff age for voting. Once we had settled on an age of enfranchisement, however, it might initially seem that the electoral disempowerment that the vote-centered model teaches comes with disenfranchisement is inevitable for children below that age. But there is a simple expedient that would allow vote-centered expression of children's interests: parents could be given extra votes on account of their children. Parents regularly make all manner of important decisions for their children. That power, founded on powerful psychological attachments, is sanctioned both by longstanding tradition and law.[4] There is no apparent reason why surrogate voting might be thought less justified than the myriad other decisions that parents make as surrogates for their children. Indeed, it is widely assumed that parents cast the single votes they now receive in part in the interests of their children.[5]

There no rush to embrace the idea of extra votes for parents on account of their children; in fact, only a handful of people have even taken note of the idea. Inattention to the extra votes idea, and more generally to the political invisibility of children, presents the second puzzle of American democracy—the solution of which is advanced by a conversational perspective.[6] The puzzle is a deep one, and in this chapter I try to expose its complexity before turning to the conversational solution.

Children and the Apportionment Base

If the electoral status of children was invisible before the Supreme Court's legislative apportionment cases of the 1960s, one might have thought that those decisions would have put the problem in plain sight. The seminal cases, *Wesberry v. Sanders,* and *Reynolds v. Sims,* came in quick succession in the early 1960s. *Wesberry* held that the Constitution requires intrastate districting for the House of Representatives according to population, and *Reynolds* that population-based apportionment is similarly required for *both* houses of state legislatures. The Court found different textual homes for the congressional and state legislative requirements, the former in Article I's provision that "[t]he House of Representatives shall be composed of members chosen . . . by the people of the several States," and the latter in the Equal Protection Clause of the Fourteenth Amendment. In both contexts, however, the requirement was encapsulated by the Court with the slogan "one person, one vote."[7]

The slogan seems to address a problem that never existed and is awkward in a number of other respects. Both before and after the Court interceded, each voter in the typical American, geographically defined, single-member districting system had one vote. The problem the Court was really addressing was interdistrict equity in the distribution of population,[8] but even in addressing that problem, the slogan shrouded ambiguity about parts of the population without the vote. For the slogan does not tell us what population is to be distributed "equally." Is only the voting population to be included in this apportionment base that must be divided equally, or are we to include one category or another of the population that is not eligible to vote?[9] Among residents of any given state, these nonvoters would typically include children as well as felons and both legal and illegal aliens. In various states, the population ineligible to vote might also include categories of ex-felons and the mentally incompetent.[10]

In *Wesberry*, the Court said that "as nearly as is practicable one man's vote in a congressional election is to be worth as much as another's."[11] In isolation, this assertion suggests that those ineligible to vote were not to be included in the apportionment base. But the Court also spoke in the same decision of "the fundamental goal" of "equal representation for equal numbers of people . . . ."[12] And in *Wesberry* and *Reynolds*, the Court used the words *voters, citizens, persons,* and *inhabitants* (*inter alia*) essentially interchangeably to refer to the relevant population.[13]

This was not an ambiguity about an incidental matter. *In toto,* the ineligible population is quite substantial in relation to the eligible population. The children who are the focus in this chapter make up a large fraction of the population themselves; when other groups of ineligibles are included, the population left in apportionment base limbo by *Wesberry* and *Reynolds* could easily exceed 30 percent of the total across the country.[14] To be sure, for any group of nonvoters that is dispersed among states and districts within states in proportion to its numbers in the entire population, the decision to include or exclude need not affect the drawing of district lines.[15] In fact, the "proportion of the census population [ineligible] . . . to vote . . . varies substantially among the States and among localities within the States."[16] The disparities are probably greater for noncitizens, but among states the percentage of the population consisting of children runs from just over 23 percent in Massachusetts to almost 34 percent in Utah. Within states, citizen children are even more heavily concentrated in some legislative districts than in others.[17]

Given this pattern of disproportionate distribution of children and others ineligible to vote, the decision of whether to include them in the apportionment base when "equality" is required becomes important—in the drawing of district lines, and in the consequent alignment of political wherewithal. To illustrate this with a hypothetical example, assume that in a given state there are two equally populated electoral districts—district A and district B—each with fifty thousand people and each entitled to one representative in the state legislature (because the allocation is based on total district population). District A, however, has twenty thousand eligible voters and thirty thousand ineligibles, while district B has forty thousand voters and ten thousand ineligibles. The franchise is then distributed between the *voters* of A and B not equally but with each of A's voters receiving twice the ability of B's voters to influence electoral outcomes. In a two-way race, for instance, with all voters going to the polls, a voter in A need attract only ten thousand additional votes for his or her choice to prevail, while a voter in B requires twenty thousand.[18]

Two years after first insisting on "equality" in apportionment, the Supreme Court explicitly treated the apportionment base question, and it remained puzzlingly indecisive. In *Burns v. Richardson*, Hawaii had apportioned its state legislature using the population of registered voters as its base. In answer to a claim that total population was the only appropriate basis for apportionment, the Court said:

> Neither in *Reynolds v. Sims* nor in any other decision has this Court suggested that the States are required to include aliens, transients, short-term or temporary residents, or persons denied the vote for conviction of crime, in the apportionment base by which their legislators are distributed and against which compliance with the Equal Protection Clause is to be measured. The decision to *include or exclude* any such group involves choices about the nature

of representation with which we have been shown no constitutionally founded reason to interfere.[19]

This passage does not mention children explicitly, but children were not included in Hawaii's apportionment base, and the decision thus clearly suggests that they need not be.

At the same time, the Court has not treated the population distribution question loosely in other respects. For congressional apportionment, it has held that the state must "make a good-faith effort to achieve *precise* mathematical equality."[20] State consideration of other "legitimate" concerns is not entirely precluded, but "absolute population equality" remains the "paramount objective."[21] For state and local legislative apportionment, the Court has provided considerably more leeway in deference to state interests in respecting internal political boundaries and the commonality of electoral concerns that may be associated with those boundaries.[22] But even in that context, the Court scrutinizes deviation from equality to make sure that it is based in "rational" state concerns.[23] Given this general stance, the almost studied avoidance by the Court of questions concerning the inclusion and exclusion of children and other groups in the apportionment base is truly stunning.[24]

It would be a mistake to think that this inattention to the question of the apportionable population was solely a problem of the Supreme Court's making. Equally populated districts (or districts equally populated with voters) have long been an ideal in American democracy, in many cases an ideal written into state constitutions at least for one house in bicameral state legislatures. It was the failure of state legislatures to live up to that ideal that brought the Court into the picture. Because they proved unwilling to confront apportionment problems more generally, there is no reason to think that the states might have confronted questions of how to deal with the anomalous political treatment of children more forthrightly than has the Court.[25]

Despite the leeway afforded by *Burns*, the usual practice in intrastate apportionment has been to use total population. I will return to possible reasons for this practice, but the result is that children *are* usually included in the apportionment base. Such inclusion means that *votes are in effect being cast on their behalf*, or at least on account of them. But those votes are cast by the district voting population as a whole. If the entire ineligible population in the hypothetical districts A and B consisted of children, for instance, the voters in A would wield enhanced voting power as a result of the higher proportion of children in the district. Given the general practice, the puzzle from a vote-centered perspective is deep indeed. In including children in the apportionment base, their vote-centered importance is seemingly affirmed, but they are without the vote-centered mechanism—the vote—for making those interests count.

Why, then, is there no rush to embrace an obvious solution, in vote-centered terms, to the dilemma of the political status of children? Why should the extra voting power on account of children that is usually dispersed among the district population as a whole not be assigned to the parents of those children? Under a vote-centered way of thinking, three steps seem required to establish a case for extra votes for parents on account of their children. First, children must be entitled to political regard. Second, the assignment of votes to parents must be a reasonably effective mechanism for providing the regard that is due. Third, the problems caused by that assignment must not be so great as to argue decisively against the extra votes route.

For present purposes, however, we need not establish anything like an ironclad case for the extra votes idea. The puzzle with which we grapple is the inattention paid to the extra votes idea as a solution to the anomalous political treatment of children. There are a great many popular movements in the United States built on debatable intellectual foundations, even putting UFO sightings to the side. If there is a plausible case to be made for the extra votes idea, that should suffice to frame the puzzle. Before inquiring more closely into the three steps along the way, however, it will be helpful to take a closer look at the point of representation in American democracy.

Representation in American Political Thought

In chapter three I discussed republican and liberal ideals in relation to the franchise. I took note of the intractable question of whether a representative government that aspires to emulate what would be expected from a meeting of the whole would conceive of that meeting in liberal or republican terms. To understand the extra votes possibility, we can now look a bit more closely at the way those republican and liberal ideals have played out in the evolving political reality of American democracy.

Although both liberal and republican visions played prominent, and intermingled, roles in the American political imagination from the start, by most accounts the republican vision was especially influential in our constitutional beginnings. For the most part, the ability to vote was given only to free, white, propertied adult males—a policy that was frequently rationalized on the ground that it was only these men who were thought capable of approaching decisionmaking in good, self-denying republican fashion.[26] Government was representative in form, to be sure, but there was revolutionary fervor with attendant sense of community, and the population of the country was minuscule compared to that of today: at the time of the revolution, the entire population approximated the current population of my hometown of Chicago. Philadelphia was the largest city, reaching a population of about forty thousand by the time it played host to the Constitutional Convention. Virginia was the most populous state, with a total free population of less than three hundred thousand according to Thomas Jefferson's 1782 estimate. Of that three-hundred thousand, fewer than sixty thousand were males twenty-one years or older, and fewer still met the property qualifications for voting.[27] In such a setting, it may well have been possible to imagine that the processes of government, even if representative in form, involved the great bulk of the voting population in an ongoing and active way, and in a spirit of republican self-sacrifice.[28]

But the tensions in a representative republicanism are not easy to contain or hide. They were on display front and center in the disputes between England and the colonies. With the colonists' battle cry of "no taxation without representation," they were objecting not simply to an inability to explain why the particular taxation of which they complained was substantively unfair; the "representation" they craved entailed not only a chance to be heard, but to vote. Their lament assumed the relevance of particular interests, not just that of the whole, that the particular interests of some would often clash with those of others, and that the particular interests of some could not simply be entrusted to the republicanism of some (or even all) of those others.

The great British statesman Edmund Burke appreciated the tension. As a devoted republican, Burke believed that there is in "*one* interest, . . . the general good," but he simultaneously sympathized with the colonists' complaint that they were unrepresented.[29] Burke tried to hold the package together, as republicans had before him, with the notion of "virtual representation": "Virtual representation is that in which there is a communion of interests and a sympathy in feelings and desires between those who act in the name of any description of people and the people in whose name they act, though the trustees are not actually chosen by them."[30]

But what would explain why virtual representation would suffice for some, but not for the colonists? Burke's answer was that virtual representation had to be based in real attachments, which were absent in the case of the "representation" afforded the nonvoting colonists. That move, however, served to highlight that distributed representation served some purpose. The purpose might conceivably be informational. Representative districts might be employed to ensure that useful information from the entire country was available as decisions were taken. But the representatives who did sit in Parliament were allowed to vote, not just speak. This fact made it hard to deny that more than information was being provided, that the representation of separate interests served more fundamental goals, that interests quite often conflict rather than coalesce around some unitary common good. Once representation is employed in the service of potentially antagonistic interests, what individuals other than those whose interests are at stake are to say that some interests can be represented virtually whereas others require actual representation? Given the American experience, the possibility of virtual representation—initially advanced in aid of the republican project—may in this fashion have helped expose its frailty.[31]

We can catch glimpses of both republican and liberal visions—and of some of the tensions between them—in early American thinking about politics and governance. In debates about the length of legislative terms, for instance, shorter terms found their defense in a liberal desire to bind representatives to constituents through the electoral mechanism, whereas longer terms were embraced by republican sentiment as fostering dispassionate and unpressured deliberation about the public interest. In parallel fashion, the direct election of members of the House of Representatives "by the people" would provide liberal responsiveness, while a Senate chosen by the state legislatures would foster republican deliberativeness.[32]

In his classic study of early American political ideology, Gordon Wood captures the confused intermingling of liberal and republican themes in debates about legislative apportionment and extension of the franchise—the matters that, in contemporary guise, bear most directly on the political status of children:

> if men were compelled to think about it some sort of conception of virtual representation was a necessary concomitant of their republican ideology and their Whig belief in the homogeneity of the people's interest. Yet ironically those who were most radically Whiggish, most devotedly republican, were at the same time most committed to the characteristics of the concept of actual representation—equal electoral districts, the particularity of consent through broadened suffrage, residence requirements for both the elected and the electors, the strict accountability of representatives to the local electorate, indeed, the closest possible ties between members and their particular constituents—characteristics that ran directly counter to the central premises of virtual representation and all that they implied about the nature of the body politic.[33]

American electoral politics has undergone great change since these beginnings. The increase in population and the growth and diversification of the economy have been of profound significance. No longer is it possible in most governmental contexts in the United States to think of the entire population, or even of some substantial subset of it, as reasoning together toward solutions to the problems of the whole "community." Our government is representative, in form and in fact. There have been other changes of surpassing importance. Slavery has, of course, been eliminated, and over time the franchise has been gradually but vastly extended to the great bulk of the adult citizenry. The U.S. Senate, originally to be selected by state legislatures, is now chosen by that expanded electorate. So, effectively, is the president. Since these two in combination choose the members of the federal judiciary, even the holders of that "nonpolitical" office are tied more closely to a broadly based popular election process than was the case in the original scheme of things.[34]

The extension of the franchise is usually—and rightly—depicted as affirming the competence and dignity of all individuals in American democracy.[35] But although efforts are made to reconcile the changes with a republican vision, this development is, as Wood suggests, much more comfortably assimilated to a liberal one instead. When virtually all adults take part in decisionmaking, it is difficult to maintain that participation in decisions is in the hands of those identified because of their capacity for republican self-denial. It is simply not credible that a large mass of decisionmakers produces decisions that systematically reach out for the interests of the whole. When virtually all adults count, to put the point somewhat differently, and count for a large sweep of decisions affecting people who are mostly strangers, decisionmaking at the electoral level must increasingly seem to be a matter not of selflessly reasoning together but of doing the counting, of aggregating interests at a minimum conceived much more locally.[36]

Even if a republican throws in the towel on any claim of a self-denying electorate focused on the good of the whole, he or she might cling to a hope that the representatives chosen would be capable of such public spirited deliberation. James Madison held that a representative legislature might "refine and enlarge the public views by passing them through the medium of a chosen body of citizens, whose wisdom may best discern the true interest of their country." But this possibility suggests weak ties between legislators and constituents, whereas the move toward an ever greater sweep for popular elections insinuates a strengthening of those ties.[37]

And strengthened ties between electorate and representatives are what the apportionment decisions seemed to take as ideal. According to the Court in *Reynolds*, "each and every citizen has an inalienable right to full and effective participation in the political processes of his State's legislative bodies," which is to be achieved "through the medium of elected representatives."[38] Again, it might be possible to put a republican gloss on such language. Representatives still might view their task not as responsiveness to constituents but rather as refining and enlarging "the public views." The service of republican reasoning at the legislative level, however, is a most unlikely prop for assigning constitutional importance to equal distribution of the franchise. The Court's reasoning in *Reynolds* conjures up an image of the popular vote as a mechanism by which representatives are tamed by members of the electorate—for why else be so overwhelmingly concerned about the equal measure? Taming representatives in the interests of their constituents, rather than freeing them from what are taken to be the narrow interests of those constituents, is to bend representative government to a liberal rather than a republican form.[39]

This is not to say that republican ideals have been banished from American political discourse. We can cling to ideals no matter how much they have been outrun by what happens on the ground. There is a lively contemporary literature explicitly trumpeting republican themes.[40] And the republican vision leaves room not available in a pure liberal one for the possibility that some part of the population is not admitted to the vote but still entitled to political regard.

The Case for Extra Votes for Parents

Step One: Entitlement to Political Regard

If the ascendant contemporary ideal in American democracy resembles the liberal vision more closely than the republican one, is it possible to conclude that disenfranchised children are entitled to political regard? The answer, I think, is "yes," but only after the liberal theorist acknowledges that no more than republicanism can the liberal ideal sit alone astride American representative government.

As a first step, the liberal should rather easily come to appreciate that there is room in the liberal vision for consideration of the interests of others. We are social beings, defining ourselves and our interests in significant part in terms of relationships with others. Given this root fact of social existence, the interests of those not charged with decisionmaking may enter into the most self-regarding contribution to the liberal calculus. At the same time, the republican may sense that it is not simply some disembodied "public interest" that is caught up in the public decisions to be made, but rather the real, and varying, interests of discrete individuals. In that case, republican self-denial might seem to be an ability to subjugate one's own private interest not so much to a community interest with an integrity all its own, but to the deserving private interests of others. It then begins to seem that the distinction between the two ideals is considerably fuzzier than it initially appeared. The liberal and the republican alike would appreciate that representative decisionmakers necessarily are dealing with the interests of individuals other than themselves and not just of some idealized whole.

The move to representative government reinforces the interpenetration of the two themes. How does the liberal imagine that there can be effective representation of the interests of citizen voters who are mostly absent when the decisions are made? This is a problem not only of the absent citizens but of the present ones. If individuals engaged in liberal self-government are assumed to pursue self-interest, the liberal must worry that representatives would pursue not their constituents' interests but their own—the "agency cost" problem discussed in chapter three. The electoral mechanism is, of course, one part of the answer, but far from a complete one, as we also saw in chapter three. The liberal might come to see that a measure of republican behavior by representatives is essential if there is to be any fuller answer.

In the midst of these invitations to intermingle the two themes, there is the overwhelming fact of regard for children, accompanied by no little rhetoric about their importance. The children we are discussing are citizens, a status strongly suggestive of entitlement to regard.[41] The inclusion in the apportionment base also signals regard. Indeed, the only indication that children are not entitled to regard is their disenfranchisement, but in the case of children (and perhaps the mentally incompetent as well) the liberal assumption that only the individual is in touch with—and through the vote is the only one who can represent—that individual's own interests meets the most severe challenge. There may be considerable doubt about the right cutoff age, but at least the youngest children could not plausibly be allowed to vote, no matter how overwhelming their claim to regard. For these children, there is no real option of enfranchisement, so that if the liberal regime has any give in it at all in this respect, disenfranchisement of at least young children tells us nothing about their entitlement to regard. With republican themes allowed through any crack in the door, it is clear that children are so entitled.[42]

To be sure, inclusion in the apportionment base is a more ambiguous signal than it might at first seem. The base typically includes noncitizens as well as citizen children, including aliens residing illegally in the country, for whom the case for political regard is probably quite tenuous.[43] Moreover, the process of counting population for apportionment purposes is a precarious business for a whole host of reasons. Given the mobility, fertility, and mortality of the population, any count, no matter how precise, is out of date even before it is publicly available; and it rapidly deteriorates from there.[44] Given this basic fact of apportionment life, even the most committed liberal theorist might find it hard to get exercised about counting inaccuracies produced by slippage between the apportionment base and entitlement to regard.

The liberal might also hold back concern about apportionment counts since dependable counting is done for the national census. This comes only once a decade and is focused on counts of total resident population because of its constitutional attachment to interstate apportionment of the House of Representatives—which the Constitution seemingly mandates be based on total population.[45] If some more limited base were thought ideally appropriate for intrastate apportionment purposes, further imprecision could often be expected from an effort to quantify that base.[46]

In the face of the array of apportionment counting problems, in other words, the liberal theorist might become resigned to basing apportionment on total population, even if some or all of the total was not thought to be entitled to political regard. Given these difficulties, the inclusion of ineligibles—children along with the rest—might be seen not as principled but simply as the path of least resistance.

Still, the inclusion of some noncitizens in the apportionment base seems a fragile basis on which to call into question the entitlement to regard of citizens. In any event, once we are working within a liberal framework that acknowledges the impossibility of a complete purge of republican elements, the indications that children are entitled to regard in American politics are all about us, making the claim much more than plausible—all that we require for this step in the identification of the puzzle.

Step Two: Parents as the Repository of Extra Votes

The liberal is then faced with an accounting problem, a mechanism for counting each regarded person as one. That call is answered partially by inclusion of children in the apportionment base, because it assigns voting power on their behalf. From a republican vantage point, the fact that this voting power is assigned to the district voting population as a whole might seem fair enough. In liberal terms, however, surrogate voting on behalf of children by the district population at large would represent fundamental surrender to an extreme republican way of thinking, republican representation without any real concern that it be "virtual." If the point is to see that entitled children receive their regard, the liberal would at least want to entertain the possibility of a more finely tuned way of providing it.

The way to ensure such entitlement is, as we saw at the outset of this chapter, rather straightforward. In terms of liberal accounting, concentrating the extra voting power in parents seems preferable to the present dispersion among parents and nonparents alike in the district voting population. To be sure, parents might not be perfect vehicles for factoring their children's interests into the electoral calculus. But in the vote-centered way of thinking about American democracy, parents would have to be counted as decidedly superior to other possibilities, including the present inattention to the problem.[47]

Here, the contrast with other categories of ineligibles is stark. The problems in providing some form of virtual representation for adult ineligibles vary from one category to another, but for each they are substantial. Who is to say, for instance, what category of voters might have the requisite attachment to incarcerated felons to make it appropriate (in virtual representation terms) to assign extra votes on account of those felons? The usual practice of assigning that voting power to the voting population in the district containing the place of incarceration seems particularly perverse in virtual representation terms. But in the absence of an obvious substitute, the liberal might well write that problem off as relatively minor in attempting to craft a satisfactory system of representation. The only category of adult ineligibles that seems at all comparable to children in the search for surrogate voters is the mentally disabled, for whom there can be appointed guardians. But the number of disenfranchised mentally disabled is minuscule in comparison to children, and the dependability of genuine attachment and empathy by guardians would seem considerably more problematic than we regularly assume for parents and their children.

The Final Step: The Possibility of Overwhelming Problems

No matter how congenial to liberal theory, the extra votes idea might be rejected because of serious problems in implementing it. There certainly would be adjustments required in the electoral system by the extension of extra votes to parents. But the most obvious adjustments seem less than overwhelming. Verification of parenthood (or, presumably, legal guardianship) would be necessary, but registration of children and identification of their parents (or parent substitutes) is done routinely for school and other matters. Dividing the votes between two parents might also be required, but half-votes could do the trick. For divorced or legally separated parents, there is the possibility that one parent would vote in a jurisdiction where the child did not live and hence was not a part of the apportionment base. But that problem would likely pale into insignificance compared with the presently tolerated disjunction between the apportionment base site and voting jurisdiction, for instance with college students and government employees.[48]

A series of "political" problems seems more serious—even apart from resistance to providing some voters with "more" votes than others. There are citizen children of noncitizen parents—indeed even of illegal alien parents.[49] Any suggestion that votes might be cast by that alien population would surely be controversial. Perhaps even more troubling would be the assignment of extra votes to public officials in the case of "wards of the state," children in the custody of public institutions.[50] Once the anomalous treatment of children was on the table, the problems of adult ineligibles included in the apportionment base might then seem more pressing. Still, to the liberal imagination these problems should seem trivial in the face of the potential for substantially more sensitive "liberal" voting for a full quarter of the nation's population.

Here, then, is the normative appeal of extra votes for parents on account of their children. Such a policy would provide meaningful representation for a population the entitlement to regard of which seems broadly taken for granted. It is grounded in the liberal vision and its basic belief that politics is about adding up private interests, although it is republican in its faith that at least part of the accounting can be accomplished by the representation of the interests of some by others. Problems of implementation are not trivial, but neither do they seem overwhelming. In the liberal terms that dominate apportionment jurisprudence, and a great deal else that is said about contemporary American democracy, extra votes for parents on account of their children at least seems to merit serious consideration, if not immediate adoption. But not only has it not caught on, it is still hardly noticed. How could it be that a suggestion with such normative appeal—and one with great potential to change the pattern of public policy decisions—is ignored or, worse, unnoticed? Inattention to the extra votes idea, and indeed the political invisibility of children more generally, has a comfortable conversational explanation.[51]

The Political Status of Children in Conversational Perspective

The conversational incentives of candidates for office are fed by the desire to garner votes, and for this reason, it is enfranchisement and disenfranchisement that has immediate conversational implications. The pattern of inclusion and exclusion in the apportionment base has no obvious conversational importance. The usual practice of dividing up the entire population would seem satisfactory, but so would the exclusion from the base of one or another group of ineligible voters. Indeed, a group of *eligible* voters might be excluded from the apportionment base with no necessary conversational consequences. Something like this already effectively happens when certain eligible voters—such as college students—are counted for census, and thence apportionment purposes not where they vote but on the college campuses where they live.[52]

This is not to say that the apportionment process is conversationally irrelevant. It was apparent when the Supreme Court first held apportionment to be justiciable in *Baker v. Carr* that a large part of the apportionment problem that the Court perceived was the self-interest of legislators in maintaining the status quo. In his concurring opinion about the Tennessee apportionment practices involved in that case, Justice Clark suggested that incumbent protection was a large part of what troubled him:

> I would not consider intervention by this Court into so delicate a field if there were any other relief available to the people of Tennessee. But . . . . [t]he majority of the voters have been caught up in a legislative strait jacket. . . . This is because the legislative policy has riveted the present seats in the Assembly to their respective constituencies, and by the votes of their incumbents a reapportionment of any kind is prevented.[53]

When such a "legislative strait jacket" results in the service of some substantive interests to the exclusion of others, conversational problems may be brewing.

The problem is not interdistrict inequity as such, for voters in districts disfavored in apportionment terms may still have strong conversational relationships with their representatives. But, as noted in chapter four, if the apportionment disadvantage persists over time, it might result in substantive marginalization at the policymaking level that could then feed back to the district level and make conversational relationships ring hollow. In *Reynolds*, the Court referred to the apportionment practices under review as constituting a "rural strangle hold" on legislative policy, suggesting just such chronic marginalization of urban interests.[54] The result could then be popular cynicism and detachment, even if mingled with something of a sense of involvement. If this is a fair way to think about the problem, then the net effect of the Court's intervention may have been to unsettle a conversationally precarious environment.[55]

The cynicism that may follow from substantive marginalization is, however, produced not by rigidity of district lines but by rigidity of political alignments that the lines help translate into legislative decisionmaking. When populations as well as the economy are in motion, stable district lines (as in the case of the U.S. Senate) can *deprive* incumbents of a tool of control. Stable lines, in other words, can unsettle rather than reinforce political alignments. Conversely, where district lines are not fixed, incumbent control of districting remains a potential "conversational" problem even after the apportionment decisions. For even when most stringently applied, the Court's requirement of equality in apportionment leaves plenty of room for incumbent protection and partisan gerrymandering. The Court's apportionment jurisprudence may actually help camouflage the continuing prevalence of partisan gerrymandering and the consequent chronic favoritism of some interests to the exclusion of others. For the Congress, however, that is more of a problem in the case of the House, where district lines can be moved, than of the Senate, where they cannot.[56]

A conversational perspective readily accommodates the disenfranchisement of children and also provides a basis for understanding why the idea of extra votes for parents on account of their children does not excite attention. The reckoning of the conversational effects on children of their disenfranchisement is a bit complicated because of the spectrum of ages involved. Very young children are preoccupied with more immediate gratifications and uninterested in receiving communication about matters of public policy. As children mature and crave communication about matters in the public realm, they are likely to find it available and adaptable to their interests and needs, even as they remain without the vote. The vote is in prospect for older children, so that candidates have a measure of incentive to communicate with them even before they become eligible to vote. And children seem likely to be drawn to public conversation initially as a part of learning about public affairs, a first step on the road to a sense of fuller involvement. For these initial purposes, children may find a good measure of satisfaction from the public conversation about them, even if it is not particularly targeted their way.

To be sure, some older children may come to feel conversationally neglected, as politicians continue to talk mostly to their parents. The

Twenty-Sixth Amendment to the Constitution now guarantees the right to vote to those eighteen and older.[57] This may miss disaffection among those seventeen and younger, but in the final analysis there is no practical way to accord the vote only to those who could be made to feel more involved by democratic conversation. Some cutoff age for eligibility to vote seems inevitable, and that will always leave the possibility of disaffection by a precocious few who are below the cutoff.

Potentially disaffected parents are far more numerous, but the conversational perspective suggests why the idea of extra votes for them excites no particular interest. The one vote that adult parents each receive as citizens provides officials and candidates—as well as media of communication—with ample incentive to engage parents conversationally. Extra votes would do no obvious harm in this respect, but neither would extra votes appreciably heighten the candidate incentive, as long as parents of underage children represent—as they do—a substantial portion of the electorate. Because they are interested in the welfare of their children in addition to themselves, parents might already be thought to have more incentive to vote than others, and more incentive to pay attention to things when candidates speak their language. If candidates respond to such a perception, this response only heightens their interest in communicating with parents, even with no extra votes in the picture. In addition, parents are dispersed broadly among legislative districts. There is thus no problem of chronic disdain for the interests of parents (including their interest in their children) that might feed back into conversational frustration.[58]

I do not want to exaggerate the point. Extra votes would provide some incremental incentive to candidates to talk parent talk. We certainly observe differential attention by candidates to well-organized groups and to those that vote either in larger numbers or more reliably. But that incremental incentive is likely to be modest when parents already represent a large portion of the voting population. The conversational perspective thus comfortably accounts for the inattention to the extra votes idea that seems so puzzling from a vote-centered perspective.

Judicial Review and the Sense of Difficulty

The United States Constitution might have been treated as advisory, or even as binding but not judicially enforceable. In the latter case, for instance, legislators would generally recognize an obligation to follow constitutional dictates, but the only sanction for failing to do so would be political. In cases of doubt about the meaning of a constitutional provision, interpretation would then be up to legislators or other affected officials and not the judiciary. The Constitution, however, declares itself "law," indeed part of the "supreme law of the land." Relying in part on this declaration, the Supreme Court held in 1803 in the great case of *Marbury v. Madison* that the Constitution must be treated by the courts as enforceable by them in an adjudication where its strictures are applicable.[1]

In the intervening years, this holding has become a staple of American governance, and federal courts now more than occasionally hold "unconstitutional" some statute or practice at the state or federal level. On occasion, a party injured by operation of such a statute or practice may even have an affirmative cause of action for redress of the injury. State courts assert a similar authority, not only in vindication of the federal constitution but also in clashes between state constitutions and state statutes or the actions of state officials. At the level of the state or federal judiciary, the practice of giving legal effect to constitutional provisions in this way is typically referred to as "judicial review."

Once a peculiarly American phenomenon, judicial review has been embraced by numerous democracies around the world (albeit with important variations from the American pattern). As judicial review has become a commonplace over the years in the United States and elsewhere, there has been no gainsaying that the exercise of discretion is involved, that judicial review entails judicial "policymaking." There is no metric by which the policymaking impact of judicial review in the United States can be compared with that of the Senate or of the political impotence of children (to invoke the subjects of the last two chapters). But there is little doubt that the practice is an important policymaking element in the American system of governance. Despite widespread acceptance, however, judicial review has been the subject of repeated pangs of doubt in the land that gave birth to it. As its policymaking implications have become clear, persistent questions have been posed about the compatibility of judicial review with the precepts of democracy.

The contemporary framework for discussing the democratic *bona fides* of judicial review can be traced to Alexander Bickel's 1962 book, *The Least Dangerous Branch.* Bickel there claimed that judicial review is "a deviant institution in the American democracy," creating what he called a "counter-majoritarian difficulty." As Bickel elaborated the difficulty:

> when the Supreme Court declares unconstitutional a legislative act or the action of an elected executive, it thwarts the will of representatives of the actual people of the here and now; it exercises control, not in behalf of the prevailing majority, but against it. . . . [This] is the reason the charge can be made that judicial review is undemocratic.[2]

Although Bickel was neither the first to express concern about judicial review nor the first to associate that concern with the non-democratic nature of the courts, it is Bickel's talk of a "countermajoritarian difficulty" that has stuck. The unease about judicial review, and the readiness to discuss it in terms of majoritarianism and its "counter," are now widespread, particularly among lawyers and legal scholars. Whereas some of the scholarship is critical of Bickel's terminology, there is also an extraordinary quantity of work that continues to grapple with a democratic "difficulty" defined by a standard of majoritarianism.[3]

It is this ongoing "countermajoritarian" commentary that poses our third puzzle. As we saw in chapter three, American democracy cannot sensibly be described as majoritarian. If the courts' constitutional decisionmaking presents a difficulty for American democracy for no reason other than their "countermajoritarianism," then we must wonder why a great deal about the rest of the system is not difficult as well. The question of whether or not judicial review presents a "difficulty" in a democratic society—and in the United States in particular—involves a large normative inquiry that would take us far beyond the explanatory power of the conversational approach. Our puzzle is not some difficulty with judicial review as such but rather the persistence of unease with the practice—the felt tension with democracy—in the face of the impoverishment of the terms in which that tension is usually discussed. The first two puzzles we discussed were products of the failure to take seriously the implications of the majoritarian dogma. This third puzzle is produced by a large number of sophisticated commentators—largely, though not exclusively, law professors and lawyers—taking it all too seriously.

The Difficulty as Counterconversational

The courts' classical self-conception is as resolvers of disputes between identifiable parties. The disputes are to be resolved according to "law." The sources of that "law" are complex (and in many ways controversial), but there is little doubt that some of the law's content may be formulated by the deciding judges in the very decisions where it is initially to be applied. This is so, even when the ostensible basis for decision is a statute or constitutional provision, for even in those contexts many questions arise for which the bare words of the governing instrument provide no single clear answer. The courts in this sense "make" law as an integral part of the adjudicatory process. This judge-made law involves the discretion in policy choices already mentioned.[4]

In constitutional and nonconstitutional contexts alike, it is often said that a minimum condition for such judicial policymaking is that the law it helps form be "principled." According to a well-known formulation of what it means for judge-made law to be "principled," judicial decisions must rest

> with respect to every step that is involved in reaching judgment on analysis and reasons quite transcending the immediate result that is achieved. . . . [There must be] grounds of adequate neutrality and generality, tested not only by the instant application but by others that the principles imply.[5]

The appeal of this requirement of "principle" is clear. It tends to ensure an evenhandedness in what the courts do in the name of the law as well as a degree of predictability for the future. But the emphasis on neutrality, and particularly on generality, means that judicial "lawmaking" may have broad societal reach, just as does legislative (and administrative) lawmaking.

At the same time, the conversational behavior of the courts is very different from that found in these other contexts. Although it is typically mediated by lawyers and couched in the language of the law, judicial conversational attention is importantly focused on the parties to the dispute to be resolved. Through the filing of briefs and the presentation of oral argument, each party will have an extensive opportunity to advance (and receive) views about matters of interest in play when a case is before a court. This arrangement is in contrast to the essentially passive conversational role of most interested people when legislative and executive officials are making the decisions. Although deep in this way, in democratic terms this party-focused conversation is also extremely narrow. In the court context, there is no decision-making competitor vying for attention and, more generally, nothing comparable to the behavior of executive and legislative officials in figuring out what might be of interest to those more broadly affected by decisions, and then in taking the initiative to talk to them. The constrained conversationalism of the courts is a product not simply of malleable custom but of deeply ingrained professional norms borne of that dispute-resolving self-conception and backed up by disciplinary procedures to which judges may be subjected.[6]

Nonparties are not excluded entirely from court conversationalism. Formal submission of argumentation by a nonparty as *amicus curiae,* friend of the court, was once quite rare, and the receptivity of the courts to such presentations has waxed and waned over the years. As the importance of court decisions for nonparties has become increasingly difficult to deny, however, the last half century has seen a steady and dramatic increase in *amicus* submissions, and the contemporary practice in the U.S. Supreme Court is freely to allow them. Although once received only as "neutral" aids to the court, moreover, *amicus* submissions are now welcomed in the Supreme Court even when they provide open advocacy of one position or another. There has also been a marked increase in citation or discussion of *amicus* presentations in the opinions of the Supreme Court. By the decade ending in 1995, one or another opinion in Supreme Court cases where any *amicus* briefs were filed contained reference to at least one such brief more than 35 percent of the time.[7]

Not only do the courts hear from nonparties through *amicus* submissions, they also *speak* to many more nonparties through publication of court opinions (and through secondary writing about those opinions in professional and popular journalism). These are not just opinions for the entire court but rather concurring and dissenting opinions as well, which I occasionally lump together as "dissonant" opinions. Like *amicus* participation, the routine practice of dissonant opinion writing is a fairly recent phenomenon. John Marshall was the great Chief Justice who authored *Marbury v. Madison,* among other important early decisions. *Marbury* was a unanimous decision, and on Marshall's Supreme Court, dissenting or even concurring opinions were the rare exception. Over the years, the practice has changed, and dissonant opinion writing is now routine. Indeed, the dissenting judge is frequently lionized in popular and professional commentary about the law.[8]

No doubt these bits of conversational outreach occasionally provide affected nonparties with something of a sense of involvement in the system of judicial decisionmaking. An *amicus* brief is likely to have been submitted by nonparties with a good deal at stake, and, as mentioned, it stands a decent chance these days of explicit notice in a court opinion.[9] Still, an *amicus* must take the initiative, the cost of filing a brief is significant, and not all courts are as receptive to *amicus* filings as is the Supreme Court.[10] For these reasons, the *amicus* submission does not usually provide anything like the breadth of conversational interactions on particular issues—even with seriously affected people—that is found in the world of democratic politics.

The sense of involvement fostered by the publication of opinions is a good deal broader. The costs of obtaining court opinions, or commentary about them, is sufficiently modest that popular conversational participation of this sort is much more accessible than is participation as *amicus*. Particularly at the Supreme Court level, moreover, opinions often provide more extensive discussion of the issues than is typically found in the political realm. Such discussion may make for engaging reading (and something of a consequent sense of involvement) for those sufficiently interested to absorb judicial opinions. But opinions are not typically crafted with broad-based consumption in mind. And even the secondary commentary on court decisions is not likely to be nearly as vigorous or extensive as coverage of issues in the political realm, precisely because it is not fed by the incentive structure of ordinary elective politics.[11]

Court opinions, moreover, are published only after a decision is made. I will return to the possibility that a judicial decision will be overruled by the same court that initially decided it. Given this possibility, disappointment of some nonparties may be softened by a dissonant opinion (and again, secondary commentary) that holds out hope for a judicial change of heart in the future.[12] Even for those who do not entertain the possibility of later change in a judicial stance, however, there may be satisfaction in knowing that a dissonant view is being voiced. Like the receptivity to *amicus* submissions, the robust contemporary tradition of dissonant opinions may thus be an important conversational phenomenon, and we will return to this possibility in chapter nine.[13] Still, the timing difference is likely to dampen severely the sense of involvement. An affected person wakes up one day to find that a court has touched his or her life with an apparently final and authoritative pronouncement of which he or she had no forewarning. Surprise can also attend legislative or administrative action, of course, but the conversational incentives in those contexts make it much more likely that an affected person would have heard something beforehand and would consequently be more likely to accept the decision as a product of a decisionmaking process in which he or she felt involved. In an adaptation of Bickel's phrase, we might for this reason call the courts "counterconversational" in contrast to the political branches of government.[14]

Unlike the asserted countermajoritarianism, judicial counterconversationalism characterizes a real difference between court processes and those found in the political realm. If I have been at all persuasive in earlier chapters that conversation does breed a sense of involvement in democratic life, then judicial counterconversationalism is a much more plausible candidate than countermajoritarianism for explaining the observable angst about the democratic *bona fides* of judicial review. And if the counterconversational account of that angst rings true, that in turn bolsters the conversational account of what holds American democracy together. In contrast to the subjects of the last two chapters, the puzzle of the countermajoritarian commentary is about things that are said rather than left unsaid. The conversational perspective is further fortified by its capacity to account not only for the felt sense of difficulty but also for a great deal of the pattern of what is said and left unsaid in this puzzling discourse about difficulty.

Silences in the Discourse of Difficulty: The Constitution and Judicial Review

Some commentators view democratic legislative decisionmaking and the constraints of a written constitution as complementary, or at least as in "need [of] each other."[15] Even those commentators, however, do not deny the tension between the two.[16] This tension is at least as great as that between legislative processes and *judicial decision* in the name of the Constitution. For whereas a judicial stance can be influenced in subtle ways by a variety of pressures that elected officials can deploy—a subject to which I return—the constitutional text can be changed only by amendment. Amendment requires the concurrence of two-thirds of each house of Congress and three-fourths of the states, a dramatically "countermajoritarian" process, by virtually any standard.[17] Yet, for all the tension between the Constitution and decisionmaking by elected officials, we encounter little discussion of that tension in the countermajoritarian literature. Far from seeming "difficult," the Constitution is mostly an object of veneration—America's "civil religion."[18] How can it be that judicial review is a practice arousing persistent concern because of its supposed countermajoritarianism, while we hear none of that concern about a countermajoritarian Constitution?

A conversational perspective can help us make sense of the contrast. Initially the Constitution might seem to share the counterconversationalism of judicial review. The Constitution itself obviously does not reach out to generate democratic conversation about its often momentous provisions. Nor do politicians often seem moved to discuss issues posed by the constitutional text. The shared conversational reticence of judicial review and the constitutional text might be ascribed to the formalities of amendment, which, after all, present an obstacle to change in each situation. But despite that formal similarity, the nature of the issues in the two contexts, and the ways in which those issues arise, can be expected to generate very different attitudes about the conversational prospects. For ease of presentation, I concentrate on the federal Constitution, but many of the points of contrast apply in the state constitutional context as well.

First, there is only a handful of constitutional provisions that, prior to judicial interpretation, hold much potential for controversy. Many are stated at an uncontroversially high level of abstraction and track broadly shared societal values or, even though in some sense arbitrary, are easily accepted as necessary for the effective functioning of the system. Who can object, for instance, to an insistence on "equal protection of the laws"? And what would be the point of quarreling with a four-year term for the president, even for someone who thinks that five would have been a better idea?[19] Other provisions, although perhaps questionable by the light of abstract theory, typically fail to attract conversational attention unless and until they impinge with some immediacy on people's lives. (I return to some examples later in the chapter.)

In sharp contrast, judicial decisions of unconstitutionality are controversial almost by definition. When a statute is held unconstitutional, it is usually a recent one, in which case there would at a minimum have been a recent legislative "majority"—and whatever popular sentiment was behind that majority—in favor of the position that was rejected. The litigant opposing the statute would have felt sufficiently strongly about his or her position to have expended substantial time and resources on the litigation. That one litigant felt so strongly on the issue often suggests that a variety of others feel strongly as well, just offstage. In the contemporary United States, these judicial decisions keep coming. At present, for instance, the U.S. Supreme Court is working out a new jurisprudence of federalism. In pursuit of this new approach, the Court has held congressional statutes to be unconstitutional that responded, *inter alia*, to perceived problems with firearms, with religious freedom, and with discrimination against the disabled. The prospects are for many more similarly controversial decisions before the development of this one chapter of contemporary judicial review will have spent its force.[20]

In addition, judicial review produces policy determinations with an abruptness that is seldom worked by the constitutional text. For this reason, judicial review is more likely to impinge meaningfully on the lives even of nonparties. In 1995, for instance, the Supreme Court held state-dictated term limits for the House and Senate unconstitutional.[21] Although this did not deprive anyone of a material benefit, it did overturn the results of recent political battles in which many people's energies—including conversational energies—had been engaged. In contrast, most constitutional provisions, even those few with seeming potential for arousing resentment, have been on the books for a long time and have settled comfortably into the background reality of American life. I suggested in chapter five that there is a possible conversational explanation for satisfaction with the Senate; however, each state has been entitled to two senators for our entire constitutional history, so it is also the case that the apportionment rule upsets nothing about people's accustomed ways of doing things.

This contrast can perhaps be brought home by considering the constitutional requirement that the president be a "natural born citizen." There are many foreign-born American citizens who surely have cause to quarrel with that provision. Were the requirement to be imposed by judicial decision today, foreign-born citizens would no doubt be outraged. But the provision works no present change, and likely for that reason seems to be either unnoticed or simply accepted as part of American political life.[22]

Thus, while the amendment possibility provides something of a common conversational environment for those potentially dissatisfied either with a constitutional provision or with a judicial determination of unconstitutionality, the two environments are in other respects very different. The only constitutional provisions likely to affect people with an immediacy similar to judicial review are recent amendments. The prohibition amendment, for instance, wreaked societal havoc in the years following adoption. At the federal level at least, constitutional amendments are exceedingly rare, and when they are made, they have typically been preceded by extensive and broad-based conversation, probably even more than accompanies ordinary legislation.

More longstanding constitutional provisions only rarely become controversial, although that can certainly happen. I should not be surprised, for instance, if the presidential qualification mentioned earlier attracts attention one day. But longstanding provisions have not been thrown up by a conversationally exclusionary process. In their day, they will likely have attracted quite robust democratic conversation.[23] This fact may be little solace to today's citizens who took no part in that conversation. But no constitutional provision will have been produced through counterconversationalism akin to that of judicial review. Only judicial review poses and often resolves contemporary policy issues through processes that decisively draw a conversational distinction between the welcome few of those affected and the unwelcome many.

Silences in the Discourse of Difficulty: Statutory Interpretation and Judicial Review

Democratic difficulty is regularly said to be a feature of judicial review, but it is hardly mentioned for judicial decisions on matters of statutory interpretation. The contrast is not entirely unnoticed, but

once noticed it seems to go down easily with a minimum of ratio-
nalization. Bickel's explanation is typical: "[U]nlike constitutional
doctrines," he insists, "[statutory] construction leave[s] . . . other institutions, particularly the legislature, free—and generally invite[s]
them—to make or remake their own decisions. . . ." In statutory
cases, there has, again in Bickel's words, been no checking of the "will
of other institutions of government by means of a judge-made rule."[24]

On its own terms, this dismissal of "difficulty" in the case of statutory interpretation moves a good deal too fast. Statutory decisions create a burden of overcoming legislative inertia. The inertia is not
nearly as great in the statutory context as it is for constitutional decisions. Putting aside the possibility of a judicial change of heart, a
statutory decision is much more easily supplanted by a new statute
than is a constitutional decision by amendment. But legislative inertia is far from trivial. The courts generally indulge in a "super-strong
presumption of [the] correctness" of their own prior statutory decisions. Those presumptively correct decisions then bump up against
impediments to change, many of which we examined in chapter
three. The net effect is a substantial systemwide *de facto* favoritism
of the court-defined statutory interpretive *status quo.*[25]

In this way, judicial construction of a statute often determines the
real-world effects of that statute for a long time. If institutions can
have "will," then, Bickel to the contrary notwithstanding, both statutory decisions and constitutional ones may check the "will" of the
system, while neither type of decision checkmates that will. If the
courts were really taken to be democratically "deviant" because they
are countermajoritarian when constitutional decisions are in issue, it
seems a bit strange that we encounter virtually no concern about a
"countermajoritarian difficulty" in statutory decisions. It will not do
to say that the judicial interpretation of statutes is so central a part of
the judicial function that there could be no sustained controversy
about it. Just such a justification is advanced in favor of judicial review, but in that context the doubts have not been quelled.

This seeming anomaly is largely dissipated by a shift to a conversational perspective. Whereas statutory cases are fully as party-focused as constitutional ones, in the statutory context the courts have
purported to act in the name of the legislature, and unhesitatingly
concede that the matter may, indeed should, be pursued further in

that forum. As a consequence, there is little *conversational* inertia in the system for what all acknowledge is core legislative business.[26] The ability to talk to a legislator is surely not a perfect substitute for speaking one's mind to the body that initially decided. But legislators and executive officials are usually available to discuss what might be done, and they may even come calling.

This dynamic is all in marked contrast to constitutional decisions. In the next section I turn to several features of constitutional adjudication that may breed conversational frustration. Even focusing on the formalities of constitutional amendment, however, the process requires the concurrence of multiple bodies at the state and federal levels. Amendment was intentionally made difficult, and it should not be surprising if legislators and constituents—and countermajoritarian commentators—sense that in comparison to statutory decisions, constitutional decisions are considerably less inviting of further conversation and of the sense of involvement that conversation may bring.[27]

Sounds in the Discourse of Difficulty: The Turn to Interpretation

Some of the commentators who worked within the majoritarian frame of reference found no "difficulty," basically because they thought that the courts' countermajoritarianism was a good thing, preserving individual prerogatives that might otherwise be smothered in a world of unconstrained majoritarianism.[28] Of those who struggled with the difficulty, it is useful to distinguish two strands of commentary, for a conversational perspective can make some sense of each in a way that a majoritarian perspective cannot.

One strand turns inward on the courts, exploring approaches to constitutional interpretation that would hem in the courts and thus confine the difficulty. That was Bickel's own tack. In *The Least Dangerous Branch*, Bickel argued that the courts' countermajoritarianism could be salutary, on two conditions. First, constitutional interpretation must be "principled," seemingly more or less in the sense discussed earlier. We are, Bickel assured us, "a nation committed to the rule of principle as well as to majoritarian democracy." He taught that judicial review was of value because the courts are "an institution which stands altogether aside from the current [democratic] clash of interests, and which, insofar as is humanly possible, is concerned only with principle." Second, even when judicial review is principled, according to Bickel it must be used sparingly in undoing what majoritarian processes have done, for a democracy made consistently to hark to "principle" might not be able to stand it. "[N]o viable society," he warned, "can be principle-ridden."[29]

Others who took this inward turn found the notion of "principle" quite unconstraining and for that reason incapable of taming the difficulty. Writing in 1980, John Ely attempted to yoke constitutional interpretation closely to a majoritarian ideal. He argued that, for the most part, the courts act appropriately in the name of the Constitution only when they shore up the processes of majoritarian democracy. For Ely, the Supreme Court's constitutionalization of abortion rights, for instance, was misguided, whereas the apportionment decisions that we discussed in chapter six were largely exemplary exercises of the power of judicial review, precisely because by Ely's calculus they furthered majoritarianism.[30]

Still more wary of the practice of judicial review have been constitutional "originalists." Prominent among them is Robert Bork, who tells us that we live with a "'Madisonian dilemma' [with] two opposing principles that must be continually reconciled." The first is that "in wide areas of life majorities are entitled to rule . . . simply because they are majorities." The second is that there are "areas of life in which the individual must be free of majority rule." The reconciliation is worked by the Constitution—by it alone, and properly understood. For Bork, appropriate constitutional interpretation does not mean according to "principle" (as for Bickel) or reinforcing majoritarianism (as for Ely), but rather "adherence to the Constitution's original meaning."[31]

No doubt each of these commentators, and others who took the turn to interpretation, were reaching for a sensible route to constitutional meaning. But it is striking how much of the effort seems to emerge from the felt sense of difficulty. John Ely, of course, explicitly tried to fashion interpretation as a direct answer to a difficulty taken to be countermajoritarian. Bickel and Bork retreated instead to fallback commitments—to principled interpretation in Bickel's case, to originalist interpretation in Bork's—but in each case the fallback seems an almost apologetic response to the specter of difficulty conceived in majoritarian terms. None of the three seemed terribly sensitive to the irony in responding in this way to the call of "majoritarianism" in implementing a decidedly countermajoritarian Constitution. And none seemed to appreciate that the rest of American democracy makes it quite awkward to talk of court processes as somehow peculiarly problematic because "countermajoritarian."[32]

Although those who took the turn to interpretation were not explicitly thinking in conversational terms, their fevered activity can be seen in some measure as a response to the courts' counterconversationalism. We have just seen that, far from arousing a sense of "difficulty," the Constitution is in general an object of veneration in American politics. If the difficulty is conceived in conversational terms, and as a feature of judicial review and not of the Constitution, then the turn to interpretation might be understood as an attempt to provide judicial review with the Constitution's conversational cover. If constitutional interpretation were done right, judicial review might achieve the conversational repose into which the document itself seems comfortably to have settled.[33]

Assimilating interpretation to the Constitution itself—and using the connection to insinuate that the need for conversation is thereby ended—has a distinguished pedigree. John Marshall is often associated with the necessity for a flexible Constitution, and thereby with a world of discretionary judicial choices in the name of judicial review. The desirability of an expansive approach to interpretation is taken to be the significance of his warning in *McCulloch v. Maryland* that "we must never forget, that it is a constitution we are expounding." But Marshall presented a very different face in initially arguing for judicial review in *Marbury,* conjuring up instead a conception of law that eliminated the difference between the Constitution and what the courts might do in its name.[34] He invoked several examples of constitutional questions that were more than straightforward. They were constitutional violations *by definition,* by virtue of reasonably precise constitutional language and stipulated fact.

The Constitution declares that "no tax or duty shall be laid on articles exported from any state." "Suppose," Marshall asked, "a [statutory] duty on the export of cotton, of tobacco, or of flour; and a suit instituted to recover it. . . . Ought the judges to close their eyes on the constitution, and only see the . . . [statute]?" Or, he asked, what of the Constitution's prohibition of legislative punishment known as a "bill of attainder"? "If . . . such a bill should be passed, and a person should be prosecuted under it," Marshall inquired, "must the court condemn to death those victims whom the constitution endeavors to preserve?" Finally Marshall invoked the Constitution's requirement that "[n]o person . . . shall be convicted of treason unless on the testimony of two witnesses . . . or on confession in open court." Could it be, he said, that in the case of legislation holding that one witness would suffice, "the constitutional principle [must] yield to the legislative"? Marshall's clear suggestion was that the constitutional questions courts would decide were nothing more than what the Constitution had already decided.[35]

If constitutional interpretation could be consistently fashioned in this image, we would see little if any judicial review. Litigation might be pursued to resolve factual disputes and, with that opening, for delay or other reasons of strategy. But once the facts were determined and the legal issues joined, constitutional questions would answer themselves. No party would have much to gain by insisting on any answer but the obvious one. There would then be limited incentive to seek judicial review in the first place, and hence few occasions for those exclusionary official proceedings that characterize the practice. The counterconversational difficulty would be brought to heel.

To be sure, the effort is doomed to failure. This is not simply because there has been no rally around a single interpretational approach. Even within each of the various approaches, there is little conversational repose to be found. When the constitutional text is not "plain" as applied to a question that arises, no approach to interpretation is likely to replicate the certainty of Marshall's examples, and hence do away with the need for conversation. The American adjudicatory system is an adversary one, in which each party has an incentive to marshal the information and argumentation that will put its case in the best light. It is designed to bring out countervailing considerations, and the turn to interpretation cannot do much to tame the tendency to do so.[36]

The commentators surely appreciated that they had no full solution to a difficulty with judicial review reconceived in conversational terms. Bickel, for instance, knew that the "principles" he insisted on were not self-defining, to say nothing of their sensitive deployment. Nor do the "representation-reinforcing" guidelines of Ely's approach provide any route to certain answers. All the ambiguities and uncertainties discussed in chapter three's criticisms of the vote-centered model would beset interpretation tied to a representation entitled to be reinforced. Resolution would then require searching discussion. The only approach to interpretation containing anything approaching explicit claim that constitutional questions can be made to answer themselves is constitutional originalism.[37] In the appendix, I explain why even originalism is no more up to the task. But the turn to interpretation might still have derived much of its inspiration from the felt, even if unarticulated, possibility that it might contain, even if it could not fully eliminate, the counterconversationalism of judicial review.

Sounds in the Discourse of Difficulty: Placing the Courts in a Democratic Context

Alexander Bickel was not oblivious to some of the criticisms of the vote-centered model examined in chapter three. He acknowledged that the characterization of American democracy as "majoritarian" might initially seem to imply too much:

> no democracy operates by taking continuous nose counts on the broad range of daily governmental activities. . . . [E]lected officials . . . are expected to delegate some of their tasks to men of their own appointment, who are not directly accountable at the polls. The whole operates under public scrutiny and criticism—but not at all times or in all parts. What we mean by democracy, therefore, is much more sophisticated and complex than the making of decisions in town meeting by a show of hands. . . . [M]yriad decisions

remain to govern the present and the future despite what may well be fluctuating majorities against them at any given time.

Despite the complications, however, Bickel concluded that the impediments to realization of the majoritarian norm were relatively minor. Although the legislature and the executive represent different constituencies, Bickel assured us that this "tends to cure inequities of over- and underrepresentation." In the final analysis, groups can be effective politically, he urged, only by "combining in some fashion . . . [and] constituting a majority."[38]

These passages evince a willingness to look at one part of the system to find compensation for majoritarian deficiencies elsewhere. In similar fashion, as we saw earlier, Bickel and others fixated with the countermajoritarianism of the courts found no difficulty with court decisions in statutory cases, because other agencies could step in to undo what the courts had done. One striking thing about *The Least Dangerous Branch* is the absence of any sustained attention to the parallel possibility that judicial review might not present much difficulty at all if other parts of the system could bring the countermajoritarian tiger under majoritarian control.

A second strand of the majoritarian commentary did take up this possibility. Perhaps the leader in this tradition has been the venerable political theorist Robert Dahl. Dahl's thesis holds that because of the many political checks on the judiciary, "the views of a majority of the justices of the Supreme Court are never out of line for very long with the views prevailing among the lawmaking majorities of the country."[39] Dahl first sounded this theme in 1957, even before *The Least Dangerous Branch* appeared, and he and others have returned to it repeatedly since.[40] The most notable recent example is a provocative thesis advanced by Bruce Ackerman. Ackerman argues that the courts are able to make far-reaching changes in constitutional understandings only when they have a "mobilized majority" of the American people behind them. In between these "constitutional moments" an "ordinary" form of politics prevails, and the courts must be content with the mundane business of consolidating the "momentous" changes and integrating them with what has gone before. Ackerman calls his a "dualist" theory of American constitutionalism.[41]

Those like Dahl and Ackerman who write in this vein emerge relatively unconcerned about difficulty, because they see majoritarian parts of the system as deflecting or compensating for the counter-majoritarianism of judicial review. Ackerman says that he has "dissolve[d]" the difficulty.[42] There is surely a good deal of bravado in any such claim, even assuming that the rest of the system might sensibly be characterized as "majoritarian." Dahl's estimate of not "very long" for the courts to come around to approval of what the legislatures might wish could, as we have seen, turn into a good stretch of time. And even Ackerman's ingenious analysis seems to acknowledge that countermajoritarianism is a feature of judicial review when only "ordinary politics" are at work. In any event, other commentators have not been won over. Again, a conversational perspective can help explain both the appeal and the limitation of this strand of commentary.

We saw earlier that the amendment procedure opens up limited conversational possibilities. But amendment is not the only recourse for those upset with a judicial decision of unconstitutionality. Most obvious is the possibility of continuing the battle in court. Just as constitutional language gives rise to multiple questions of what it means as legislative, social and economic developments pose fresh questions, so what is said in judicial decision must itself be interpreted when questions arise of its implications for some new problem. More generally, although *stare decisis*—the judicial doctrine of adherence to an earlier decision—is not an inviolable rule for courts in any sorts of decisions, it is typically thought to have least force for a holding that a statute or practice is unconstitutional.[43] For these reasons, disappointed nonparties can envisage future judicial proceedings in which strangers to the original proceeding might be welcome. In and of themselves, these proceedings entail only constrained conversation. But they form the backdrop against which more freewheeling conversation becomes possible.

There are, for instance, formal levers of political influence over the judiciary, such as legislative control over judicial budgets, court jurisdiction, and even the number of judges and justices.[44] Attempts to employ these powers because of dissatisfaction with court decisions can become occasions and stimulus for involving conversation. However, two other possibilities are probably of greater contemporary significance. One is executive and legislative power over judicial appointments. A court decision may be overruled or changed more subtly by the same judges who decided it initially, but some such adjustment is much more likely to come from a different mix of decisionmakers.[45] The executive power of nomination and the legislative power of confirmation of new judges thus provide powerful levers over that route to change. In recent times, this executive power has led to discussion of whether it is appropriate to employ "litmus tests" for judicial appointees.[46] Nominees may be impeded by professional norms in what they can discuss, but senators and other politicians are not.[47] In contrast to legislative elections, federal judges are appointed only one at a time. For purposes of assessing conversational possibilities, however, Senate confirmation hearings for at least each of the highly visible Supreme Court appointments can, through the involvement of senators and other elected officials, open the way to varied political conversation about questions that are subject to judicial review.[48]

Second, and often of even greater conversational import, is the possibility of chipping away at a disfavored decision by the passage of legislation violating the spirit, and sometimes even the letter, of the decision. Such chipping away can nudge courts toward reconsideration. Even short of that, the sobering reality is that legislative and executive branches have substantial ability to thwart implementation of a constitutional decision. Political reaction to the Supreme Court's abortion decision in *Roe v. Wade* provides an extreme but instructive example of chipping away, all the way up to flirting with disobedience. According to one commentator, there were more than three hundred state anti-abortion laws enacted in the sixteen years after *Roe*. More than five hundred pieces of legislation dealing with abortion were introduced in Congress in the decade after the decision. Each of these provided a focused occasion for democratic conversation about abortion.[49]

These occasions for democratic conversation are not confined in separate packages. For almost forty years, for instance, the Supreme Court used its power of judicial review to stifle congressional attempts to keep the products of child labor out of interstate commerce. The saga eventuating in approval of such legislation saw various attempts at legislative end-runs around adverse court decisions, attempts at constitutional amendment, and the influence of the appointment power—all accompanied by active discussion in the popular press (and no doubt on the political hustings as well).[50]

Viewing the courts in their larger democratic context thus brings into view an array of conversational possibilities in the wake of judicial review. But as we saw in the contrast between the Constitution and judicial review, the counterconversationalism of judicial review works to dampen conversational enthusiasm. In addition, the courts claim that they have the final say in constitutional interpretation, short of the amendment possibility.[51] Although this judicial claim is decidedly controversial,[52] the stance does mean that attempts to do something about a constitutional decision short of amendment must contend with a Court that says no such thing is permitted, and with the bleak reality that the chance of even chipping away at a decision remains a remote and time-consuming possibility. For these reasons, it is not surprising from a conversational perspective that a sense of difficulty persists even after our attention has been called to the fact that judicial review cannot fully be isolated from a larger conversational milieu in which it is embedded.

Sounds in the Discourse of Difficulty: The Choice between the Strands of Commentary

Because this contextual approach brings the range of conversational alternatives into view, a conversational perspective might suggest that such an approach should be ascendant in the literature of difficulty. Instead, those who take the turn to interpretation and those who place the courts in a larger democratic context have managed largely to ignore each other. One possible explanation is that the respective commentators have different standards for what counts as "real" conversation.

Consider the pioneers, Bickel and Dahl—the first largely unwilling, the second eager to take the larger context into account. Bickel was a law professor and most of those who have taken the turn to interpretation have been as well. Even Robert Bork, who came to public attention in his days as a public official, had an earlier life in the law professoriate.[53] Law professors, and lawyers more generally, tend to talk the language of the courts, and they may well find particularly unsatisfying the discussions of constitutional matters that surface in the political realm. Excluded as nonparties from the court discussions they understand, and unsatisfied by political substitutes, they may be peculiarly sensitive to the conversational difficulty that the courts in isolation present. Dahl, in contrast, is a political scientist, as have been many of those who were prepared to view the courts in their larger democratic context. Even Ackerman, whose primary identification is as a law professor, also holds an appointment in Yale's political science department. Political scientists seem much less likely than law professors to find something special about the language in which the courts address problems.

My point is not to place law professors and political scientists in separate, hermetically sealed boxes, for the two strands are not entirely oblivious to each other. We saw that Bickel himself paid glancing attention to the possibility of placing the courts in a larger context. Nor is the sense of difficulty confined to those who observe from behind academic walls, or to lawyers. If lawyers and law professors do resist accepting political discussion as a substitute for the language in which courts discuss constitutional matters, we would expect more concentrated attention by them to "difficulty" in statutory decisions than we observe. The point, rather, is that there may be some degree of explanatory power in different inclinations to view political conversants as real substitutes for judicial ones. The contradictory signals that the institutions of government send out about the allocation of decisionmaking power on constitutional questions is probably as much a cause of the separate strands as is any isolation of academic disciplines.

In any event, from a conversational perspective what the strands have in common is more compelling than what separates them. Each is impressed with a democratic difficulty that requires the most serious attention. Each gravitates to discussion of that difficulty in terms of a phantom majoritarianism. And in each case, we are helped to understand that discussion by viewing it in a conversational perspective.

Rational Choice Theory and the Paradox of Voting

Ianticipate that some who have come this far may wonder whether any seeming power of the conversational approach is a function of the weakness of the competition. It may seem that I have erected a straw man in majoritarianism and then provided the vote-centered model as an initially plausible—but easily demolished—mechanism by which that straw man might be held together. I do not think such a charge would be fair, for the commonplace characterization of American democracy as majoritarian is not my doing. But if the prevalence of majoritarianism and the vote-centered model that I have taken as my foil are real, it is nonetheless true that they are not much competition. As I mentioned in chapter two, I am by no means the first to point out that that particular emperor is scantily clad. For that reason, I discuss a fourth puzzle in this chapter that simultaneously introduces what might be taken to be stronger competition.

The puzzle is the so-called *paradox of voting*—why it is that so many people vote when that vote has so little potential to benefit them as individuals. The puzzle is not confined to American democracy, but rather extends to democracies generally, indeed to virtually all electoral settings with a large electorate. Although the puzzle presented by widespread voting was apparently first noticed by Hegel,[1] the modern perspective associated with the paradox is rational choice theory, probably the dominant contemporary theory of politics among American political scientists. The basic rational choice premise is that "individuals in the political arena as in the marketplace behave rationally and in their own self-interest."[2] It thus represents an effort to apply the liberal assumption of self-regarding behavior across the range of political phenomena. Unlike the liberal political ideal that we discussed in chapter three, however, rational choice makes no particular claim of normative appeal. Its ambitions are explanatory only.

Rational Choice Theory

Starting with the work of Mancur Olson, the activity of interest groups in the political process that caused problems for the vote-centered model has been one locus of concern for rational choice theorists. The premise of rational pursuit of self-interest implies that individuals join in collective action only if the costs of doing so are less than the incremental benefits to be expected from bearing those costs. Political action on behalf of a set of individuals with common interests may then die aborning, as each individual calculates that his or her individual contribution to any collective effort would make no discernible difference. Olson noted that each individual might as well "ride free" on the efforts of the others, with the result that none would be willing to join any collective effort. This might be so, even if each individual would have been better off making his or her proportionate contribution to a group effort.[3]

Another locus of rational choice concern has been the behavior of public officials and candidates for public office. Rational choice theorists have typically assumed that the self-interest at work for these people is attaining or retaining office. In the electoral context, this self-interest means that candidates focus single-mindedly on being elected in the first place and then, once elected, on reelection. The efforts of organized groups provide one tool that candidates can seek to use in the electoral struggle. The interaction of candidates and interest groups, each in pursuit of self-interest in the defined ways, has suggested to some rational choice theorists that the pre-political views and interests of public officials are irrelevant to public policy outcomes. In one well-known version, "legislation is [simply] supplied to groups or coalitions that outbid rival seekers of favorable legislation."[4]

Rational choice theory was subject to a scathing attack in 1994 by Donald Green and Ian Shapiro, two political scientists at Yale University.[5] The attack prompted a series of responses, and the exchange has enriched our understanding not only of the strengths and weaknesses of rational choice theory but also more generally of the process of theorizing about political phenomena.[6] The core of the attack by Green and Shapiro was that there is scant empirical support for the conclusions suggested by rational choice theorists. Contrary to interest group theory, for instance, we do see political mobilization of many people with small individual interests in the political outcomes that the group pursues. The American Association of Retired Persons is a particularly visible example in the contemporary United States. And contrary to the rational choice analysis of the behavior of public officials, most studies suggest that the individual ideologies of officials are strong determinants of the substantive positions that they pursue.[7]

In response to findings such as these, rational choice theorists have sometimes offered refinement of their theories, as in the suggestion that "entrepreneurs" may play a role in mobilizing small and dispersed interests into politically active groups. Rational choice theorists have also sometimes acknowledged that assumptions like the single-minded pursuit of reelection by elected officials are oversimplified while nevertheless insisting that that is beside the point. If the theories explain a large part of political behavior, they are useful aids to understanding, even if they are patent oversimplifications. Thus, we do observe interest groups at work in the political vineyards, often quite effectively so, at the same time that many individuals remain politically passive. We certainly see duplicity and worse by those running for office, understandable because of a willingness to put forthrightness aside in the pursuit of public office. As one of the responses to Green and Shapiro put it, "[r]esearchers . . . employ whatever theory they think has the most explanatory potential. . . . [L]ow *predictive* strength of a theory does not undermine its *explanatory* power."[8]

I do not propose here to probe those particular controversies more deeply, although I do return to some of the lessons that might be learned from the controversy about theorizing more generally. Instead, I focus—as a fourth puzzle—on the paradox of voting, yet another empirical embarrassment to rational choice theory. The paradox of voting illustrates nicely the power of a conversational perspective even in the face of what many would count as the more powerful competition of rational choice theory.

The Paradox of Voting

The paradox of voting is that so many people vote. In recent elections, approximately one half of the eligible portion of the American electorate has voted in presidential contests, some 100 million people.[9] What makes this statistic paradoxical from the perspective of rational choice theory is that the "rational" self-interested calculation that leads people to vote is not apparent. For most voters, it is difficult enough to fathom what material difference a victory by one candidate or another will make. Even if some combination of material and psychic benefits is assumed to flow to a voter with election of a favored candidate, the chance of any one voter determining the outcome of an election approaches the vanishing point in elections for which many voters turn out. It has become a favorite rhetorical move among commentators discussing the paradox of voting to suggest that an individual's chance of having his or her vote determine the outcome of an American presidential election is "about the same order of magnitude as . . . [the chance] of being killed driving to the polls."[10] Whatever the basis for the odds making on those two possibilities, it is fair enough to point out that in deciding whether to vote, a person faces a "free rider" possibility similar to that of the person deciding whether to join in some collective effort at political action. Because the voter has almost no chance of affecting the outcome of an election, he or she could ride free on the voting of others and do something else with the time required to vote. But this is not what we observe with about half of the eligible population.[11]

Perhaps one reason that the paradox of voting has attracted a large measure of attention is that both popular and professional commentary has traditionally identified as a puzzle not the fact that so many vote but that so many abstain from voting. This diametrically opposed vision of a problem emerges from the emphasis on majoritarianism and the vote-centered model. From the vote-centered point of view, abstention at the polls represents a loss of the individual's contribution to public policy decisions, a repudiation of "self-government." The vote-centered concern with abstention mixes the normative and the positive in a way that the rational choice theorist disdains. However, because about half of the relevant population votes and half abstains, the hard-headed rational choice proponent seemingly turns out to be no more clear-eyed than the romantic majoritarian.[12]

Some rational choice theorists have dealt with the paradox by abandoning, or softening, the assumption that voters are rational, self-interested actors. One commentator suggests, for instance, that voting is such a low-stakes matter—in terms of both costs and benefits—that voters are freed from the constraints of rational self-interested calculation. Others have been extraordinarily creative in manipulating costs and benefits to allow the "rational" calculus to work out. Noting that wealthier people are more likely to vote, for instance, one commentator actually speculated that those with higher paying jobs might more effectively minimize the costs of voting by thinking about the problems they are paid high wages to solve while waiting in line at the voting booth![13]

Within the rational choice framework, the single most plausible stab to date at explaining the widespread inclination to vote is probably the suggestion that voting is the product of a sense of civic duty. This is said to be consistent with rational self-interest, because people derive satisfaction from voting, much as they do from reading a novel or going to a movie. They have a "taste" for doing their civic duty, and voting satisfies that taste. In the language that rational choice borrows from economics, fulfilling one's civic duty is a "consumption good," the craving for which is satisfied by voting. One commentator in the rational choice tradition even posits that the taste for voting is a conditioned response to positive reinforcement received earlier in life from playing by the rules. Studies of voting behavior have found that both education and income are positively associated with a likelihood of voting. This same commentator argues that these correlations are consistent with the conditioned response possibility, because "[i]ncome, like a graduation certificate, is a mark of success at playing by certain rules of the societal game."[14]

This all seems terribly far-fetched. It is possible to rescue voting from irrationality by retreating to tautology. Any activity could be understood as "rational" by positing a taste for it, the satisfaction of which outweighs the costs associated with obtaining that satisfaction. If tautology obviously will not do, however, positing an early learned response seems implausible as a basis for escape from the "rationality" calculus. Of course we have learned responses, but it seems unlikely that we learn to vote because we receive positive reinforcement when we follow rules early in life. There are rules we learn in school, such as coming to class and handing in homework on time; and some of us learned that we must do the dishes at home and turn off the television until that homework is done. But there is no rule specifically about voting that is learned early. In fact, in the United States there is no rule that ever requires voting. Dutiful voting, then, seems an unlikely candidate for something learned specifically as a part of learning generally to follow rules. In addition, one might have thought that education and higher income were correlated with successfully choosing among rules to follow rather than rotely following them all. If that is so, the "rational" payoff from voting remains a mystery.[15]

If voting is done out of a sense of civic duty that is somehow learned early, the lesson is learned selectively. Voter turnout is affected both by the offices that are in play and apparently by the perceived closeness of the election. It is easy enough to understand the intuitive appeal of each as affecting turnout, but neither is comfortably assimilated to a sense of public duty as the explanation for why people vote. It is not obvious why there is less of a "public duty" to vote for dogcatcher than for president. Green and Shapiro enlarge the point about pursuit of "civic duty":

> [I]t is a peculiar brand of civic duty that explains why people turn out to vote by the tens of millions but also accounts for the comparative dearth of letter writing to local officials or of enthusiasm for jury service. If the fulfillment of one's civic obligations . . . [is a] consumption good . . . that citizens wish to enjoy, it is not clear why there should be pent-up demand for voting in national elections, given the myriad opportunities to do one's duty or show one's colors.[16]

At the same time, it seems that those who vote are *more likely* to engage in publicly dutiful behavior—just the opposite of the consumption pattern that we would expect if doing one's public duty were an ordinary "consumption good."[17] Of course, the taste we satisfy by voting, and for specified other things, might be a taste for voting and for those other things, rather than for fulfillment of civic duty more generally. This explanation would return us to tautology, however, unless the tastes involved could be explained rather than simply asserted. For me, the most plausible explanation of why people vote in large numbers is grounded in the importance that conversation plays in democratic settings, including the American one.

The Conversational Explanation of the Taste for Voting

In the rational choice literature that depicts voting as paradoxical, voters cast their votes to command some discernible benefit for themselves. Although the literature does not focus on potential voters' attentiveness to discourse on public issues, such attentiveness would presumably be an aid to voting, and equally as paradoxical. With voting reconceived as the pursuit of civic duty, attentiveness to the conversation is presumably a means to the end of informed voting. It would not be paradoxical if somehow the paradox of voting could be wrestled down, and if the additional burdens of paying attention to the conversation did not cast us back into paradoxical waters. This way of thinking about democratic conversation has one thing in common with majoritarianism and the vote-centered model. With the vote as the center of attention, each model views the conversation as secondary. The democratic conversation is there to help us vote, and we pay attention to it only because we anticipate the vote.

This conclusion seems to me to point the causal arrow in precisely the wrong direction. We vote in large numbers because we have previously been caught up in the democratic conversation, rather than paying attention to that conversation because we must vote. The sense of belongingness induced by the democratic conversation makes it natural to do our civic "duty" and vote, without necessarily feeling that we are doing anything dutiful. We vote in large numbers simply because that is one of the things one does when one feels involved in a democratic community. Indeed, voting in public elections is probably the signal act of belongingness in a democratic polity. But it is the conversation that makes us feel involved. From this perspective, there is nothing more paradoxical about voting than there is about sitting quietly in the back of the audience at the decidedly amateurish school play in which one's child has a part. Each is the product of a prior sense of involvement.[18]

This explanation for voting is akin to the suggestion of a "learned response" but considerably more plausible. They both point the causal arrow in the same direction. We are caused to vote by earlier stimuli rather than by the prospect of future gain. The learned response suggestion, however, puts those earlier stimuli much earlier and does not connect them convincingly with the act of voting. They are all just part of undifferentiated learning that one is to follow the "rules." The conversational explanation, in contrast, ties voting closely to its hypothesized causes. Although I have been at pains to deemphasize voting as governance, there is no doubt that the popular vote is the characteristic feature of democratic life. We are bombarded by democratic conversation, much of it directly stimulated—and almost all of it indirectly stimulated—by the prospect of those popular elections. We are told repeatedly, moreover, that these elections are what sets membership in a democracy apart. When the democratic conversation has stimulated a sense of involvement in the democratic whole, the act of voting is an entirely natural response.

Nor is there much problem in understanding abstention from voting. Some parents are alienated from their children, and some citizens are alienated from politics. Even quite involved parents sometimes forget to attend the play or have pressing things to do that require their presence elsewhere, just as some citizens may wish to vote but are unable to do so. Some parents may have relationships with their children that are focused on sports or academic studies or the latest fashions, and for them the play may not be that important. So it is with voters who would not miss the dogcatcher election but could not care less about weighing in at the polls on the presidency. No doubt, some of the abstention is attributable to indifference—to politics in general, to be sure, but also to the choice between the visible candidates.

This understanding of the relationship between the democratic conversation and voting integrates many real-world aspects of voting turnout. The fact that those who vote are also more likely to be publicly involved in other ways is now entirely natural rather than puzzling. A degree of involvement in some social endeavor is fully as likely to be followed by more involvement as by less. One does not routinely skip his child's play because he attended the soccer match the previous weekend. That elections for obscure offices attract fewer voters is to be expected, because those elections will have been preceded by less public discussion as well as less private interest in that discussion. Elections that are predicted to be close are likely to have produced more gripping conversation before the election and hence a larger sense of involvement, quite naturally to be followed by a greater likelihood of voting. The positive correlation with education may well be understandable if education induces more attention to the election commentary that leads to elections.[19]

I do not mean to suggest that prior involvement in conversation can explain all voting turnout. Election day weather conditions and other elements of the "costs" of voting certainly play a role. Some people may vote because of a personal relationship with a candidate or campaign worker. There may even be material inducements that bring some people to the polls. And at the margin, concern about public policy outcomes that will be produced in-between elections no doubt has an independent effect, perhaps even an "irrationally" large one. But prior involvement in the democratic conversation provides an entirely plausible explanation for a large part of the observed voting turnout.

In chapter four, I took a preliminary look at the case to be made for the descriptive accuracy of a conversational account of American democracy. At that point, only majoritarianism through the vote-centered model was available as a competitor for conversationalism. With the introduction in this chapter of the rational choice account of political phenomena, as well as the conversational resolution of the paradox of voting, we are now in a position to assess more fully the power of the conversational perspective. That is the subject of chapter nine.

Evaluating the Power of a Conversational Perspective

In chapter three, I was quite critical of both the vote-centered model and the optimistic version of pluralism. Each purports to explain majoritarian results, but there is no way to know if the results obtained are indeed what would be expected of majoritarianism. My criticism, however, was based not solely on this uncertainty but also on the absence of any plausible causal mechanism by which majoritarian results would be achieved. Majoritarian and pluralist theorists offer no account of familiar human motivations operating in the institutional environment of American democracy that would be expected to produce majoritarian results. I suggested that these theorists had likely allowed normative predispositions to shape their positive accounts. With the discussion of four puzzles of American democracy under our belts, and with rational choice theory available for further comparison, it is now appropriate to explore what it is that might ground absolute and comparative claims for the power of a conversational perspective. I start with general observations about the possibilities and limitations in descriptive accounts of complex social phenomena.

The Distinction between Positive and Normative Accounts

My purpose in advancing the conversational account is fundamentally descriptive, as opposed to prescriptive. The distinction between positive (descriptive) and normative (prescriptive) accounts of phenomena is fundamental to appreciating both the power and the limitations of the conversational approach, not the least because the line between the two is difficult to hold.

A normative account provides an ideal to be strived for, or perhaps only dreamt of, but that need not exist or even be attainable. It will often be advanced with improvement of the real world in mind, or even in justification of what is. However, aside from the fact that normative theory is produced by human beings who must let their imaginations take off from their base in the real world, there is nothing inherent in the notion of normative theory that requires resemblance to the real world. In contrast, a descriptive account tells us about existing things in the real world—not how to improve them, but what they are. It would be a contradiction in terms to claim that a theory was descriptive but that it did not truly describe or explain anything about the actual world in which we function.

We can illustrate the difference by calling on some of the commentary on the "countermajoritarian difficulty" discussed in chapter seven. Bruce Ackerman's "dualist" theory of American constitutional history is a claim that if one correctly understands what has happened over time, constitutional decisionmaking has taken two very different forms. The "people" as a whole sometimes have made fundamental decisions about the constitutional order, but only on those rare occasions when they have become "mobilized" to do so. In between these "constitutional moments," the Supreme Court has challenged elected units of government in the name of the Constitution, but these challenges have been relatively modest; in laying down these challenges, the Court was only fleshing out the earlier large-scale choices already made by the mobilized "people." I am not here concerned with whether Ackerman's depiction is accurate. For present purposes, what is important is that, at first blush at least, Ackerman advances a descriptive theory that invites evaluation for its historical and contemporary accuracy—quite apart from whether the system described is thought to be desirable or not.[1]

In contrast, John Ely's "representation reinforcement" theory of judicial review, also discussed in chapter seven, is straightforwardly prescriptive. Ely urges that the courts for the most part act appropriately in the name of the Constitution only when they shore up the processes of representative government. This normative ideal provides a stance from which Ely criticizes a good deal of what the Court has done. His effort takes much of its point from the fact that the reality of the Supreme Court's behavior is rather different from the ideal that the theory lays down. Unlike Ackerman's effort, no defect inherent in Ely's theory is provided by a showing that it inaccurately describes some present or past reality. It is both common and coherent to criticize a normative theory on the ground that it is unrealistic, but such a criticism is directed not to the theory's accuracy but to its usefulness. A normative theory is challenged more directly either by questioning its animating values or by showing that, if implemented, it would have undesirable consequences more serious than any good that it might advance.

Although clear enough in theory, the line between normative and positive accounts is difficult to heed in practice. This is so for a variety of reasons. First, there is a constant danger of what happened with majoritarian and pluralist theorists—the seduction of positive accounts by normative visions. This danger can in turn be traced, in part at least, to the fact that a complete description of anything is impossible. Something as simple and "objective" as a table, for instance, can be described in terms of its material, its shape, the number of its legs, the manner of its manufacture, its age, or its owner. If one set out with the goal of "comprehensive" description of a table, all these things would presumably have to be included, as would the chemical composition of the table, its molecular structure as well as spatial and time dimensions—for starters, the table's placement today and yesterday and the day before in the houses or show windows or alleys where it was found. Sooner or later in this effort at comprehensive description, it would become apparent that there is no place to stop.

Nor would there ever be much sense in being as comprehensive as possible. Any discussion of a particular table, or of tables in general, will be directed to some purpose or purposes, and those purposes will suggest the descriptive dimensions of concern. If a family is worried about whether it can afford to buy a table, then it will focus on price; if worried about aesthetics, then it may focus on a variety of things, but not on molecular structure. Once we know the purpose of the discussion, it will impede rather than advance that purpose to range beyond relevant descriptive dimensions.

The impossibility of comprehensiveness is even more obvious for complex social phenomena like American democracy. Do we, for instance, include the contrasting senses of humor in Texas and Massachusetts? A useful model of a complex phenomenon must be brutally selective if it is "to bring salient order to the blooming, buzzing confusion of human experience."[2] Any theory about politics will necessarily miss some of "the richness and diversity of political institutions"; but if we do not have some simplifying theory, "we may be overwhelmed by fascinating facts and unable to orient ourselves."[3] At the same time, the purpose of some discussion of democracy is often more diffuse and elusive than with tables. The result is to introduce a good deal of uncertainty about the right dimensions on which to focus. In particular, if we seek to "understand" this complex thing, but without any concrete goal in mind (akin to whether we can afford to buy the table), we have relatively little to guide us in the process of inclusion and exclusion as we make our retreat from comprehensive description.

It is precisely in such an environment that normative visions are quite likely to intrude. Most of us carry around normative judgments of commonplace and relatively simple things—if not of tables, then of cell phones or broccoli, cocker spaniels or roaches. Even more so for complex social phenomena like American democracy, "value commitments" are typically "embedded in the very institutions and practices analyzed," and "biases are built into the very languages and concepts employed." The result is that, often at least, "if we think that what we are describing and explaining consists of value-neutral 'brute facts' . . . we are on the brink of misunderstanding. . . ."[4] A second consequence of selectivity is that the resulting shortfall can be depicted as inaccuracy; something—indeed an infinity of things— about the phenomenon described will unavoidably fail to be captured by the description. The inclination to challenge a depiction and the terms of the challenge will, again, often reflect the contestant's normative stance or presuppositions.

The line between the normative and the descriptive is also difficult to hold if one's account is normative in inspiration. Although accounts consciously designed as normative can be largely divorced from reality, they are likely to have substantial points of attachment to a reality they seek to instruct. "[P]olitical theorists . . . begin from where . . . [they] are. . . ."[5] They could hardly do anything else, and what is more, if the distance between what is and what they conceive ought to be is too great, the task of bridging it may well seem too substantial to justify the bother. Normative theories conceived with betterment in mind will thus usually have many points of connection with the portion of the reality that is thought to require improvement. If the instruction takes hold, and the reality moves closer to the normative ideal, the points of connection will increase. Or if the instruction does not take hold, or does not seem likely to, the normative theorist may make further concessions to reality by introducing additional connections to increase the chances of bringing reality around. For these reasons, there will typically be a high degree of correspondence between normative accounts and the portion of the real world in view, and the normative may easily be mistaken for description—by the consumers of commentary, but also on occasion by the commentators.[6]

Ackerman's and Ely's efforts provide instructive examples of the mingling of the positive and the normative. While Ackerman clearly invites (and has received) criticism that the theoretical framework he provides, combined with the facts on which he relies, misconstrues history, his was a "reflective study of the past," aimed simultaneously at mining that history for the lessons it holds about how we now should proceed. Ackerman acknowledges that he sees "the bright side of the American constitutional achievement . . . to call his fellow Americans to live out its dream. . . ."[7] And while Ely's normative stance allows him to criticize certain Supreme Court decisions, he holds others up as entirely appropriate, even exemplary. The theoretical case he makes is clearly the more powerful for being able to point to real-world elements that could be followed on the road to normative advance. If the Court were to be drawn to the instruction Ely offered, for instance, it would have tested examples on which to build, as well as comfort in the thought that its better future could be built on at least a part of its past.[8]

Those forces no doubt often operate without explicit acknowledgment, or perhaps even understanding. Even when understood, it is entirely possible—as with Ackerman's effort—that a theoretical account will both describe and praise the way things are, will be designed to be descriptive *and* normative at once. Thus, it is not surprising that "one can find in . . . models of democracy an intermingling of the descriptive and the normative."[9] It might even be tempting to say that there is no difference between descriptive and prescriptive theories, but that would surely be wrong as well. For even if "tacit evaluations are built into [the] . . . very framework [of social description],"[10] positive and normative projects have different inspirations, and the tendencies toward coalescence can be resisted, even if they cannot be entirely overcome.

In evaluating competing accounts of American democracy, it is important to keep in mind the power and subtlety of the forces pushing the positive and the normative together. I have little doubt that a mingling of the normative with the descriptive has worked its way into my conversational account of American democracy, just as I have noted it in the work of others. By acknowledging the problem—to myself and to my gentle readers—I hope to contain the possibilities of confusion.

The Distinction between Bare Description and Explanation

Within the realm of positive theories, there is a further distinction to be noted between bare description and a richer form that might be called "explanation." By drawing attention to some characteristics to the exclusion of others, even quite spare description allows us to focus on what is chosen, but explanation helps us "*see*" much more.[11] It is an observable fact that both whales and tuna inhabit the sea, for instance, but it takes richer explanation for us to "see" that whales are closer relatives of elephants than they are of those tuna. Explanation is the furthering of understanding. It provides an "organizing framework" that draws causal connections between discrete aspects of complex phenomena.[12] Explanation brings "order and connectedness in our view of the world."[13] An explanatory model, in Ronald Coase's words, helps "us to understand what is going on by enabling us to organise our thoughts."[14] Then, "by unifying apparently diverse phenomena . . . [explanatory models] can change the way we look at the empirical world. . . ."[15]

Success in explanation will not be comprehensive. Precisely because explanatory theories of complex phenomena are simple and selective, there are aspects of the larger reality they address that theories will fail to explain. Evolutionary theory, for instance, has no particularly convincing explanation of why so many human beings live well past the age of reproduction. The result is that two "competing" theories may each enjoy a large measure of success—either because they explain different things about the complex phenomenon or because they each partially explain the same things. Nor need there be any metric for judging which has the larger success. The competition will then be judged, *inter alia*, on the simplicity of the explanation, the range of phenomena explained, and the plausibility of the causal connections posited. The choice may be easy, as in the case of evolutionary theory, in which the mystery of a designing creator seems to be the only serious competitor that the human mind can conceive at present to explain the diversity of living things. Or the choice may be difficult, as I am prepared to acknowledge is the choice among explanatory theories of American democracy.

It might be asked what is so all-fired important about explanation, or even understanding, particularly when, as in the case of conversationalism, an effort is made to insulate that explanation from normative infestation. As I proceeded with earlier phases of this project, I encountered occasional puzzlement about what the point of analysis is if there are no normative lessons to be learned, because an effort is made to keep the explanation free of normative edge. One part of the answer is that there may well be normative lessons to be learned, because positive understanding can be put to use in normative inquiry.[16] With understanding comes the possibility of change, including change toward normative advance. If that understanding is clouded to begin with, the route to improvement is likely to be clouded as well. In chapter ten, I return to possible normative uses of the positive account I have offered. However, there is a more fundamental response to the point of reaching out for explanation and thence understanding, for which I quote Albert Einstein: "[t]here exists a passion for comprehension, just as there exists a passion for music."[17]

Evaluation: The Power of Conversationalism

It is as an explanation of American democracy that I believe the conversational perspective succeeds. At least at the level of the nation-state, genuine contemporary democracies are characterized by competitive elections. The exercise of a high degree of authority by officials chosen in a competitive electoral environment may well be the essence of representative democracy; and competitive elections are what power the democratic conversation. For this reason, any contemporary democracy worthy of the name will be characterized by a large degree of conversationalism. Beyond that generalization, however, democracies do vary greatly in features with conversational implications, and there is reason to believe that American democracy in particular is a highly conversational one.

Thus, as we saw in chapter four, the conversational perspective nicely incorporates a number of features of American democracy: the near universal extension of the franchise to the adult population, which broadly extends the democratic conversational reach; bicameralism and federalism, which provide a rich mix of conversants and conversational topics for the voting population; the move over time to popular election for the Senate and the national executive, which provide conversational incentives for aspirants to those prominent offices; geographically defined legislative districts, which define special relationships between candidates and constituents that then provide focus for their conversational energies; loose political party discipline, which allows freer reign for those conversational relationships to develop; and the central role that the First Amendment protections of speech and press have come to play in American law and politics. Except for the first, each of these features of the American form of government is, more or less, unusual among the world's democracies;

the combination, however, is probably unique to the United States. The conversational account of American democracy is, of course, not comprehensive, but the ease with which it can account for so many important and unusual features of that democracy is just the "order and connectedness" that successful explanatory theories provide.

The causal mechanism producing this American conversationalism is basically an evolutionary one. American democracy has certainly known its moments of instability, but by most accounts it is the most long-lasting of the world's democracies. The conversational account posits that democratic conversation helps explain this endurance because it is adaptive for the enterprise as a whole. The sense of involvement in the public enterprise produced by the conversation fosters reconciliation to decisions taken with which there might otherwise be substantive disagreement. When sources of discontent are dampened in this way, challenge to the system as a whole becomes less likely. By this account, conversation-enhancing features could emerge for a variety of reasons, but they tend to endure because they allow American democracy to "weather its storms."

The sense of involvement and consequent reconciliation cannot be observed or measured directly—at least in any satisfactory way that I have been able to imagine—but neither direct observation nor measurement is determinative of the success of explanatory theories. The involvement and reconciliation become plausible because they can be assimilated readily to familiar everyday phenomena—to our commonplace experiences with private conversation as a way of fostering and facilitating a sense of involvement in, and satisfaction with, private relationships. If there is initial appeal to this commonsensical mechanism of involvement and reconciliation, the order and connectedness that the conversational account brings to far-flung features of American democracy is powerful indirect evidence that involvement through conversation is at work on the larger public stage.

Evaluation: Solving Puzzles

Since I have started "seeing" American democracy in conversational terms, I have come to see as well connections I had not previously appreciated, to understand old phenomena in new ways. Thus, the order and connectedness extends beyond institutional features to attitudinal and behavioral phenomena. The four puzzles we explored in chapters five through eight are all of that sort, and they are puzzles that I gradually came to think about *after* I had first come to see American democracy in conversational terms.[18] This ability to open up new insights very substantially fortifies the power of the conversational approach. If there were only one puzzle that had lent itself to a conversational solution, there might be little interest in that fact. But that there are four, and that they come from disparate parts of the American democratic reality, shows far-ranging explanatory power.

Moreover, although I have chosen four puzzles to explore in some detail, it is quite easy to identify additional puzzling features of American democracy that might be clarified by the conversational perspective. Indeed, puzzles come in various shapes and sizes, and the discussions thus far have actually uncovered many more than four. In chapter seven, for instance, we dealt with the insistent sense of "difficulty" with judicial review. But exploration of that subject uncovered subsidiary puzzles along the way, like the silences about the similarly "countermajoritarian" Constitution and statutory interpretation.

There are further puzzling things about American democracy for which conversationalism might provide a satisfactory account. Many members of the American electorate, for instance, simultaneously have relatively positive views of their own representatives and relatively negative views of legislative institutions as a whole. This might seem puzzling, but only from a vote-centered perspective, through which it is legislative outcomes that matter. From that perspective, the individual representative is basically a vehicle for transmitting constituent interests to and through the legislative process. Failure of the process to give a voter his or her vote-centered (i.e., equal) due seems at least as plausibly ascribed to the representative's failure as to that of the institution as a whole. From a conversational perspective, however, there is nothing puzzling about the differential attitudes. An individual voter's conversational attention is focused on his or her own representative. Representatives try hard to direct conversation to constituents that will be pleasing to them. It is, then, natural rather than puzzling that constituents develop a sense of involvement with their representatives that is more attenuated for the legislative bodies in which those individual representatives function, or for the system as a whole.[19]

There is also a ready conversational explanation for the apparent desire of many members of the Black citizenry in the United States to have legislative representatives of their own race. From a vote-centered perspective, the desire is perhaps puzzling, because that population might be thought better served in its substantive interests by constituting a large minority in several districts, so that a larger number of representatives, whatever their race, would cater to those substantive interests. The conversational explanation, of course, is that a representative of one's own race might prove particularly satisfying as a conversational companion. In chapter four, we distinguished "deep" and "broad" conversational interactions at the district level, and it could well be that a Black representative would provide "deep" conversational interactions in a predominantly Black district in a way that a non-Black representative could not.[20]

An interesting contrast is provided by the constitutional requirement I mentioned in chapter seven that the president be a "natural born citizen."[21] That provision seems to have all sorts of potential to raise hackles for foreign-born citizens, yet there is almost no discussion of it, let alone evidence of umbrage taken. This too seems puzzling, not so much from a vote-centered perspective, but because the requirement flies in the face of the ideology of American democracy as a place of opportunity equally open to all its citizens. From a conversational point of view, however, the function of the president is to produce and direct involving conversation to the citizenry, including the foreign-born citizenry. Being a "natural born citizen" does not at all foreclose talking the talk the foreign-born citizenry values hearing. A president or presidential candidate cannot embody within himself all—or even many—of the politically salient characteristics of his many constituencies, but he can give voice to themes that appeal to a great many of the sentiments of those constituencies. Indifference to the natural-born citizen requirement might then be attributable in part to the fact that candidates for the presidency can and do reach out conversationally to the foreign-born citizens who might otherwise seem ripe to take offense.

There is obviously some tension between these last two examples. Why is it that Blacks might find conversational satisfactions in having representatives of their own race, while the foreign born want for no conversational satisfaction when native-born candidates for president speak to them? The most obvious explanation is that there can be only one American president, and only two or three genuinely competitive challengers for the office. In contrast, there are 435 members of the House of Representatives, leaving plenty of room for members to embody politically salient characteristics of large numbers of constituencies. A representative represents only one district, of course, but it seems understandable that the large size of the body as a whole arouses conversational yearnings that might otherwise remain dormant. The intermediate case of the Senate tends to reinforce the importance of this distinction. In this century there have been very few Black senators. This seldom seems to arouse resentment on the part of Black constituencies, perhaps due in part to the fact that it is obvious that for almost all constituencies Senators who can "talk the talk" across a broad spectrum of constituencies are the most that can be expected.[22]

There are also distinctions between Blacks and the foreign born that may have some explanatory force. The foreign-born disqualification lasts only a generation, whereas Blacks might foresee no end to conversational frustrations they might feel. In addition, for historical and cultural reasons, Blacks form a cohesive minority in American politics in a way that the foreign born do not. The latter seem more likely to identify with those who share ethnicity, ancestral country, or even language with them than they are with the foreign born more generally. It seems unlikely, for instance, that recent immigrants to the United States from Mexico would relate more easily to Henry Kissinger because he, too, was foreign born. To put that point another way, it may just be that Black representatives can provide "deep" conversational interactions with a cohesive constituency in a way that foreign-born candidates for president never could.

One further example of a puzzle susceptible to conversational solution brings together some of these themes. We saw in the discussion of judicial review (see chapter seven) that dissonant opinion writing, although an apparently secure feature of contemporary practice on the U.S. Supreme Court, is a relatively recent phenomenon.

There was relatively little dissonance before 1941, when there was a veritable explosion of separate opinion writing. Dissonance increased sharply thereafter until about 1948 and has since remained at levels that are extraordinarily high by historical standards. The leadership style and preferences of Harlan Fiske Stone, who acceded to the Chief Justiceship in 1941, is often cited as the reason for the shift, but there is an interesting question of whether the staying power of the change might find a conversational explanation.[23]

It is hard to credit a conversational explanation for the production and publication of majority opinions. Those opinions are, to be sure, conversational after a fashion, but as we saw in chapter seven, their involving capacity is limited by the fact that opinions are made public only after a decision has been reached. More importantly, the practice of publishing majority opinions has a compelling justification *internal* to the Court's processes. Publication is a way of informing the populace of the law with which it must contend. There is no apparent reason why that internal justification does not suffice to explain the routine practice of publicizing majority opinions.

Publication of dissonant opinions raises different and instructive questions. Within the judicial context, there is an obvious but at present little discussed difficulty with dissonant opinions, whether they take the form of open dissent or only of difference with the rationale provided by the majority. By definition, the dissonant opinion asserts a position on the law that is known to have lost at the time it is announced. It seems fair to ask why dissenters (or even those who concur on grounds rejected by a court majority) are free to quarrel in this way. In chapter seven, we also encountered the ongoing debate about whether nonjudicial democratic actors should feel free to act on views on constitutional questions that diverge from what the courts have announced. Even if an affirmative answer is given to that question, dissenting judges are different. They are a part of the very institution that is shown to have decided against their position no later than the time the position is announced.

Still, there is also a plausible "internal" justification for producing and publishing dissonant opinions: They may have a salutary effect on the majority's work product. By putting the court majority on guard that it must deal carefully with the issues presented, the possibility of a dissonant opinion may regularly produce more carefully reasoned statements of the law.[24] This salutary effect might be produced (without public "lawlessness") by the pre-publication exchange of views.[25] It seems likely, however, that the possibility of published dissent is an important element in keeping a court majority on its toes. By this reasoning, the dissent is tolerated despite its surface disregard of the "law" because it serves to improve the process by which that law is produced.

The same cannot be said, however, of the common practice of repetition of dissonant positions the second and subsequent times that an issue is taken to arise. Dissenting and concurring judges do not routinely persist in dissonant positions, but they evidence no great compunction about doing so. A classic example is Justice Stevens' repetition of dissent (on behalf of an identical set of four dissenters) in the second "flag burning" decision, acknowledging that the issue was essentially identical to what was decided the first time around.[26] Whatever the "internal" justification for dissonance the first time an issue arises, that case is diminished close to the vanishing point for persistence in a dissonant position that is already on the books. The first opinion will by then have exerted most of whatever benign pressure on the majority is to be expected. Rather than serving an institutional purpose, the repetition of a dissonant position (or dissonance by a newly appointed judge) might, from an internal point of view, seem self-indulgent at best and "lawless" at worst. The fact that legislators feel free to "dissent" anew when legislation is reconsidered is no answer to this argument from the internal vantage point. The legislative context is one of avowed ongoing discretion, whereas the judiciary insists that its decisionmaking is externally constrained by the "law."

Despite the weakness of the internal justification, there is almost no visible criticism of the judicial practice of persistence in dissonance. This silence is yet another puzzle that might be solved with a conversational perspective. Repetition of dissonance may help soothe the ongoing pain of loss, particularly for *nonparties* who thereby can see that someone is voicing what in their view needs to be said. The dissonant opinion, in other words, shows affected nonparties a sympathetic and ongoing public voice, not unlike the voice their elected legislators and executive officials so often provide. The conversational balm of dissonance does, to be sure, come after an adverse decision, not before. But the fact that it is a repetition of an earlier dissonant position demonstrates that the issue remained alive despite having already been decided. The repeated dissonant position may thus help communicate to the external audience the ongoing possibility of later overruling.

This conversational explanation for dissonant stubbornness is one I came to appreciate only after I began to think about American democracy in conversational terms. I had earlier written an article contrasting an "individual" and an "institutional" style of judging, calling attention to the "internal" questions that might be raised about the repetition of dissenting positions. I did not then appreciate or "see," as I now do, that those questions might not rise to the level of salience because of the conversational dynamics at work.[27]

Evaluation: Conversationalism and the Vote-Centered Model

Even if there are phenomena for which majoritarianism and the vote-centered model come up largely empty, that fact need not be decisive in preferring conversationalism. For one thing, like any simple descriptive model of a complex reality, conversationalism also fails to account for much of the observable reality of American democracy. Although conversationalism might help us understand why the move toward popular election in the choice of the president of the United States seems irreversible, why there is no controversy about the requirement of natural born citizenship, why the common judicial practice of repetition of dissonant positions goes unquestioned, I have no particularly convincing *conversational* explanation, for instance, for what causes the retention of the electoral college to be controversial at some times and not at others (apparently including in the wake of the 2000 election).[28] Conversation might help explain the appeal of bicameralism, but not simultaneously Nebraska's apparent contentment with unicameralism.[29] At least in the latter case, there is no doubt simple inertia at work, but it is also patently obvious that conversationalism is not the only force currently shaping either the large institutions or the fine details of American democracy.

Most fundamentally, the substance of decisions matters greatly to various actors in American democracy, and we cannot account fully for many developments if we ignore the importance of substantive outcomes. Indeed, the importance of substance provides much of the incentive for conversational interactions. Writing almost fifty years ago, Robert Dahl argued that American democracy is put in peril when highly committed and large minorities of the population are sharply divided on an important issue. It was just such a situation that led to the Civil War. That observation seems entirely sound, and is not made less so by the fact that the sharp divisions would surely be accompanied by incessant public conversation on the subjects that divided.[30]

The sensible comparison between the vote-centered model and conversationalism is not in explanatory shortfall but in explanatory success—or perhaps in some judgment of the balance of failure and success. Majoritarianism is not without some explanatory power. The protections of speech and press, for instance, can easily be rationalized in vote-centered terms as contributing to intelligent voting. In similar fashion, the disenfranchisement of children is at least understandable in a vote-centered context. Whatever one might think about surrogate voters, it is not hard to understand why vote-centered self-government would be subverted by asking two-year-olds to vote. Majoritarianism can certainly account better than conversationalism for all the talk of American democracy as majoritarian.

This being said, in any accounting of the explanatory power of the two, conversationalism seems to win hands down. To be sure, the comparison is not straightforward, in part because the explanatory energies of the two are aimed most directly at different things. The vote-centered model is focused on public policy outcomes, which conversationalism ignores. Conversationalism, in contrast, is concerned with the stability-enhancing power of a feeling of involvement. There is no objectively verifiable basis for saying that one rather than the other has described the "right" thing. Moreover, in neither case is success in explanation readily quantifiable. There is no common metric by which to judge one more "accurate" than the other. In such a setting, the relative appeal of the vote-centered model and of conversationalism will necessarily rest not on some systematic basis for choice but on informed intuition about whether they focus on important things and provide coherent accounts of diverse phenomena. It is on this basis that conversationalism succeeds. The conversational account points the way to connections among large and important features of American democracy as well as many more incidental ones. The vote-centered model both misses or muddles those connections and provides scant compensation with the insights it does provide.

The comparison may not seem all that earth shattering. In chapter eight, I introduced a third competitor in large part because the vote-centered model provides such frail competition in furthering an understanding of American democracy. Not only does the entry of that third competitor—the rational choice approach—make the comparative judgment considerably more difficult, it also serves to illuminate what we are looking for in successful positive theories of complex social phenomena.

Evaluation: Conversationalism and Rational Choice

It would be entirely too facile to cite the shortcomings of rational choice highlighted by Green and Shapiro and discussed in chapter eight to conclude that conversationalism must be better than rational choice. For this comparative judgment at least, those shortcomings seem to me to be neither as serious nor as decisive as might at first seem. The comparative judgment between conversationalism and rational choice is more complex and considerably closer than that between conversationalism, on the one hand, and majoritarianism via the vote-centered model, on the other.

To Green and Shapiro, rational choice theorists have gone astray because they cling to universalist pretensions for their theory in the face of serious empirical failings. The predictions of the theory about legislator behavior, effective political organization, and voter behavior (see chapter eight) are simply not borne out by the facts. Rather than genuinely explaining "phenomena that arise in the world," rational choice theorists have, according to Green and Shapiro, allowed their efforts to focus on substantiating the rational choice dogma. They have engaged in a "method-driven" approach rather than the more appropriate "problem-driven" research. Green and Shapiro urge, instead, "a synthesis of different theoretical perspectives," even if that "entails a sacrifice in terms of theoretical parsimony."[31]

This criticism associates a quest for theoretical parsimony and universalist pretensions when the two can more instructively be treated separately. For reasons suggested earlier, parsimonious explanation can be a great aid in understanding. At a minimum, the factors on which a theory focuses have the "special" status of association with that theory. By drawing our attention to an explanatory vehicle, that special status allows us to "see" new things, or old things in new ways. A synthesis of different theoretical perspectives, in contrast, raises the danger of providing a hodgepodge of explanations that does little more than replicate the "blooming, buzzing confusion of human experience." To insist that every problem be addressed from a variety "of different theoretical perspectives" raises the danger of keeping us from *seeing* with any one of them.

Take voter turnout. It is quite plausibly affected by the weather, the quality of candidates, the level of voter satisfaction with the present state of affairs, the proximity of polling places to where people live, and recent dramatic events, to name a few besides the rational pursuit of self-interest and conversational involvement. But we would understand turnout much less well if our theory told us that it was affected by these factors as well as a hundred and one other things that surely do play some role. There is no doubt a place for studying each of these contributors, but not all at once. Both rational choice theory and conversationalism are better aids to understanding, because each allows us to see and understand important aspects of voter turnout in ways that simultaneous engagement with a multiplicity of perspectives would not. A point made more than once in the responses to Green and Shapiro was that it was not until rational choice theory came along that voting rather than abstention was a phenomenon of interest.[32]

In reply to their critics, Green and Shapiro suggest that the shift in emphasis to the reasons for voting rather than for abstention was a wrong turn, a "wild goose chase."[33] But that conclusion does not seem fair. It is entirely plausible that a good deal of voter abstention *is* grounded in exactly the kind of calculation that rational choice theory posits—I won't vote in today's election, in part at least, because my vote isn't going to make any difference anyway, and I have other things to do. We can now "see" that logic more clearly because the theory drew our attention to the possibility. Commentators nonetheless still routinely ignore the rational choice explanation of abstention and engage in gnashing of teeth about voter apathy.[34] From a normative perspective, criticizing voter apathy is entirely appropriate, but if voting theorists really wish to change the world, they ignore the rational choice explanation at some peril to their cause. The importance of any change that lowers the cost of voting—bringing polling places closer to where people live, for instance—comes into clearer focus from a rational choice perspective than it does from a vote-centered one. The fact that the rational choice explanation captures only a part of the totality of voting behavior—and indeed a rather small part—is important as well. At least for complex social phenomena, however, real insight is achieved by theoretical inquiry that comes up short empirically, as all such inquiry surely does. Despite the shortcomings of rational choice theorizing, the rational actor assumption has helped bring a semblance of order to a great many political phenomena.

There can, of course, be no greater failure of an explanatory theory than that it explains nothing. But Green and Shapiro's standards are awfully high. If Mancur Olson's work on collective choice fails to account for much collective activity, it is highly suggestive about why "the full spectrum of economic interests is not equally represented by interest groups."[35] When the empirical failings of the theory cause other theorists to posit the importance of entrepreneurs, and we then observe the crucial role that seems to be played by such entrepreneurs, that result consists of one part empirical failure and another part success—which adds up to a good deal more than nothing.

It seems to me that it is not the theoretical parsimony that gets rational choice theorists in trouble, but the universalist pretensions. When rational choice theory "predicts" voter turnout near zero, its theorists are well aware that no such thing is true. But rather than suggesting that factors other than rational pursuit of self-interest might be at work, the theorists strain for explanations in rational choice terms. To the extent that these explanations fail, there is no place to hide, save insistence on "paradox." If rational choice theorists had instead acknowledged that many influences on voting behavior are not captured particularly well with notions of rational pursuit of self-interest, they need not have gone on to spell out what those are. They could have pursued their "method-driven" inquiries, milking them for the understanding they can bring, without the claim that their method occupies the field. Without the universalist bravado, empirical shortfall seems much less of a failing. The minimum empirical test for a successful theory should be a fair degree of empirical support, not the complete absence of empirical failure. A successful theory must have the empirical glass partly full, but that need not mean that the glass cannot remain in greater part empty.

In any event, a degree of explanatory power suggests the standard by which conversationalism succeeds. In pursuing a conversational explanation of voter turnout, for instance, I have openly acknowledged the causal contribution of things other than the involving effect of conversation. And a great many of my criticisms of the vote-centered model in chapter three were grounded in rational choice assumptions about the incentives that people pursue. I explicitly assumed candidate concern with winning, for instance, and individual disinclination to organize into politically active groups unless a "free rider" problem could be overcome. Indeed, I have abjured the words *theory* and *model* to characterize the conversational approach, precisely because these words seem to me to suggest more reach and precision than I have wanted to claim. I have opted instead for *perspective, approach,* and *account.* At the same time, I have not allowed myself to be diverted to a "synthesis of different theoretical perspectives," which I am sure would have delayed, and perhaps even scuttled, the possibilities of understanding a great many things in conversational terms.

Green and Shapiro sometimes seem to align themselves with those who urge that the only valid criterion for the validity of a theory in the social as in the physical sciences is its capacity to provide predictions about the future. But such an assumption is surely wrong. If an explanatory theory can repeatedly predict the future, that predictive power will provide powerful substantiation of the theory. If predictions can be tested in measurement, that too may provide evidence of the theory's power. But neither prediction nor measurement is determinative of the success of explanatory theories. Particularly for large and complex phenomena, controlled experimentation is often very expensive or entirely unavailable, thereby allowing scant opportunity for testing the predictive power of an explanatory theory. Measurement too, at least useful measurement, is often unavailable.[36]

Darwinian evolutionary theory must be counted one of the great successes of scientific inquiry, but there is little experimentation to back up its most ambitious claims, and its power was evident long before the experimentation that has bolstered it. Darwinian theory also has little to tell us about the future configuration of the plant and animal species about which it purports to explain so much.[37] Rather, the power of evolutionary theory resides in its capacity to draw together disparate phenomena of plant and animal species with a relatively coherent and simple explanation that can be related to other phenomena with which we are familiar. This power survives—perhaps even thrives on—the possibility that causal factors not readily assimilated to natural selection—meteors, volcanic eruptions, unusual weather, and the like—have also shaped the history and the present configuration of plant and animal species. There may well be lessons about the future that Darwinian theory provides,[38] but the interest for us of Darwinian theory is surely in greater part independent of any such predictive potential.[39] The simple truth is that, as Einstein said, understanding is satisfying in and of itself.

Green and Shapiro's response to the example of natural selection seems particularly weak:

> evolutionary theory can and does produce testable predictions. For instance, a variant of evolutionary theory might generate the hypothesis that there was a gradual expansion of the cranial capacities of a given species during a particular period. This, in turn, would issue in predictions that could be falsified if larger skulls were subsequently discovered that could be shown (by independent dating methods) to be older than smaller, younger skulls from the specified period. If evolutionary theory produced no falsifiable predictions of this kind, there would be little reason to take it any more seriously than creationism.[40]

Aside from a seemingly hypothetical example about how the "power" of an overwhelmingly accepted scientific theory might be demonstrated, this response uses "prediction" in the sense of finding new data about the past, rather than foretelling the future. It thus seems to narrow, if not eliminate, the difference between prediction and explanation. Green and Shapiro could have made a stronger case in their own terms had they focused on the real-time, small-scale evolutionary change that can be observed.[41] In truth, however, the explanatory power of evolutionary theory is largely independent of predictions about the future. Indeed, that explanatory power is so great that the fact of phenomena for which it does not account very well (such as the easy survival of humans well past the age of reproduction) has not proved much of an embarrassment at all.[42]

The problem of voter turnout discussed earlier also demonstrates the limits of measurement. Measurement can certainly undermine a theory or provide a degree of support for it. Thus, I can conceive of interesting investigations of voting patterns that might help undermine or bolster the conversational explanation that I advanced in chapter eight. It appears, for instance, that voter turnout increases in elections that are projected to be close.[43] The conversational explanation for this is that close elections make for more intense and engaging preelection conversation.

It then seems fair to ask whether in a presidential election one would expect the relevant "closeness" to be national or state by state. The vote that "counts" is state-by-state, but much of the conversation takes place across state borders, often nationwide. If the conversation causes voting, then the projected closeness of the nationwide vote should have some effect on turnout that is independent of the state-by-state vote. But neither the presence nor absence of such a correlation would be decisive about the conversational perspective, since voting behavior is a product of many causes. A theoretical "explanation" isolates some causes to the exclusion of others. Although measurement where feasible can help in evaluation of explanation, it is neither necessary nor sufficient for such evaluation. For better or worse, conversationalism, like most social theory, must find its justification in plausibility without much help from measurement.

Rational choice would look a lot more successful if its ambitions were scaled back to resemble more closely those of the conversational approach that I advance. If forced to choose between the two, the contest would, in my judgment, be a lot closer than that between majoritarianism via vote-centeredness and conversationalism. If choice were required, a good case could be made for conversationalism as the more powerful theory. In the only head-to-head battle for explanatory power between the two, I explained in chapter eight why conversationalism more readily accounts for the pattern of voter turnout that we observe. Both approaches account for some of the pattern—conversationalism for the turnout, and rational choice for the abstention. That might be counted a standoff. But conversationalism also accounts for details of turnout much more persuasively than does rational choice. Thus, conversationalism comfortably explains why voter turnout is greater among the educated, whereas rational choice strains for an explanation.[44] Similarly, conversationalism explains why a candidate can bring out voters of common racial or ethnic background, whereas rational choice cannot. More generally, conversationalism seems the more powerful because it has something to teach about such a diversity of American phenomena, many of which are commonly seen as fundaments of the system.

In the final analysis, however, it is not necessary to choose between conversationalism and rational choice theory. Each brings considerable explanatory power to the table, and each does so in reasonably coherent and simple terms. If we appreciate that descriptive and explanatory accounts of complex phenomena are necessarily selective, there is nothing anomalous about the possibility of two—or more—simultaneously "accurate" accounts. Conversationalism and rational choice emphasize different aspects of a complex reality; and while the phenomena they purport to explain sometimes overlap—as in the case of gross voter turnout—they are by no means identical. The phenomena that rational choice explains are mostly behavioral—interest group formation, politician public policy choices, voter turnout—whereas those of conversationalism are mostly institutional—federalism, bicameralism, single-member legislative districting—or attitudinal—contentment with the Senate, indifference to the political status of children. Both approaches, however, can claim a good deal of explanatory power over an important part of the whole.

Conversational Explanation and Its Normative Use

S uppose that legislators were chosen not by election but by lot from among the entire electorate. The resulting legislature could well resemble the microcosm of the electorate that, as we saw in chapter two, a number of Federalists envisaged for the new national legislature in their arguments in favor of ratification of the Constitution. Given the present expanse of that electorate, the lot-chosen legislature might be thought to have substantial advantages over our system of geographically defined representative districts in effectuating the liberal democratic "majoritarian" ideal examined in chapter three. The idea of choosing legislators by lot actually has a handful of contemporary sympathizers.[1]

Despite these smatterings of interest, the idea of a legislature chosen by lot seems even more of a political nonstarter than a proposal to give extra votes to parents on account of their children, and perhaps for related—conversational—reasons. There would be little in the way of felt personal relationship between lot-chosen legislators and constituents. Conceivably, such legislators would view it as their responsibility to seek information from their constituencies, but those constituencies would not be differentiated along any defined dimensions. It seems quite possible that ideologists of lot-chosen legislatures, and perhaps the legislators themselves, would view efforts at interaction with constituents as likely to introduce "distortions" into "democratic" decisionmaking. Reaching out to the "electorate" would risk disproportions in influence that their manner of selection had been meant to combat. If the point was to provide the microcosm, then lot-chosen legislators might best proceed with their legislating as if they embodied within themselves all the information and sentiments necessary for the task.

A competitive electoral system structures incentives for candidates, and secondarily for all manner of mass (and not so mass) media, to communicate with members of the electorate. If that competition takes place in a series of geographically defined districts, as in the United States, it serves to set up relationships between constituents and representatives that can focus the attention of each in ways that make the resulting conversation involving for the constituents.[2] If those geographically defined districts come in multiple and overlapping shapes and sizes with differently defined substantive areas of concern—again, as they do in the United States—the result is a diverse menu of conversational possibilities. The real possibility that a lot-chosen legislature would be cut off in this way from conversational interactions with the population at large may help account for the fact that the idea has never been taken seriously.

The conversational realities of American democracy have a large degree of explanatory power for observable facts about the operation of the system. I have concentrated in this text on four "puzzles" of American democracy. Two are puzzles of attitude and sentiment that elude understanding in terms of the prevailing majoritarian ideology. Given its apportionment by states, it would seem that the U.S. Senate should be offensive to liberal majoritarian sensibilities; yet there is no evidence of widespread concern about that apportionment. Even less evident is concern with the anomalous treatment of children in our representational system, despite the fact that majoritarian ideology leaves them in a representational no-man's-land. There is, in contrast, considerable angst about the democratic legitimacy of judicial review, particularly among law professors. The puzzle of judicial review is how that sense of difficulty persists in the face of the obvious fact that the majoritarian *bona fides* of judicial review are not obviously more deficient than those of the uncontroversial Senate or of the system as a whole. Finally, there is the paradox of voting, identified as such by those who take seriously the liberal insistence that political actors—including voters—pursue self-interest, even in the public realm.

Each of these puzzles has a reasonably comfortable conversational solution. From a conversational perspective, it is easy to understand voter turnout, popular attitudes toward the Senate, inattention to the electoral status of children, and at least lawyer and law professor views toward judicial review. A conversational perspective also serves to bring into focus many other aspects of American democracy, including the almost complete disinterest in choosing legislators by lot.

None of this discussion establishes conversation as a normative beacon for American democracy. The conversational approach is an attempt to explain and understand, rather than to justify. If democratic conversation were simply an opiate, lulling the populace into going along while substantive outrages are committed in the name of democracy, the most complete understanding that a conversational perspective might provide would carry no intimation of approval. If the democratic conversation produces a sense of involvement in and commitment to the larger enterprise, such a role does not free us from the necessity for judgment about the worthiness of the enterprise. But a conversational perspective does bring many things about American democracy into clearer focus. It does so much more clearly and fully than does the common characterization of the system as majoritarian. And it does so at least as clearly and fully as rational choice theory, which must be considered the prevailing contemporary descriptive account of the operation of American democracy.

At the same time, normative inquiry into American democracy would do well to take conversationalism into account. If conversationalism gives us insight into some of the satisfactions that have helped form America's present-day democratic reality, it should also help us appreciate consequences that may attend change. Moves toward improvement by the lights of one normative vision or another will be put at peril if they ignore real-world forces that continue to impinge on a changed reality. I have tried to steer clear of normative inquiry, and for present purposes I continue to hold back from normative conclusions that conversationalism might be thought to suggest. But there are contemporary normative debates about democracy in the United States where conversational insights can clearly be brought to bear.

In recent years, for instance, there has emerged a vigorous movement for legislative term limits. The Supreme Court has held that term limits are constitutionally impermissible for federal legislative officers, but that has not completely dampened the enthusiasm of proponents of the idea. Many states have adopted term limits for state and local offices, and some states have experimented with devices that might nudge even federal legislators toward the support of a federal constitutional amendment that would allow limits at the national level.[3] There are conversational implications of term limits, cutting in different ways. Term limits might be thought to dampen the democratic conversation. Because it is the prospect of election that provides the primary incentive for legislator involvement in conversation, a legislator facing his or her final term has greatly diminished incentives.[4] Those who seek to succeed him or her will continue to reach out conversationally, but constituents will likely not be able to identify and follow those conversants nearly as well as they could the incumbent. At the same time, it may be that some incumbents have such nonconversational advantages in seeking reelection that they neglect conversational interactions.[5] Because term limits upset the incumbent advantage, they might be thought to stimulate more conversation. The tradeoff between these conversational effects will depend on complicated judgments about incumbency that often vary with context.

Even if the conversational tradeoffs are confidently understood, or even measured, they might influence but not necessarily settle the term limit debate. Quite apart from conversational effects, for instance, we might oppose term limits because experienced legislators produce better substantive decisions; or we might support term limits on the opposite assumption (particularly given concerns about incumbent advantages). If our normative vision of legislating is "republican" in the sense discussed in chapter three, we might be prepared to sacrifice a degree of responsiveness to constituents that the prospect of reelection might induce in order to gain a measure of fresh public interest idealism that could come with periodic insistence on a change of personnel.

A second contemporary problem with conversational dimensions is that of obstacles placed in the way of ballot access for candidates, typically taking the form of requirements of minimum demonstrations of support on petitions.[6] Here, again, there are both conversational and nonconversational dimensions of the problem posed by the requirements. Excluded candidates are not foreclosed from initiating conversation with the electorate, but they may find such efforts impeded by the cynicism and resulting alienation from the system of their natural constituencies, thereby complicating both the ability to attract monetary contributions and to command attention for what they say. Against this conversational loss must be weighed the virtue—usually taken to be some degree of manageability and orderliness in the electoral system—that might be thought to inhere in electoral competition that is limited to two, or at least a relatively small number, of parties and candidates.[7] This orderliness itself might have direct conversational implications, if conversational interactions are facilitated when there is only a manageable number of candidates vying for electoral attention.

These examples could be multiplied manyfold. The campaign finance debate has obvious conversational dimensions, as does the racial districting problem discussed in chapter nine. Conversationalism might illuminate some of the virtues and drawbacks in electing a variety of executive officials (as is done in some U.S. states), the consequences of changes in the lines of geographically defined legislative districts, and just what we should be looking for in a "good" public official. The use and timing of presidential primaries in the various states, the choice between treaties and ordinary legislation as instruments for ratification of international agreements,[8] the use of an executive line-item veto,[9] and the willingness to assign important decisionmaking powers to foreign or international tribunals[10] are just a few of the additional contemporary problems that have important conversational dimensions.

Beyond these more immediate questions, conversationalism might usefully inform the discussion of issues of normative democratic theory. The conversational perspective might help us appreciate, for instance, why representative democracy seems to work—to all appearances, even thrive—on a large scale, such as that found in the United States and other populous democracies. At the time that the U.S. Constitution was adopted, the antifederalists argued that a legislature made up of a tiny proportion of the population, such as made sense for an extended republic, could not sensitively represent the interests of a large population.[11] From a vote-centered perspective, they certainly had a point, for voting, even when supplemented by open communication thereafter, cannot make the legislature into a mechanism for processing the sentiments of a large population. Indeed, if the vote is taken as the mechanism of self-government, then, other things being equal, the degree of the individual's self-governing power necessarily diminishes as the size of the electorate grows, approaching the vanishing point with an electorate of any substantial size.[12] The democratic conversation, in contrast, has attributes of a "public good" in the economist's sense, in which participation by one person does not correspondingly diminish the capacity of others to participate—as long as it is appreciated that by far the largest portion of participation will be passive rather than active. To the extent that the democratic conversation is the linchpin of the system, and participation in it by the electorate is largely passive, the conversational perspective suggests that there is no obvious maximum size for districts in a stable democracy, nor for the democracy as a whole.[13]

This point may be missed by the most sophisticated of commentators operating outside a conversational framework. In discussing an alleged virtue of single-member, geographically based plurality systems as creating "a direct linkage between the elector and its elected representative," for instance, Giovanni Sartori asks whether the linkage can be "meaningful" in populous districts. He states that those who vote for the loser "simply lose their vote. . . . [and are] not represented at all."[14] Once the possibility of passive participation in conversation is recognized, however, it is not clear that there need be a loss of "linkage" in large districts. Indeed, since the largest part of the democratic conversation proceeds without the representative, deals with a multitude of different subjects, and contemplates eventual rather than immediate effect on the representative, it is not even clear that *active* conversational participation by one member of the electorate does that much to crowd out *active* participation by others.

I have not attempted any real comparative inquiry into the operation of the democratic conversation. It seems clear that the conversation is considerably more didactic, constrained, and stilted—and hence considerably less productive of a sense of involvement—in nondemocratic contexts. This fact seems almost self-evident, but it also finds support from a rather different sort of inquiry—the linguistic parsing of political speech in different contexts:

> Despots, whether traditional dynasts or modern dictators, customarily address the public in a speech sharply distinguished from the vernacular or vernaculars spoken by the population living under their rule. Democraticizing leaders begin and electoral politicians complete a rapprochement with the vernacular, addressing the population in ordinary language.[15]

The variations among democracies, on the other hand, are not likely to be nearly so stark. All politicians subjected to electoral pressures in genuinely competitive contexts tend to reach out conversationally. At the same time, it seems likely that a number of features of the American system probably produce more, and more involving, conversation than is found in many other democratic contexts. These include single-member districts, bicameralism, federalism, an independently elected executive, and wide-ranging protection for speech. These features are not all limited to the form of democracy found in the United States, but the combination is—which leads me to suggest that conversation may play more of a role in inducing fidelity to the system in the United States than it does elsewhere. I stress, however, that I have not examined such questions with any detail, and I offer the suggestion in a speculative spirit.[16]

Trusting that I have at least said enough to suggest the power of a conversational account of American democracy, I close with a comment that is at once personal and extraterrestrial. In the early part of the nineteenth century, astronomers assumed that there were seven planets in our solar system. The eighth, which we now call Neptune, was discovered initially not because it was observed directly, but because it caused Uranus, then assumed to be the outermost planet, to move in ways that were considered aberrant according to the prevailing Newtonian conception of planetary movement. In similar fashion, the vote-centered conceptualization of the operation of American democracy helped me see things that were necessary to make that conceptualization work. In particular, it first showed me that something was amiss in the apparent satisfaction with the U.S. Senate, and then that there was something even more mysterious in the political treatment of children. Further inquiry was necessary, but then the astronomical precedent broke down. For Neptune turned out to be there, whereas no phenomena surfaced to explain why, from the prevailing majoritarian conceptualization, the Senate was uncontroversial and children politically invisible. The Newtonian conception held, but the vote-centered one could not.[17]

The reason is fairly apparent. The vote-centered conception of American democracy is essentially a normative conception that has been put to descriptive service. Descriptive accounts of large-scale social phenomena are never perfect, and that fact has helped disguise the deficiencies in the vote-centered account. But the Senate is too central a phenomenon of American democracy to have its easy embrace dismissed as just a small blur in an otherwise clear picture. The Senate, and then the problem of children, pointed me to still other problems with the vote-centered account, and then to alternative ways of depicting American democracy, and from there to problems with those alternatives as well. The result was an appreciation of democracy as involvement in conversation.

Even with the conversational account in hand, there remains an important difference between attempts to capture planetary movements and American democracy. Unlike planetary movements, American democracy can be unsettled by normativity that will not be denied. In its normative guise, the vote-centered vision may yet inject life into a movement for change in the apportionment of the Senate or even attention to the possibility of extra votes for parents on account of their children. Our Neptune may, in that way, be caused to appear. Until it does—or even after it does—we will still do well to notice the deficiencies of the vote-centered account and the power of a conversational alternative, for in all likelihood there are many more lessons to be learned.

Appendix: Originalism and the Enduring Need For Conversation

In chapter seven I discussed various approaches to constitutional interpretation, including what is called "originalism." Originalists insist that only the Constitution's "original meaning" provides a basis for application to contemporary problems.[1] Interpretational theorists may be drawn to one approach or the other by the prospect of answering constitutional questions without the messy need for conversation. Originalists in particular sometimes suggest that their approach to interpretation will severely limit the possibilities for dispute and hence the desire for conversation about constitutional questions.[2] However, originalism cannot realize any such ambition.

Aside from reliance on text, originalism depicts constitutional meaning as revolving around a defined historical inquiry, and for purposes of this discussion, I assume that it is right to do so. There are varieties of originalism. Some originalists search for the intentions of the framers, or the ratifiers, of the constitutional provision in issue, whereas for others it is the understanding of those to whom the provisions were addressed that is the key to constitutional meaning.[3] For present purposes, I also assume that those controversies are settled—which way it matters not. These historical inquiries seriously curtail the need for conversation only if the historical answers are clear—and that they will seldom be, for a variety of reasons.[4]

Whether the originalist inquiry is focused on framers, ratifiers, or addressees, there will have been more than one person involved. The sheer number of actors with official duties in the formulation and adoption of the Constitution—to say nothing of the population that constituted the addressees at the time—makes unsurprising Jack Rakove's conclusion with regard to the original Constitution:

> It is entirely possible—even probable, indeed almost certain—that the intentions of the framers and the understanding of the ratifiers and their electors diverged in numerous ways, on points both major and minor. Given the highly charged and intensely political character of the ratification campaign, no other outcome was possible.[5]

Rakove may actually underestimate the problem. Those responsible for enacting the Constitution may not have thought at all about a particular question of meaning. Unless there is evidence about what each and every one of them (or at least of enough of them to ensure adoption) thought on some question—and that they thought the same thing—controversy is possible. For there is no historical answer to the question of how we are to count the intentions of the different actors: those who took the lead as opposed to those who followed in some voting body with the authority to decide, those who gave thought to a question as opposed to those who did not, or those who spoke out as opposed to those who kept silent.[6] The same is obviously—indeed even more clearly—true for addressees.

Even a single individual, moreover, may have thought different things at different times. An individual may even have thought two (or more) things at once that point in different directions with regard to some question that comes to be in issue. The classic example of this, illuminated in the work of Ronald Dworkin, is the varying levels of concreteness and generality that an individual may have entertained that could be thought to bear on a discrete problem.[7] If to a contemporary judge those different levels cut toward different results, there is no historical answer to the question of which is to be used.

Finally, no actor involved in the promulgation of a constitutional provision—or seeking to understand it once promulgated—will have given any thought to phenomena he could not foresee. In a real sense, he could not foresee much at all about the future, for even superficially similar phenomena can take on meaning from the different social and economic settings in which they arise. One cannot, as Heraclitus taught, "step into the same river twice."[8] A contemporary problem could thus be solved unproblematically by reference to what some person or people thought at an earlier time only if the present problem differs in no arguable normative way from the one originally considered. Because of all these sources of uncertainty, moreover, constitutional adjudication requires a doctrine of precedent, what to do with decisions that come to be seen as mistaken. History provides no answer to that question either.

This is not to deny that there may be better and worse originalist answers to constitutional questions, nor that originalism—or, for that matter, any of the competing approaches to interpretation—is the right approach. It is only to say that if the sense of difficulty is produced by the courts' counterconversationalism, no more than other approaches to interpretation can originalism still that sense. Even if the answers to constitutional questions left open by the text are rooted in historical data as originalism would have it, there is plenty of material for controversy, which then provides an opening for normative concerns into which there will be no reluctance by the parties to adjudication to rush. As long as courts do the deciding under conventional procedures, the counterconversational difference in their approach to decisionmaking will have ample material with which to feed a sense of difficulty.

Notes

Preface

1. Alexander M. Bickel, THE LEAST DANGEROUS BRANCH (Bobbs-Merrill Co. 1962).
2. Robert W. Bennett, *Democracy as Meaningful Conversation*, 14 CONSTITUTIONAL COMMENTARY 481 (1997), selections reprinted by special permission of the University of Minnesota Law School; Robert W. Bennett, *Should Parents Be Given Extra Votes on Account of Their Children?: Toward a Conversational Understanding of American Democracy*, 94 NORTHWESTERN UNIVERSITY LAW REVIEW 503 (2000); Robert W. Bennett, *The Senate of the United States, in* ROLE AND FUNCTION OF THE SECOND CHAMBER, PROCEEDINGS OF THE THIRD CONGRESS OF THE EUROPEAN ASSOCIATION OF LEGISLATION (EAL) 141 (Ulrich Karpen ed., Nomos Verlagsgesellschaft 1999); Robert W. Bennett, *Counter-Conversationalism and the Sense of Difficulty*, 95 NORTHWESTERN UNIVERSITY LAW REVIEW 845 (2001), selections reprinted by special permission of Northwestern University School of Law; Robert W. Bennett, *Response: On Substantiation of Positive Social Theory*, 95 NORTHWESTERN UNIVERSITY LAW REVIEW 977 (2001), selections reprinted by special permission of Northwestern University School of Law.
3. My doubts on this score grew gradually, but they were substantially reinforced when Barry Friedman made the point in criticism of my

discussion in *Counter-Conversationalism, supra* note 2. *See* Barry Friedman, *The Counter-Majoritarian Problem and the Pathology of Constitutional Scholarship,* 95 NORTHWESTERN UNIVERSITY LAW REVIEW 933, 951 (2001).

Chapter 1. The Explanatory Reach of Democratic Conversation

1. William N. Eskridge Jr., *The One Senator, One Vote Clause, in Constitutional Stupidities: A Symposium,* 12 CONSTITUTIONAL COMMENTARY 159, 161–162 (1995); Suzanna Sherry, *Our Unconstitutional Senate, id.* at 213; Daniel A. Farber, *Our (Almost) Perfect Constitution, id.* at 163, 164–165. Senate apportionment also received mention in J. M. Balkin, *The Constitution as a Box of Chocolates, id.* at 147. The idea for the symposium was apparently brought to the journal by Sanford Levinson and William Eskridge; *see* Sanford Levinson and William N. Eskridge Jr., *Introduction, id.* at 139. For a few other jibes at the Senate *see* Stephen M. Griffin, *The Nominee Is . . . Article V, in* CONSTITUTIONAL STUPIDITIES, CONSTITUTIONAL TRAGEDIES 51, 53 (William N. Eskridge Jr. & Sanford Levinson eds., New York University Press 1998); Michael Stokes Paulsen, *Someone Should Have Told Spiro Agnew, in* CONSTITUTIONAL TRAGEDIES, *supra,* at 75, 79–80 n.8; Martin S. Flaherty, *Are We to Be a Nation? Federal Power vs. "States' Rights" in Foreign Affairs,* 70 UNIVERSITY OF COLORADO LAW REVIEW 1277, 1308 (1999).
2. Robert D. Putnam, BOWLING ALONE 21, 31–133 (Simon & Schuster 2000).
3. *See, e.g.,* Richard Flacks, *Strike, Spare and Scratch,* L.A. Times, July 16, 2000, Book Review Section, at 5; Margaret Talbot, *Who Wants to Be a Legionnaire?,* N.Y. Times, June 25, 2000, § 7, at 11; Christopher Farrell, *Bring Back the Quilting Bee,* Business Week, June 26, 2000, at 26.
4. Putnam, *supra* note 2, at 134–137.
5. *See, e.g.,* Farrell, *supra* note 3 ("Crime rates are dropping. . . . [U]rban centers are enjoying a renaissance. . . . Alcoholics Anonymous, gay and lesbian support groups, evangelical religion, and other social movements are thriving.").
6. Putnam, *supra* note 2, at 31–33, 35, 46, 336.

Chapter 2. Majoritarianism and the Vote-Centered Model

1. *See* Alexander M. Bickel, THE LEAST DANGEROUS BRANCH (Bobbs-Merrill Co. 1962). Bickel's most celebrated academic precursor was James

Bradley Thayer. The influence of Thayer's article, James Bradley Thayer, *The Origin and Scope of the American Doctrine of Constitutional Law*, 7 HARVARD LAW REVIEW 129 (1893), has been noted widely, *see One Hundred Years of Judicial Review: The Thayer Centennial Symposium*, 88 NORTHWESTERN UNIVERSITY LAW REVIEW 1 (1993), including by Bickel who calls it "a singularly important piece of American legal scholarship" (Bickel, *supra*, at 35). Concern with the tension between American democracy and judicial review, however, long preceded Thayer. *See* Jesse H. Choper, JUDICIAL REVIEW AND THE NATIONAL POLITICAL PROCESS 4 (University of Chicago Press 1980). The term *judicial review* is also sometimes used to refer to review of action by administrative agencies, in which there can arise questions of compliance with statutes as well as with the Constitution. I use the term only in the narrower sense suggested in the text.

2. In what is by now a classic work of political theory, Robert Dahl, invoking Jefferson, Lincoln, and de Tocqueville, among others, says that "the whole history of democratic theories [has seen] . . . the identification of 'democracy' with . . . rule by majorities." Robert A. Dahl, A PREFACE TO DEMOCRATIC THEORY 34 (University of Chicago Press 1956). *See* Abner J. Mikva, *Foreword: Symposium on the Theory of Public Choice*, 74 VIRGINIA LAW REVIEW 167 (1988): "I am still one of those . . . who believe . . . that majorities in effect make policy in this country. . . ."; Robert H. Bork, THE TEMPTING OF AMERICA 139 (Free Press 1990): American "self-government . . . means that in wide areas of life majorities are entitled to rule . . . simply because they are majorities"; Steven G. Calabresi, *Textualism and the Countermajoritarian Difficulty*, 66 GEORGE WASHINGTON UNIVERSITY LAW REVIEW 1373, 1382–1383, 1391 (1998): "the Court's recent movement . . . toward. . . . enforc[ing] textually prescribed structural constitutional allocations of power. . . . does not suffer from the countermajoritarian difficulty . . . because it is engaged only in choosing which majority should govern on which issue. . . . [D]emocracy is simply a regime where there is majority rule. . . ."; Frederick Schauer, FREE SPEECH: A PHILOSOPHICAL ENQUIRY 41 (Cambridge University Press 1982): "The more we accept the premise of the argument from democracy, the less can we impinge on the right of self-government by restricting the power of the majority."; Kathleen M. Sullivan, *Law's Labors*, THE NEW REPUBLIC, May 23, 1994, at 42, 44 (reviewing David J. Garrow, LIBERTY AND SEXUALITY: THE RIGHT TO PRIVACY AND THE MAKING OF *Roe v. Wade* [Macmillan 1994]): associating "imperfections in the political marketplace" with "thwart[ing] . . . vindication of . . . majority preferences"; Frank H. Easterbrook, *Textualism and the Dead Hand*, 66 GEORGE WASHINGTON

UNIVERSITY LAW REVIEW 1119, 1122 (1998): "Today's majority accepts limits on its own power. . . ."; Mark Tushnet, RED, WHITE, AND BLUE 16 (Harvard University Press 1988): "In general [in our society] the choice made by a majority is to be respected"; Mary Becker, *Conservative Free Speech and the Uneasy Case for Judicial Review*, 64 UNIVERSITY OF COLORADO LAW REVIEW 975 (1993): "countermajoritarian . . . judicial review" identified with "judicial interference with quality democratic deliberations."; Christopher J. Peters, *Adjudication As Representation*, 97 COLUMBIA LAW REVIEW 312, 419–420 (1997): "The process of judicial review may not be *majoritarian,* but it is *democratic* in a sense closely akin to that of majoritarian lawmaking" (emphasis in original); Choper, *supra* note 1, at 9–10: "the procedure of judicial review is in conflict with the fundamental principle of democracy—majority rule under conditions of political freedom"; William H. Rehnquist, *The Notion of a Living Constitution,* 54 TEXAS LAW REVIEW 693, 695–696 (1976): "those who have pondered the matter have always recognized that the ideal of judicial review has basically antidemocratic and anti-majoritarian facets that require some justification in this Nation, which prides itself on being a self-governing representative democracy"; Guido Calabresi, A COMMON LAW FOR THE AGE OF STATUTES 101–102 (Harvard University Press 1982): urging that unenforced statutes may lose their claim on us, because they only "commanded a majoritarian basis" at some time in the past; Rebecca L. Brown, *Accountability, Liberty, and the Constitution,* 98 COLUMBIA LAW REVIEW 531, 541 (1998): "Common wisdom paints the twentieth century as simply one continuous movement toward a majoritarian paradigm. . . ."; *cf.* Richard John Neuhaus, *Rebuilding the Civil Public Square, in* THE END OF DEMOCRACY? II 3, 8, 14 (Mitchell S. Muncy ed., Spencer Publishing Co. 1999): criticizing "judicial usurpation of politics" through judicial review on the ground that "a Constitution . . . increasingly pitted against the majority will, in time, become an ineffectual instrument in protecting minorities."; William N. Eskridge, Jr., *Dynamic Statutory Interpretation* 135 UNIVERSITY OF PENNSYLVANIA LAW REVIEW 1479, 1528 (1987): "public choice theory predicts that . . . [legislator] incentives will lead them away from majoritarian preferences and that, in any event, the rules created by a legislature will often fail to reflect majority preferences because of procedural manipulations."; Tracy E. Higgins, *Democracy and Feminism,* 110 HARVARD LAW REVIEW 1657 (1997): associating democracy with "majoritarian rule" and discussing the tension with constitutionalism; Steven P. Croley, *The Majoritarian Difficulty: Elective Judiciaries and the Rule of Law,* 62 UNIVERSITY OF

CHICAGO LAW REVIEW 689, 710 (1995): making the association, though not particularly approvingly; Daniel A. Farber & Philip P. Frickey, LAW AND PUBLIC CHOICE, A CRITICAL INTRODUCTION 147 (University of Chicago Press 1991): judicial review called a "countermajoritarian authority," a characterization that is particularly jarring in a book devoted to discussing the theoretical underpinnings of many qualifications on the reign of majorities, *see, e.g., id.* at 8, 57; Frances E. Lee & Bruce I. Oppenheimer, SIZING UP THE SENATE 116, 120 (University of Chicago Press 1999): referring to apportionment of the Senate as having "countermajoritarian" effects. For a sample of the majoritarian assumption in opinions of U.S. Supreme Court Justices, *see* San Antonio Independent School Dist. v. Rodriguez, 411 U.S. 1, 28 (1973); Schweiker v. Wilson, 450 U.S. 221, 243 (1981) (Powell, J., dissenting); Central Hudson Gas & Electric Corp. v. PSC of New York, 447 U.S. 557, 598 (1980) (Rehnquist, J., dissenting); United States v. Raddatz, 447 U.S. 667, 704 (1980) (Marshall, J., dissenting); United States v. Richardson, 418 U.S. 166, 192 (1974) (Powell, J., concurring); Flast v. Cohen, 392 U.S. 83, 110 (1968) (Douglas, J., concurring). Long before this contemporary commentary, Alexander Hamilton said in FEDERALIST 22 that the "fundamental maxim of republican government" is that "the sense of the majority should prevail." And in his first inaugural, Thomas Jefferson insisted that "absolute acquiescence in the decisions of the majority" is "the vital principle of republics." *First Inaugural Address* by President Thomas Jefferson (March 4, 1801), *reprinted in* I THE FOUNDERS' CONSTITUTION 140, 141 (Philip B. Kurland & Ralph Lerner eds., University of Chicago Press 1987). Both Hamilton and Jefferson were surely assuming that the United States was a "republic."

3. David Held, MODELS OF DEMOCRACY 18, 19 (2d ed. Stanford University Press 1996), quoting from Aristotle's THE POLITICS, where he contrasts this "numerical equality" with decisionmaking power "based on merit."

4. Once eligibility to vote is determined, and even assuming that formal abstention is counted as a vote, there is the further problem of what to do if not all those eligible take advantage of the opportunity. There are some electoral systems, even democratic ones, in which voting is required and sanctions imposed on nonvoters (see G. Bingham Powell Jr., CONTEMPORARY DEMOCRACIES 113–114 [Harvard University Press 1982]), but in many systems there is no such requirement. With or without a voting requirement, there may be a requirement that any matter receive approval by a majority of the entire electorate. Absent one of these mechanisms, a deciding "majority" may be a majority of those who

cast votes, but not necessarily of those who are acknowledged to be enfranchised members of the community. A quorum requirement is a common mechanism through which majoritarian systems ensure that a healthy percentage of the electorate—even if less than a majority of those eligible to vote—approves the eventual choice.

5. If the answer seems obvious that all three floors must constitute a single issue, consider that the first floor may get the most wear, the second may have had a recent soiling from an accident, and the third may have only recently been cleaned "privately" at the expense of the owners on the floor. In the real world of American politics, legislation potentially brings together issues considerably more disconnected than the quaint example of carpet cleaning in a three-story condominium. A story in the news as I was writing this chapter, for instance, depicts a tug of war between the U.S. Senate and the president about whether support for abortion programs in foreign countries and the payment of America's overdue dues for the United Nations are to be treated as one matter or two (Eric Schmitt, *Abortion Discord Holds Up U.N. Dues and U.S. Budget*, N.Y. Times, Nov. 11, 1999, at A18). Another telling example is reported in Joseph Kahn, *Horse-Trading (and Pork) on the Trade Bill*, N.Y. Times, May 11, 2000, at A6 (permanent trading rights for China and tax treatment of investment in Pennsylvania coal industry).

6. A nice discussion appears in Dennis C. Mueller, Public Choice 207–226 (Cambridge University Press 1979). *See* James M. Buchanan & Gordon Tullock, The Calculus of Consent 85–96, 131–145 (Ann Arbor Paperback 1965).

7. On the plurality choice losing in head-to-head confrontations with all other possibilities, if there were five voters—V1, V2, V3, V4, and V5—choosing among four possibilities—X, Y, Z, and W—X might be the plurality choice of V1 and V2, beating Y, Z, and W, each of which was the favorite of only one voter (V3, V4, and V5, respectively). But V4 and V5 might still join with V3 to favor Y over X in a standoff between just those two. *See* Kenneth Arrow, Social Choice and Individual Values (Wiley 1951).

8. *See* Sylvia R. Lazos Vargas, *Judicial Review of Initiatives and Referendums in which Majorities Vote on Minorities' Democratic Citizenship*, 60 Ohio State Law Journal 399, 411 (1999); *see generally* Julian N. Eule, *Judicial Review of Direct Democracy*, 99 Yale Law Journal 1503, 1508–1513 (1990). A proposal "that the President should be elected by 'the citizens of the United States,' or by the 'people' . . . [was] voted down [at the constitutional convention]." McPherson v. Blacker, 146 U.S. 1, 28 (1892). Under the scheme that was adopted, the president

is chosen by what has come to be called the "electoral college," membership in which is apportioned by states, with substantial discretion over the manner of selection of the electors reposed in the individual states. I return in chapter three to the deviations from "majoritarianism" that the electoral college creates. One commentator has recently suggested that a majority of American voters could now require Congress to convene a constitutional convention by submitting a petition to that effect "and that an amendment could be lawfully ratified by a simple majority of the American electorate." Akhil Reed Amar, *Popular Sovereignty and Constitutional Amendment, in* RESPONDING TO IMPERFECTION 89 n.1 (Sanford Levinson ed., Princeton University Press 1995). *See also* Akhil Reed Amar, *Philadelphia Revisited: Amending the Constitution Outside Article V,* 55 UNIVERSITY OF CHICAGO LAW REVIEW 1043 (1988); Akhil Reed Amar, *The Consent of the Governed: Constitutional Amendment Outside Article V,* 94 COLUMBIA LAW REVIEW 457 (1994). This is, to say the least, an eccentric view. There is not a word in the Constitution that would support such a procedure, and it is thoroughly at odds with the most fundamental assumptions of our constitutional order, including, importantly, the role of the states. Thus, the qualification to vote in federal elections was originally, and remains to a degree, within the discretion of the states, *see* U.S. Const. Art. I, § 2, cl. 1; Art. II, § 1; Am. XVII, so that there are not even the uniform national qualifications that would seem necessary to give coherence to the notion of a "simple" national majority.

9. *Cf.* Randy E. Barnett, *The Relevance of the Framers' Intent,* 19 HARVARD JOURNAL OF LAW AND PUBLIC POLICY 403, 404 (1996). There are three steps if each chamber of our bicameral national legislature is counted separately, four if the requirement of presidential approval is also counted separately, and as many as six if the popular elections are counted separately.

10. In addition to majoritarianism, the ideology of democracy—including the representative variant—recurs repeatedly to political equality and self-government or popular sovereignty. *See* Dahl, *supra* note 2, at 34. Each of these elements seem traceable to emphasis on the popular vote as the central mechanism of democratic governance.

11. *"Philanthrop" to the Public, in* I THE DEBATE ON THE CONSTITUTION: FEDERALIST AND ANTIFEDERALIST SPEECHES, ARTICLES, AND LETTERS DURING THE STRUGGLE OVER RATIFICATION 325 (Bernard Bailyn ed., The Library of America 1993); "Americanus" (John Stevens Jr.) III, *in* I THE DEBATE, *supra,* at 437, 440; Jack N. Rakove, ORIGINAL MEANINGS 203 (Alfred A. Knopf 1996). In a letter to Thomas Jefferson from Lon-

don in 1787, Adams said "We agree perfectly that the many should have a full fair and perfect Representation." John Adams to Thomas Jefferson, *in* I THE DEBATE, *supra*, at 473. (In the case of Adams at least, it is clear that he was simultaneously wary of an elected assembly and in favor of substantial countervailing power in a stable executive (*Id.*) For an antifederalist statement to the same effect, *see Dissent of the Minority of the Pennsylvania Convention, in* I THE DEBATE, *supra*, at 526, 541–542 ("the representation [by a 'legislature of a free country'] ought to be fair, equal, and sufficiently numerous, to possess the same interests, feelings, opinions, and views, which the people themselves would possess, were they all assembled. . . ."). I am using the term *federalist* here to refer to those who supported ratification of the Constitution, as opposed to the "antifederalists." At the time, there was no political party known as the "Federalists," but it was not long before there was open political competition between a Federalist and a Republican party. In that contest, the espousal of majoritarian decisionmaking was more likely to be associated with the Republicans, because a majoritarian ideal was an article of faith with Thomas Jefferson, the undisputed initial leader of the Republican Party. *See* Paul W. Kahn, THE REIGN OF LAW 49–52 (Yale University Press 1997). Still, embrace and wariness of majoritarianism did not divide predictably along either federalist/ antifederalist or Republican/Federalist lines.

12. Joseph M. Bessette, THE MILD VOICE OF REASON 2 (University of Chicago Press 1994). John Rawls advances a "principle of (equal) participation" requiring that "all citizens are to have an equal right to take part in, and to determine the outcome of, the constitutional process that establishes the laws with which they are to comply." John Rawls, A THEORY OF JUSTICE 221 (Harvard University Press 1971); *see* Frederick Rosen, *Majorities and Minorities: a Classical Utilitarian View, in* NOMOS XXXII, MAJORITIES AND MINORITIES 24, 32 (John W. Chapman & Alan Wertheimer eds., New York University Press 1990). Rawls speaks of a "right" to participate and determine outcomes that is to be distributed equally, but he quickly makes clear that it is *actual contribution* to outcomes he has in mind:

> The liberties protected by the principle of participation lose much of their value whenever those who have greater private means are permitted to use their advantages to control the course of public debate. For eventually these inequalities will enable those better situated to exercise a larger influence over the development of legislation.

Rawls, *supra*, at 225. In a similar vein, Robert Dahl explains that among the "ideal standards" of a democracy is that at "the decisive stage of collective decisions, each citizen must be ensured an equal opportunity to express a choice that will be counted as equal in weight to the choice expressed by any other citizen." Robert A. Dahl, DEMOCRACY AND ITS CRITICS 108–109 (Yale University Press 1989) (italics omitted). And Thomas Christiano elaborates on what political equality means:

> The basic principle of political equality is that in collective decision making designed for the purpose of deciding upon collective properties of society, all the relevant means to securing desired ends ought to be distributed equally. Voting power is the first important candidate for inclusion among these means. . . .

Thomas Christiano, *Political Equality, in* NOMOS XXXII, *supra,* at 153. For a selection of additional examples, *see* Douglas J. Amy, REAL CHOICES/NEW VOICES 27 (Columbia University Press 1993); Jamin Raskin & John Bonifaz, *The Constitutionally Imperative and Practical Superiority of Democratically Financed Elections,* 94 COLUMBIA LAW REVIEW 1160, 1162. *See also* Benjamin I. Page, WHO DELIBERATES? (University of Chicago Press 1996).

13. Reynolds v. Sims, 377 U.S. 533, 565 (1964) (emphasis supplied).

Chapter 3. Descriptive Shortcomings of the Vote-Centered Model

1. Joseph Ellis cautions that "the history of what might have been is usually not really history at all, mixing together as it does the messy tangle of past experience with the clairvoyant certainty of our present preferences." Joseph J. Ellis, FOUNDING BROTHERS 105 (Alfred A. Knopf 2000). The problem is, of course, infinitely worse for imagined events that could not have been.
2. *See, e.g.,* Clinton v. Jones, 520 U.S. 681 (1997).
3. For a discussion of early tensions between the two, *see* Gordon S. Wood, THE RADICALISM OF THE AMERICAN REVOLUTION 243–270 (Random House 1991). Geoffrey Brennan & Alan Hamlin, *Paying for Politics, in* NOMOS XLII, DESIGNING DEMOCRATIC INSTITUTIONS 55, 59 (Ian Shapiro & Stephen Macedo eds., New York University Press 2000) discuss contemporary issues of campaign finance in terms of what they call "rational actor" and "deliberative democracy" models. In a contribution to the same volume, John Ferejohn discusses "aggregative" and "deliberative" models (*Instituting Deliberative Democracy, in* NOMOS XLII, *supra,* at 75). Jane Mansbridge contrasts "adversary" and "unitary" democracy in Jane J. Mansbridge, BEYOND ADVERSARY DEMOCRACY (University of Chicago Press 1983). Each of these pairings, and no

doubt others as well, is derivative of the contrasting liberal and republican visions.

4. *See* Hannah Fenichel Pitkin, THE CONCEPT OF REPRESENTATION 127–131 (University of California Press 1967).

5. *See* Jack N. Rakove, ORIGINAL MEANINGS 55 (Alfred A. Knopf 1996) (characterizing the thought of James Madison).

6. It is not entirely clear why this is so for either the republican or the liberal. For the republican, the problem of rationalizing equality in the vote is acute. The republican is seeking the interest of the community as a whole, and since he or she is dealing largely with the interests of others, the republican decisionmaker has no special access to the reality of those interests. It might well be thought that some republican voters would be better than others at perceiving the community interest. In such a setting, equality in the vote of those who are entitled to vote has no obvious rationale integral to republicanism, save perhaps that any other rule might prove contentious. *See* Jeremy Waldron, *Legislation, Authority, and Voting,* 84 GEORGETOWN LAW JOURNAL 2185, 2188 (1996); Brennan & Hamlin, *supra* note 3, at 59; *but see* Mansbridge, *supra* note 3, at 28 (suggesting that in what she calls "unitary democracy," equality may help induce the empathy essential to hold the enterprise together).

For the liberal, the problem is perhaps a bit less tricky, but not much. Membership in a liberal community is coincident with the franchise, for voting is the mechanism by which those entitled to be represented achieve that representation. And the liberal voter does have privileged access to information about the interest he or she is to represent, *i.e.* one's own. To be sure, the liberal may accommodate the interests of others in deciding how to vote, either because the interests of those others are a part of what the liberal voter comes to think of as his or her own interest, or because the liberal is looking for reciprocal accommodation in turn. But the liberal voter is under no illusions that he or she is somehow *obliged* by virtue of participation in the process of voting to consider the interests of others, or of some notion of a "community." This combination might seem to make equality of voting power the obvious rule of decision, but only if there is some prior commitment to an equality ideal. For in a liberal environment, it is still unclear how or why voters concerned with self-interest would accede to equal representation for others. Again, the reason may simply be that equal regard of others is the only plausible basis on which each liberal voter may obtain cooperation in a venture in which all are seen to have a stake.

7. FEDERALIST 10.

8. "In all very numerous assemblies, of whatever characters composed, passion never fails to wrest the scepter from reason. Had every Athenian citizen been a Socrates, every Athenian assembly would still have been a mob." FEDERALIST 55. Madison was not particularly enamored of small direct democratic gatherings either. *See* FEDERALIST 10; *see also* Hamilton's FEDERALIST 58 ("infirmities incident to collective meetings of the people") and Madison's FEDERALIST 39.

9. Quite the opposite, disapproval is formalized in a large number of state constitutions through single subject rules that crimp the style of would-be traders. *See, e.g.,* People v. Cervantes, 189 Ill. 2d 80, 723 N.E. 2d 265 (1999).

10. *Cf.* Ian Ayres, *Disclosure Versus Anonymity in Campaign Finance, in* NOMOS XLII, *supra* note 3, at 19, 26.

11. *See* Kenneth Arrow, SOCIAL CHOICE AND INDIVIDUAL VALUES (Wiley 1951).

12. *See* Amos Tversky & Daniel Kahneman, *The Framing of Decisions and the Psychology of Choice,* 211 SCIENCE 435, 457 (1981).

13. *See* Saul Levmore, *Parliamentary Law, Majority Decisionmaking, and the Voting Paradox,* 75 VIRGINIA LAW REVIEW 971, 989–990 (1989). Procedural "rules can be neutral—for example, if either the chair is unaware of the individuals' preferences or, more affirmatively, there is a random process to determine voting order—but they will still determine the outcome, because there is no collective preference independent of the rules of order." *Id.* at 990.

14. We might, for instance, try assuming that the whole was small enough to make a meeting conceivable if cumbersome, and then try to extrapolate from there.

15. There are, of course, two senators for each "district," *i.e.,* state. But no state has both senatorial slots open at once, except in case of some emergency. With only one position being filled at a time, even the U.S. Senate is in this important way composed of legislators chosen from "single member" districts.

16. In theory, just over one quarter of the votes in the polity as a whole could control outcomes in a unicameral legislative assembly, assuming districting based on voting population of the districts. For "only a bare majority of the representatives in a chamber is needed to pass legislation, and each representative in the governing majority needs just over one-half of the voters in his or her district." Saul Levmore, *Bicameralism: When Are Two Decisions Better Than One?,* 12 INTERNATIONAL REVIEW OF LAW AND ECONOMICS 145, 151–152 (1992); *see* James M. Buchanan & Gordon Tullock, THE CALCULUS OF CONSENT 220–222

(Ann Arbor Paperback 1965). For exploration of the importance of the difference between equally populated districts and districts equally populated with voters, *see* Robert W. Bennett, *Should Parents Be Given Extra Votes on Account of Their Children?: Toward A Conversational Understanding of American Democracy*, 94 NORTHWESTERN UNIVERSITY LAW REVIEW 503, 506–517 (2000).

17. *See* Daniel A. Farber & Philip P. Frickey, LAW AND PUBLIC CHOICE 27 (University of Chicago Press 1991).

18. If each representative had only a handful of constituents and ongoing contact with them, the information problem might be manageable, but then we would be unlikely to find representative government.

19. Paul Kleppner, WHO VOTED?: THE DYNAMICS OF ELECTORAL TURNOUT, 1870–1980 4 (Praeger Publishers 1982).

20. For one rendition of the interest group theory, *see* Frank Easterbrook, *Foreword: The Court and the Economic System*, 98 HARVARD LAW REVIEW 4, 15–16 (1984). One consequence of differential interests is that members of the population often remain ignorant about a wide range of matters of public policy. A recent issue of the journal CRITICAL REVIEW, Vol. 12, No. 4 (Fall 1998) was devoted to the phenomenon of "public ignorance." The introductory essay asserts that the fact that "the public is overwhelmingly ignorant when it comes to politics. . . . is ['possibly *the* strongest' finding] produced by any social science." Jeffrey Friedman, *Introduction: Public Ignorance and Democratic Theory, id.* at 397 (emphasis in original). *See* Carole Pateman, PARTICIPATION AND DEMOCRATIC THEORY 3 (Cambridge University Press 1970).

21. There is a host of other determinants of outcomes ranging from input by noncitizens to the weather on election day to policy with regard to the positioning of candidates on the ballot. *See* Harry M. Bain Jr. & Donald S. Hecock, BALLOT POSITION AND VOTER'S CHOICE (Wayne State University Press 1957).

22. FEDERALIST 62.

23. Madison made this point most sharply by spurning direct or, as he put it, "pure" democracy in his classic discussion of "factions":

> a pure democracy, by which I mean a society consisting of a small number of citizens, who assemble and administer the government in person, can admit of no cure for the mischiefs of faction. A common passion or interest will, in almost every case, be felt by a majority of the whole; a communication and concert results from the form of government itself; and there is nothing to check the inducements to sacrifice the weaker party or an obnoxious individual.

FEDERALIST 10.

If anything, Madison seemed to think that large-scale direct democracy would be worse:

> In all very numerous assemblies, of whatever characters composed, passion never fails to wrest the scepter from reason. Had every Athenian citizen been a Socrates, every Athenian assembly would still have been a mob.

FEDERALIST 55.

24. *See* Harry N. Scheiber, *Federalism and the Constitution: The Original Understanding,* in AMERICAN LAW AND THE CONSTITUTIONAL ORDER 85, 92–94 (Lawrence N. Friedman and Harry N. Scheiber eds., Harvard University Press 1988).

25. Assume nine electors of whom five are Libertarians (E1, E2, E3, E4, and E5) and four are Egalitarians (E6, E7, E8, and E9). If each branch of the legislature has three members, and the House districting puts E1, E2, and E6 in house district one; E3, E4, and E7 in house district two; and E5, E8 and E9 in house district three, the House will presumably have a 2–1 Libertarian majority with the representatives from districts one and two. If the Senate districting puts E1, E2, and E3 in senate district one; E4, E6, and E7 in senate district two; and E5, E8, and E9 in senate district three, however, the Senate would presumably return a 2–1 Egalitarian majority with the senators from districts two and three. This is, of course, a function of the fact noted earlier that a majority of the entire electorate need not be reflected, even along the most politically salient of dimensions, in a body of representatives chosen in American-style single-member, geographically defined districts.

26. The quoted words are taken from FEDERALIST 51 and FEDERALIST 62.

27. *See* Frances E. Lee & Bruce I. Oppenheimer, SIZING UP THE SENATE 116 (University of Chicago Press 1999) (senatorial "apportionment has generally had a distinctly countermajoritarian effect on the partisan outcomes of Senate elections throughout the period since the adoption of the Seventeenth Amendment.").

28. The Constitution provides that "[r]epresentatives shall be apportioned *among* the several states." U.S. Const., Am. XIV, § 2 (italics supplied); *see* U.S. Const, Art. I, § 2, cl. 3. Although this is not entirely explicit, the practice has been—and the intention surely was—as stated in the text.

29. Dept. of Commerce v. Montana, 503 U.S. 442, 445 (1992). The Court was thus a little fast and loose when it said in Wesberry v. Sanders, 376 U.S. 1 (1964), that "one principle was uppermost in the minds of many delegates [to the Constitutional Convention]: that, no matter where he

lived, each voter should have a voice equal to that of every other in electing members of Congress." 376 U.S. at 10. We return to the Supreme Court's apportionment jurisprudence when I take up the puzzle of the democratic status of children in chapter six.

30. In Karcher v. Daggett, 462 U.S. 725 (1983), the Court found unconstitutional malapportionment of New Jersey congressional districts where "the population of the largest district [was] . . . less than one percent greater than the population of the smallest district"—527,472 to 523,798. 462 U.S. at 727–728. But it is entirely possible—and indeed routinely happens even since the Supreme Court's reapportionment decisions— that states entitled to *multimember* House delegations have district populations that diverge quite substantially from the national average. In 1990, for instance, by my calculation fifteen states (Maine, Rhode Island, North Dakota, South Dakota, Nebraska, Kansas, Delaware, Kentucky, Mississippi, Oklahoma, Montana, Idaho, Wyoming, Colorado, and New Mexico) with a total of forty-four representatives had average district populations that were more than 40,000 people more or fewer than the 572,466 people representing the national apportionment population divided by the 435 seats in the House of Representatives. *See* U.S. Bureau of the Census, STATISTICAL ABSTRACT OF THE UNITED STATES: 1997 (117th ed.) Washington, D.C., 1997; U.S. Bureau of the Census, PERCENT OF POPULATION VOTING BY CITIZENSHIP STATUS AND SELECTED DEMOGRAPHIC CHARACTERISTICS: NOVEMBER 1994, Washington, D.C. 1997; Michael R. Lavin, UNDERSTANDING THE CENSUS 367 (Epoch Books 1996). The Court thus moved too fast in Reynolds v. Sims, 377 U.S. 533 (1964), when it leapt from the correct observation that "only four States have less than 1/435 of the country's total population under the 1960 census" to the conclusion that "only four seats . . . are distributed on a basis other than strict population." 377 U.S. at 572 n.49.

31. FEDERALIST 62. *See also* FEDERALIST 51, where after mentioning bicameralism as a remedy for the predominance of legislative authority, Madison also extolled the fact that the two houses would be rendered "by different modes of election and different principles of action, as little connected with each other as the nature of their common functions and their common dependence on the society will admit." In addition, Madison thought that the Senate provided special protections, beyond the mere fact of differences. That is a subject to which I return in chapter five.

32. Matthew D. Adler, *Judicial Restraint in the Administrative State: Beyond the Countermajoritarian Difficulty*, 145 UNIVERSITY OF PENNSYLVANIA LAW REVIEW 759 (1997), presents an extended argument that

even assuming the majoritarian credentials of much legislation, many of the decisions of administrative agencies would not be similarly "plebiscitary."

33. U.S. Const. Art. II, § 1, cl. 2. Under the twenty-third amendment passed in 1961, the District of Columbia is provided representation in the electoral college essentially equal to that of the least populous states.

34. *See, e.g.,* this assumption in Noah Webster's *A Citizen of America in* I THE DEBATE 129, 135 (Bernard Bailyn, ed. The Library of America 1993).

35. *See* Lawrence D. Longley & Neal R. Peirce, THE ELECTORAL COLLEGE PRIMER 2000 21–22 (Yale University Press 1999). Originally there was to be a single ballot for both president and vice president (U.S. Const. Art. II, § 1, cl. 3). Each elector had two votes to be cast for two separate people, with the person receiving the most votes to be president and the runner-up vice president, on the condition in each case that the winner receive a number of votes equal to a majority of the total number of electors. This policy led to the debacle of the 1800 election in which Thomas Jefferson, the Republican candidate for president, and Aaron Burr, the Republican candidate for vice president, tied, each with the necessary majority. In the case of a tie, as in the case of a plurality, the election was then remitted to the House of Representatives, where Jefferson eventually prevailed, averting disaster. *See* Longley & Pierce, *supra,* at 26–27.

36. "In practice, the people of the states have been given the power to choose the electors in statewide elections since the 1830s. The last scattered instances in which a legislature chose the electors directly were in South Carolina until 1860, in the newly reconstructed state of Florida in 1868, and in the newly admitted state of Colorado in 1876." Longley & Peirce, *supra* note 35, at 102.

37. *See id.* at 26–36.

38. *See id.* at 142–144.

39. On the constitutional jurisprudence, *see, e.g.,* Kimel v. Florida Bd. of Regents, 528 U.S. 62 (2000).

40. I join a large variety of others in reaching this conclusion. *See, e.g.,* Daniel A. Farber & Philip P. Frickey, *The Jurisprudence of Public Choice,* 65 TEXAS LAW REVIEW 873, 890 (1987); Jon Elster, *Introduction, in* CONSTITUTIONALISM AND DEMOCRACY 4 (Jon Elster and Rune Slagstad eds., Cambridge University Press 1988); Frank Michelman, *Foreword: Traces of Self-Government,* 100 HARVARD LAW REVIEW 4, 75 (1986); Barry Friedman, *Dialogue and Judicial Review,* 91 MICHIGAN LAW REVIEW 577 (1993); Barry Friedman, *The History of the Counter-*

majoritarian Difficulty, Part One: The Road to Judicial Supremacy, 73 NEW YORK UNIVERSITY LAW REVIEW 333, 334–343 (1998); Robert C. Post, CONSTITUTIONAL DOMAINS 191 (Harvard University Press 1995); Erwin Chemerinsky, *Foreword: The Vanishing Constitution,* 103 HARVARD LAW REVIEW 43, 64 (1989); Rebecca L. Brown, *Accountability, Liberty, and the Constitution,* 98 COLUMBIA LAW REVIEW 531 (1998); Stephen M. Griffin, AMERICAN CONSTITUTIONALISM 107 (Princeton University Press 1996); Henry Paul Monaghan, *We The People[s], Original Understanding, and Constitutional Amendment,* 96 COLUMBIA LAW REVIEW 121 (1996); Julian N. Eule, *Judicial Review of Direct Democracy,* 99 YALE LAW JOURNAL 1503, 1531–1533 (1990).

41. *See* Robert Bellah, *Civil Religion in America, reprinted in* AMERICAN CIVIL RELIGION (Russell E. Richey & Donald G. Jones eds., Harper & Row 1974). Some version of this point has been made by a large number of commentators. *See, e.g.,* Max Lerner, *The Court and Constitution as Symbols,* 46 YALE LAW JOURNAL 1290 (1937); Thomas Grey, *The Constitution as Scripture,* 37 STANFORD LAW REVIEW 1 (1984); Mark Tushnet, TAKING THE CONSTITUTION AWAY FROM THE COURTS 50 (Princeton University Press 1999); Sanford Levinson, CONSTITUTIONAL FAITH (Princeton University Press 1988). Alexander Bickel mentions Supreme Court Justice George Sutherland's belief since childhood that "the Constitution 'was a divinely inspired instrument.'" Alexander Bickel, THE SUPREME COURT AND THE IDEA OF PROGRESS 14–15 (Yale University Press 1978).

42. Alexander M. Bickel, THE LEAST DANGEROUS BRANCH 18 (Bobbs-Merrill Co. 1962); *see also id.* at 193 (discussing "differently weighted constituenc[ies of American political institutions] . . . with the executive's normally being the most straight-out majoritarian"), 197 (suggesting that "even the Supreme Court may enter the 'political thicket' in states where no branch of government, not even the executive, rests on the majoritarian principle").

43. *See* Farber & Frickey, *supra* note 17, at 13 (quoting Arthur F. Bentley, THE PROCESS OF GOVERNMENT 258–259 [Principia Press 1908]) (alteration in original).

44. Robert A. Dahl, DEMOCRACY AND ITS CRITICS 295 (Yale University Press 1989); *cf.* Mansbridge, *supra* note 3, at 267.

45. This time speaking in his own voice, Robert Dahl says that the institutions of democracy "make it unlikely . . . that a government will long pursue policies that deeply offend a majority of citizens." Dahl, *supra* note 44, at 223. *See also* Ian Shapiro, *Three Fallacies Concerning Majorities, Minorities, and Democratic Politics, in* NOMOS XXXII, MAJORITIES AND MINORITIES 79, 108 (John W. Chapman & Alan Wertheimer

eds., New York University Press 1990) ("pluralism was thought to distribute political satisfaction . . . widely. . . . [so that no] particular group will lose so often as to have no commitment to the system and nothing to lose but its proverbial chains").

46. E. E. Schattschneider, THE SEMI-SOVEREIGN PEOPLE: A REALIST'S VIEW OF DEMOCRACY IN AMERICA 35 (Holt, Rinehart and Winston 1960).

47. *See* Peter Schuck, *Against (And For) Madison: An Essay in Praise of Factions,* 15 YALE LAW AND POLICY REVIEW 553, 564 (1997).

Chapter 4. Democracy as Involvement in Conversation

1. I do not mean to deny that the motivation for much interelection communication between constituents and elected officials is to provide useful information to the one and the other. At the same time, there can be little doubt that much of that communication is generated by electoral incentives. In addition, what is said in the text requires minor qualification for candidates who run for symbolic reasons (or otherwise have no hope of winning), and who consciously appeal to a constituency that is assumed to represent less than a majority (or plurality) of the vote. To simplify exposition, however, henceforth I assume a two-candidate race and that a majority is required for election.

2. Lewis A. Dexter, *Standards for Representative Selection and Apportionment, in* NOMOS X, REPRESENTATION 155, 158 (J. Roland Pennock & John W. Chapman eds., Atherton Press 1968). *Cf.* John Ferejohn, *Instituting Deliberative Democracy, in* NOMOS XLII, DESIGNING DEMOCRATIC INSTITUTIONS 75, 86 (Ian Shapiro & Stephen Macedo eds., New York University Press 2000) ("decisions that emerge from . . . an open process might very well enjoy a kind of legitimacy that is partially independent of the content or effect of the decisions themselves"); Richard D. Anderson Jr., *The Place of the Media in Popular Democracy,* 12 CRITICAL REVIEW 481, 493 (1998). Aside from occasional passages such as these, the connection between a feeling of involvement among a democratic citizenry and the stability of their democracy has typically been part of normative work and has been focused on a more active form of involvement than the democratic "conversation" that I have in mind. *See* Amy Gutmann & Dennis Thompson, DEMOCRACY AND DISAGREEMENT 41–42 (Harvard University Press 1996); Stephen Earl Bennett & David Resnick, *The Implications of Nonvoting for Democracy in the United States,* 34 AMERICAN JOURNAL OF POLITICAL SCIENCE 771, 773–774 (1990).

3. Nebraska is the only state that does not have a bicameral legislature.

The peculiar system for choosing the president (and vice president) in the United States (*see* chapter three) illustrates the occasionally complex interaction of electoral incentives and other conversational influences. Whereas the decisive popular vote counts are taken separately in each state, the conversation that accompanies presidential elections (and indeed presidential politics between elections) pays relatively little respect to state lines. Many issues on which presidential candidates stake out positions engage portions of the population not defined by geography, and electronic media coverage in this day and age harks very little to state lines. Those who study voter turnout find that in general close elections lead to a higher rate of voting (Dennis C. Mueller, Public Choice II 358–361 [Cambridge University Press 1989]). At the same time, this correlation seems to be less clear in presidential elections on a state-by-state measure of closeness—the closeness that counts as a legal matter in presidential elections. *See* Carroll B. Foster, *The Performance of Rational Voter Models in Recent Presidential Elections,* 78 American Political Science Review 678 (1984). A plausible explanation for this disparity is that conversational intensity increases voter turnout rather than the formalities of the ways in which votes are counted. Because presidential politics commands nationwide attention and the competition in it results in conversation directed to large segments of the voting population of the country as a whole, it is possible that the relevant correlation of closeness is with nationwide turnout rather than on a state-by-state basis. My rough and ready calculation of turnout and closeness on a nationwide basis in presidential elections suggests a positive correlation, but the small number of events and the complexity of possible determinants (combined with my methodological ineptitude in this area) make me stop short of any firm conclusions.

4. For the U.S. Senate, each "district" (*i.e.*, state) has two "representatives," but in conversation-inducing respects these are very much like single-member districts. *See* chapter five.

5. The First Amendment—and what the courts have done in its name— is of course crucial here. But there are other manifestations. Administrative agencies are, for instance, required to apprise the public of proposed action and to receive and consider comment. *See* 5 U.S.C. § 553 (1994).

6. Ralph Nader is frequently cited as a conversational entrepreneur, a private individual who through force of personality and energy was able to bring issues of auto safety to the public attention in the 1960s. *See* Jay Acton & Alan LeMond, Ralph Nader: A Man and a Movement (Warner 1972). Rachel Carson's 1962 book Silent Spring is often cred-

ited with advancing environmental issues on the national agenda. *See* Zygmunt J. B. Plater, *From the Beginning, A Fundamental Shift of Paradigms: A Theory and Short History of Environmental Law,* 27 LOYOLA OF LOS ANGELES LAW REVIEW 981 n.1 (1994).

7. Because of the Supreme Court's apportionment decisions in Reynolds v. Sims, 377 U.S. 533 (1964) and Wesberry v. Sanders, 376 U.S. 1 (1964), and their progeny, the courts are often involved in legislative apportionment, but legislative bodies retain initial responsibility and a great deal of real power in apportionment decisions. By one recent estimate "perhaps as few as a tenth of the Congressional districts . . . [had] truly competitive races" in the 2000 elections. *See* Robin Toner, *Willing Contenders at a Premium in Fierce Fight to Rule Congress,* N.Y. Times, Jan. 3, 2000, at A1. On the districting problem, *see* Davis v. Bandemer, 478 U.S. 109, 174 (1986) (Powell, J., concurring in part and dissenting in part). On the problem of incumbent advantage generally, *see* Justice Thomas's discussion in dissent in U.S. Term Limits, Inc. v. Thornton, 514 U.S. 779, 845, 922–923 (1995). It is possible that representatives of one district may communicate with constituents of other districts because fundraising takes place out of the district; because representatives enjoy the battle; or simply because, given the frequent impossibility of finely tuning intended audiences, they cannot help themselves. Such out-of-district communication may then soften minority disenchantment borne of conversational neglect in homogeneous districts. But there is relatively little incentive for targeted out-of-district communication, and thus such communication can be expected to contribute only modestly to the breadth of conversational attention within a given electoral district.

8. "In the practice of our democratic politics, communicating by sound bite, competing by character assassination, and resolving political conflicts through self-seeking bargaining too often substitute for deliberation on the merits of controversial issues." Gutmann & Thompson, *supra* note 2, at 12. *See generally* Jeffrey Friedman, *Introduction: Public Ignorance and Democratic Theory,* 12 CRITICAL REVIEW 397 (1998). It is possible to put even simplistic and petty parts of the conversation in a favorable light:

> If the media emphasize contests rather than issues, attract attention to politics by dramatizing it, make learning about politics easier by simplifying and condensing it, help citizens pick out some issues as important from the welter of possibly important ones, and generate feelings of intimacy with politicians by attending to their personalities, the media may make politics more interesting and accessible, helping to include people who might otherwise

> think it remote from their personal concerns. . . . If inclusion rather than de-
> liberation produces the desirable consequences of democracy, maybe the me-
> dia effects that corrode deliberation should be praised, not damned.

Anderson, *supra* note 2, at 493.

Of course real-world politicians may have a more complex set of goals than election and reelection, but simplification is often an essential step to understanding—and this particular simplifying assumption has become standard in the rational choice literature at least since Anthony Downs, AN ECONOMIC THEORY OF DEMOCRACY (Harper & Row 1957).

9. Gordon S. Wood, THE RADICALISM OF THE AMERICAN REVOLUTION 294 (Random House 1993). In the first competitive presidential race, that of 1796, "[n]one of the candidates campaigned or as much as lifted a finger to win the election" (James Roger Sharp, AMERICAN POLITICS IN THE EARLY REPUBLIC 138 [Yale University Press 1993]). It was not until somewhat later that "blatant electioneering and . . . competitive campaigning" supplanted a republican ideal (Wood, *supra*, at 297). *See* J. R. Pole, POLITICAL REPRESENTATION IN ENGLAND & THE ORIGINS OF THE AMERICAN REPUBLIC 165 (St. Martin's Press 1966).

10. *See* G. Edward White, *The First Amendment Comes of Age: The Emergence of Free Speech in Twentieth Century America*, 95 MICHIGAN LAW REVIEW 299, 300–301 (1966).

11. Learned Hand, THE BILL OF RIGHTS 73–74 (Harvard University Press 1958).

12. *See, e.g.,* Paul Kleppner, WHO VOTED? THE DYNAMICS OF ELECTORAL TURNOUT, 1870–1980 4 (Praeger Publishers 1982). ("Despite its limited informational capability. . . . [v]oting is an important source of diffuse support for the political system.")

13. Benjamin R. Barber, STRONG DEMOCRACY: PARTICIPATORY POLITICS FOR A NEW AGE 136 (University of California Press, 1984), *quoted in* Robert C. Post, CONSTITUTIONAL DOMAINS 185 (Harvard University Press 1995).

14. *See, e.g.,* Frank I. Michelman, *Foreword: Traces of Self-Government,* 100 HARVARD LAW REVIEW 4, 19 (1986); Michael Sandel, DEMOCRACY'S DISCONTENT (Harvard University Press 1996); Cass R. Sunstein, THE PARTIAL CONSTITUTION (Harvard University Press 1993); *see also, e.g.,* Thomas Christiano, *Deliberative Equality and Democratic Order, in* NOMOS XXXVIII, POLITICAL ORDER 251 (Ian Shapiro & Russell Hardin eds., New York University Press 1993); Gutmann & Thompson, *supra* note 2.

15. Post, *supra* note 13, at 185–187.

16. An exception is Barry Friedman, *Dialogue and Judicial Review*, 91 MICHIGAN LAW REVIEW 577, 584 (1993).

17. Post, *supra* note 13, at 187.

18. *See, e.g.,* Edwin Chen, *Crisis in Yugoslavia: Clinton Approval Rating Drops*, L.A. Times, May 1, 1999, at A17.

19. *See* Bennett & Resnick, *supra* note 2, at 777–787; *cf.* Jack C. Doppelt & Ellen Shearer, NONVOTERS 13, 25–30 (Sage Publications, Inc. 1999).

20. Much of the work is discussed in E. Allan Lind & Tom R. Tyler, THE SOCIAL PSYCHOLOGY OF PROCEDURAL JUSTICE (Plenum Press 1988). *Cf.* Jerry L. Mashaw, DUE PROCESS IN THE ADMINISTRATIVE STATE 162–163 (Yale University Press 1985).

21. Lind & Tyler, *supra* note 20, at 169.

22. "[A]pplications of procedural justice in the political arena must rely on intuitions about what constitutes procedural fairness; there has been little research on what citizens view as fair in political procedures" (*Id.* at 164).

23. Henry David Thoreau, JOURNAL, 11 November 1850, *quoted in* THE OXFORD DICTIONARY OF QUOTATIONS 550 (3d ed. Book Club Associates 1980).

24. *See* Alexander M. Bickel, THE LEAST DANGEROUS BRANCH 18 (Bobbs-Merrill Co. 1962); Stephen Holmes, *Gag Rules or the Politics of Omission, in* CONSTITUTIONALISM AND DEMOCRACY 19, 35 (Jon Elster and Rune Slagstad eds., Cambridge University Press 1988); Martin Shapiro, LAW AND POLITICS IN THE SUPREME COURT 249 (Free Press 1964).

25. In similar fashion, Darwinian natural selection can explain the development of both large and small creatures (and indeed myriad other "inconsistencies") in the same environment. An example from social theory is provided in Robert D. Putnam, BOWLING ALONE 21 (Simon & Schuster 2000), in which Putnam discusses the effect of changes in American society on its "social capital," despite the fact that it is not a single "'thing'" but rather "comes in many different shapes and sizes with many different uses." Normative theorizing about "deliberation" in democracy similarly depicts that deliberation as a complex phenomenon. *See* Gutmann & Thompson, *supra* note 2, at 12–13.

26. I say "mainly" because individual legislators may have effective power over some policy decisions in their districts. Individual Chicago aldermen, for instance, can be very influential in zoning decisions.

27. Reynolds v. Sims, 377 U.S. 533, 543 (1964).

28. Even more dispiriting, of course, would be the possibility of protracted substantive and conversational inattention. That was the apparent fate of the large Black minority in southern, and some northern,

jurisdictions from the time of the end of Reconstruction until the voting rights initiatives of the Civil Rights era. Both the period of inattention and its passing were probably derivative of real-world changes in the ability to vote. Although problems of disenfranchisement can still be found today, there is apparently nothing like the systematic large-scale denial of the vote to southern Blacks.

29. It may be a bit unfair that I have used the more portentous terms for vote-centeredness, but I hereby acknowledge having done so in part to make a rhetorical point of how deficient the majoritarian perspective is.

30. *See* Robert W. Bennett, *Should Parents Be Given Extra Votes on Account of Their Children?: Toward A Conversational Understanding of American Democracy,* 94 NORTHWESTERN UNIVERSITY LAW REVIEW 503, 560–562 (2000). In this respect, conversationalism is like most evolutionary theory, providing an explanation of why some things survive and others do not, but without claiming to explain the precise pattern of what emerges.

Chapter 5. The United States Senate

1. Albeit with the important limitation produced by the fact that representative districts are wholly contained within a state, with each state entitled to at least one representative (U.S. Const., Art. I, § 2). *See* note 9, *infra.*

2. *See* U.S. Const., Art. I, § 3, cl. 1; Art. I, § 7, cls. 1–3; Art II, § 2, cl. 2. As a formal matter, concurrence in treaties—which the Constitution places along with itself and national legislation as "supreme law"—requires a two-thirds vote of the Senate but no action by the House at all (U.S. Const., Art. II, § 2, cl. 2; *see* Art. VI, cl. 2). In practice, however, the House has come to assume virtually coequal power with the Senate in endorsing (or rejecting) international agreements. *See generally* Bruce Ackerman & David Golove, *Is NAFTA Constitutional?,* 108 HARVARD LAW REVIEW 799 (1995). The Senate also has the final say in removing seriously misbehaving senior governmental officers, but both House and the Senate play important roles in the process. *Compare* U.S. Const., Art. I, § 2, cl. 5 *with* U.S. Const., Art. I, § 3, cl. 6. The House is assigned a potentially important contingent role in the selection of the president (U.S. Const., Am. XII), but no occasion for its use has arisen for more than 175 years (Lawrence D. Longley & Neil R. Peirce, THE ELECTORAL COLLEGE PRIMER 2000 31 [Yale University Press 1999]).

3. Frances E. Lee & Bruce I. Oppenheimer, Sizing Up the Senate 2 (University of Chicago Press 1999).

4. *See* 377 U.S. 533, 565 (1964) (emphasis supplied). There is, of course, specific constitutional language governing the apportionment of the Senate, whereas the Constitution is basically silent on the structure of state government, save that the states are guaranteed a "republican form of government," U.S. Const., Art. IV, § 4—the framers term for what we would be more likely to call "representative democracy." *See, e.g.*, Madison's Federalist 10. The Court based its decision not on that "guarantee," which had long been held to be nonjusticiable, Luther v. Borden, 48 U.S. (7 How.) 1 (1849); *see generally* Baker v. Carr, 369 U.S. 186, 217–225 (1962), but on the Equal Protection Clause of the Fourteenth Amendment.

5. 377 U.S. at 574–575. At least in the formation of the state of Vermont, it appears that the towns were a good deal more analogous to the states in the formation of the Union than the Court suggests in this passage. *See* Jane J. Mansbridge, Beyond Adversary Democracy 127 (University of Chicago Press 1983).

6. *See* Lee & Oppenheimer, *supra* note 3, at 225 ("equal representation of states violates the principle of one person one vote. . . . the only tenable standard for apportioning legislative chambers in democratic theory today"). Senatorial apportionment is treated with special deference by the constitutional amendment provision of Article V: "no state, without its consent, shall be deprived of its equal suffrage in the Senate." Despite the constitutional language, an argument has been made that the entrenchment could be finessed for all states by first amending Article V to eliminate the entrenchment, and then amending the senatorial representation provision. *See* remarks of Senator Bigler, Cong. Globe 36th Cong., 2d Sess. 1387, *quoted in* Douglas Linder, *What in the Constitution Cannot Be Amended?*, 23 Arizona Law Review 717, 729 n.67 (1981). Whatever the theoretical or practical possibilities of such a two-step process (about both of which I am dubious), change with the consent of overrepresented states is in any event not foreclosed. And there is nothing to prevent popular agitation about things that have only the most remote chance of being changed.

7. Federalist 62.

8. Max Farrand, The Framing of the Constitution of the United States 69 (Yale University Press 1913).

9. This is not made explicit but is clearly implied by the required apportionment of the House "among" the States (U.S. Const. Art. I, § 2, cl. 3; Am. XIV, § 2), by the stipulation that each state is to have "at least"

one representative (U.S. Const. Art. I, § 2, cl. 3), by the provision that qualifications to vote for members of the House are to be the qualifications that each state imposes "for electors of the most numerous branch of the state legislature" (U.S. Const. Art. I, § 2, cl. 1), and by the requirement that a member of the House be "when elected . . . an inhabitant of that state in which he shall be chosen." U.S. Const. Art I, § 2, cl. 2. *See* Department of Commerce v. Montana, 503 U.S. 442, 448 n.14 (1992).

10. McPherson v. Blacker, 146 U.S. 1, 26 (1892); *but see* Cook v. Gralike, 531 U.S. 510, 528 (2001) (Kennedy, J., concurring) ("Representatives in the National Government are responsible to the people who elect them, not to the States in which they reside.").

11. *See* Lee & Oppenheimer, *supra* note 3, at 133; *see also id.* at 168–169, collecting earlier work supporting the point.

12. *See generally* George H. Haynes, II THE SENATE OF THE UNITED STATES 1025–1034 (Houghton Mifflin Co. 1938).

13. Senators are probably identified with state matters as frequently in their quasiexecutive functions as in their role as legislators. Among the officials to whose appointment the Senate must by law "consent" are federal judges and higher level federal prosecutors (known as "United States Attorneys"). In both cases, the states have been used as the legal and administrative bases for assignment of these federal offices, and tradition and politics have conspired to give a state's senators special prerogatives with regard to appointments to their state's offices. Particularly when at least one of the state's senators is of the same political party as the president, this senatorial prerogative can be decisive in appointments. Terry Smith, *Rediscovering the Sovereignty of the People: The Case of Senate Districts*, 75 NORTH CAROLINA LAW REVIEW 1 (1996) advances the novel suggestion that states might create two separate senatorial districts.

14. Lee & Oppenheimer, *supra* note 3, at 8; *see id.* at 161, collecting earlier authorities that had made much the same point.

15. U.S. Const., Art. VII, cl. 1; *see* Farrand, *supra* note 8, at 3, 10–11. The original call for a convention coming out of a gathering in Annapolis had contemplated that ratification of the product of the convention would be "'by the Legislatures of every State.'" *Id.* at 10.

16. *E.g.*, U.S. Term Limits, Inc. v. Thornton, 514 U.S. 779, 792, 794, 801, 806–809, 819–822, 833 (1995).

17. *See* FEDERALIST 62.

18. FEDERALIST 51; FEDERALIST 62.

19. FEDERALIST 51.

20. FEDERALIST 51; FEDERALIST 62.

21. FEDERALIST 66 (emphasis in original).

22. FEDERALIST 62; FEDERALIST 63. *See also* FEDERALIST 64, where in discussing the Senate's role in making treaties, Jay depicts the selection of senators by state legislatures as likely to yield a body of "men . . . who have become the most distinguished by their abilities and virtue. . . ."

23. In fact "incumbent senators are far more likely than incumbent representatives to be defeated when they run for reelection." Jonathan S. Krasno, CHALLENGERS, COMPETITION AND REELECTION 1 (Yale University Press 1994).

24. *Id.* at 161–162. It was not always so. John Quincy Adams, for instance, served first in the Senate and, after a term as president, ended his career in the House of Representatives. *See* Paul C. Nagel, JOHN QUINCY ADAMS (Alfred A. Knopf 1997).

25. The federal government's commerce power has been pared back a bit by recent decisions of the Supreme Court, *see, e.g.,* United States v. Morrison, 529 U.S. 598 (2000), but few would likely quarrel with Justice Souter's comment that "the Framers . . . would be astonished by the reach of Congress under the Commerce Clause generally. The proliferation of Government, State and Federal, would amaze the Framers. . . ." Alden v. Maine, 527 U.S. 706, 760, 807 (1999) (Souter, J., dissenting).

26. In FEDERALIST 10 Madison said: "If a faction consists of less than a majority, relief is supplied by the republican principle, which enables the majority to defeat its sinister views by regular vote." Although Madison was not entirely oblivious to the possibility of coalitions (*see* note 27, *infra*), this passage does seem to neglect the possibility of a combination of minority factions to make a majority which would vote together in support of their individual agendas—what today we would call "logrolling."

27. In a particularly expansive passage about the virtues of an "extended republic," Madison said:

> In the extended republic of the United States, and among the great variety of interests, parties, and sects which it embraces, a coalition of a majority of the whole society could seldom take place on any other principles than those of justice and the general good. . . .

FEDERALIST 51. Few contemporary commentators would accede to the suggestion that the operation of faction has been stifled in either the House or Senate in the way that this passage suggests.

28. Lee & Oppenheimer, *supra* note 3, at xi. The authors do note a few exceptions, New York's Senator Daniel Patrick Moynihan among them (as well as the CONSTITUTIONAL COMMENTARY writers mentioned in

chapter one), *see id.* at 3, but the paucity of them remains quite remarkable.

29. *Id.* at xi; *see id.* at 4 ("reading the scholarly literature on the Senate might lead one to conclude that apportionment is not a particularly important feature of that institution.").

30. *Id.* at 229. They go on to suggest that the lack of awareness may be traceable to the absence of systematic study (*id.*), but on that point you can count me as dubious for reasons to which the text now turns. *See* Andrew Hacker, CONGRESSIONAL DISTRICTING 3 (Brookings Institution 1964).

31. *See* U.S. Const., Art. I, § 4, cl. 1; George H. Haynes, I THE SENATE OF THE UNITED STATES 81–86 (Houghton Mifflin Co. 1938) (hereinafter "Haynes, I The Senate").

32. George H. Haynes, THE ELECTION OF SENATORS 47–48 (Henry Holt & Co. 1906) (hereinafter "Haynes, Election").

33. Haynes, I The Senate, *supra* note 31, at 87.

34. Haynes, Election, *supra* note 32, at 133.

35. I say "purporting to bind" because the constitutionality of such requirements would be in doubt. *Cf.* Ray v. Blair, 343 U.S. 214 (1952) (discussing the status of presidential electors who cast electoral votes for candidates other than those to whom they are pledged). The availability of the popular initiative aided the early movement for reform. *See* Haynes, I The Senate, *supra* note 31, at 101.

36. In exercise of its power to preempt the states with regard to the "manner" of holding elections for senators and representatives, U.S. Const., Art. I, § 4, cl. 1, Congress has now required that elections for the House are to be held in single-member districts. 2 U.S.C.A. §2c (1997). The result is that intrastate House apportionment is required in all states entitled to more than the constitutional minimum of one House member. *See generally* Samuel Issacharoff, Pamela S. Karlan & Richard H. Pildes, THE LAW OF DEMOCRACY 1156–1160 (Foundation Press 2d ed. 2001). Election of a state's two senators is, of course, "at-large" from the state as a whole, although the elections are typically conducted at different times. Smith, *supra* note 13, presents a proposal that a state's senators be elected from two different districts.

37. *See, e.g.,* Times Mirror Center for the People and the Press, *Congressional Opinion Survey,* Nov. 3–5, 1994.

38. *See* Lee & Oppenheimer, *supra* note 3, at 46–47; *but cf.* Barbara Hinkley, *The American Voter in Congressional Elections,* 74 AMERICAN POLITICAL SCIENCE REVIEW 641 (1980).

39. Lee & Oppenheimer, *supra* note 3, at 100, 145. ("In more populous

states, senators are defined less by their face-to-face, person-to-person contacts with voters and more by the media.")

40. *Id.* at 88–90; Krasno, *supra* note 23, at 38–39.

41. Lee & Oppenheimer, *supra* note 3, at 80.

42. It seems that constituents can identify their senators at least as readily as they can their representatives in the House (Krasno, *supra* note 23, at 139). The Constitution provides that "no new State shall be formed or erected within the jurisdiction of any other State; nor any State be formed by the junction of two or more States, or parts of States, without the consent of the legislatures of the States concerned as well as of the Congress." U.S. Const., Art. IV, § 3. With regard to House districts, on the other hand, state legislatures can change district lines even without population shifts. Still, the one more typically follows the other. If the size of a state's House delegation changes as a result of the decennial census and consequent interstate House apportionment, some district lines obviously have to be changed. Even with no change in the size of the delegation, moreover, in states with multimember delegations, the Supreme Court's decision in Wesberry v. Sanders, 376 U.S. 1 (1964), applying the "one person one vote" rule to intrastate House districting, necessitates the redrawing of district lines after every census.

43. *See* Krasno, *supra* note 23, at 37 n.2, 48 n.16, 101 n.24. A particularly striking finding in Hinkley, *supra* note 38, was that voters were much more likely to identify *challengers* for senatorial positions than for seats in the House of Representatives.

44. *See generally* Paul S. Hernson, CONGRESSIONAL ELECTIONS: CAMPAIGNING AT HOME AND IN WASHINGTON (Congressional Quarterly Press 1995); Krasno, *supra* note 23; Richard F. Fenno, Jr., THE UNITED STATES SENATE: A BICAMERAL PERSPECTIVE (American Enterprise Institute 1982).

45. Krasno, *supra* note 23, at 100–101.

46. Id. at 81, 160 n.5; Alan I. Abramowitz, *A Comparison of Voting for U.S. Senator and Representative in 1978,* 74 AMERICAN POLITICAL SCIENCE REVIEW 633, 635–636 (1980).

47. Krasno, *supra* note 23, at 78. *See id.* at 12; Lee & Oppenheimer, *supra* note 3, at 84.

48. Krasno, *supra* note 23, at 88–89; Hinkley, *supra* note 38.

49. Lee & Oppenheimer, *supra* note 3, at 97; *see* Krasno, *supra* note 23, at 1, 59.

50. Lee & Oppenheimer, *supra* note 3, at 126 (quoting David R. Mayhew, CONGRESS: THE ELECTORAL CONNECTION 73 [Yale University Press 1974]); *but see* Krasno, *supra* note 23, at 25, 115–117.

51. Lee & Oppenheimer, *supra* note 3, at 58, 125. ("Senators represent-
    ing large states are more likely to turn to 'position taking' . . . or, put
    somewhat less cynically, to a strategy of policy activism on a broad
    range of national issues to further their reelection goals.")
52. Lee & Oppenheimer, *supra* note 3, at 186–222. Less clear—to me at
    least—is the normative purchase to a goal articulated by Lee and Op-
    penheimer of "equality of potential access," beyond the contribution
    the access might be thought to make to eventual outcomes. *See id.* at
    226.

Chapter 6. The Electoral Status of Children

1. No official count of this population is made. I have extrapolated from
   1996 midcensus figures, which show approximately 26 percent of the
   entire resident population of 265,000,000—including noncitizens—as
   under the age of eighteen, as well as a noncitizen adult population of
   13,000,000. *See* U.S. Bureau of the Census, Statistical Abstract of
   the United States: 1997 (117th ed.) (1997) [hereinafter Statistical
   Abstract: 1997]; U.S. Bureau of the Census, Percent of Population
   Voting By Citizenship Status and Selected Demographic Characteristics: November 1994 (1997). In any event, if the number of resident citizen children ineligible to vote were added to the total eligible
   population, the children would represent a substantial fraction of the
   whole.

   The Twenty-Sixth Amendment of the U.S. Constitution now forbids
   withholding the vote "on account of age" from those eighteen and
   older. Presumably states remain free to lower the age of suffrage below
   eighteen, but as of 1988 at least, no state had done so. *See* Thompson
   v. Oklahoma, 487 U.S. 815, 839 (1988) (Appendix A). The state determinations then govern for state and many local elections, and for federal elections as well (U.S. Const., Art. I, § 2, cl. 1; Art. II, § 1, cl. 2; Am
   XVII). There may be elections for some local bodies (like school boards
   or park districts) in which children are allowed to vote, but I have not
   encountered references to any. Children do, of course, vote for student
   councils and the like, or for captains of their school teams, and if the
   definition of "public official" were extended to such offices, the statement in the text would require qualification.
2. *Cf.* Barnett v. Daley, 32 F.3d 1196, 1200 (7th Cir. 1994). I see little basis for quarreling with this proposition, for the signs of societal concern
   for children are all about. One of the most popular versions of Indiana

license plates, for instance, proclaims "kids first." *See also* Carl E. Goldfarb, *Allocating the Local Apportionment Pie: What Portion For Resident Aliens?* 104 YALE LAW JOURNAL 1441, 1452 (1991); *but cf.* Jane Rutherford, *One Child, One Vote: Proxies for Parents,* 82 MINNESOTA LAW REVIEW 1463 (1998). Still, there is a certain awkwardness in much of the evidence that could be adduced, because a great part of the solicitousness of children takes the form of subordination to their parents, or, when that mechanism is thought likely to fail, to the state. As one example of the resulting tension (as well as the basic supposition that children are entitled to regard), here is Justice Powell struggling with a question of the legal prerogatives of adolescent girls in making the abortion decision:

> Properly understood . . . the tradition of parental authority is not inconsistent with our tradition of individual liberty; rather, the former is one of the basic presuppositions of the latter. Legal restrictions on minors, especially those supportive of the parental role, may be important to the child's chances for the full growth and maturity that make eventual participation in a free society meaningful and rewarding.

Bellotti v. Baird, 443 U.S. 622, 638–639 (1979).
3. Needless to say, I do not mean to endorse one set of decisions or the other. I only suggest that the distribution of the vote will likely influence public policy choices when the numbers are as large as they are with children.
4. *See* Nancy Goldhill, *Ties That Bind: The Impact of Psychological and Legal Debates on the Child Welfare System,* 22 NEW YORK UNIVERSITY REVIEW OF LAW AND SOCIAL CHANGE 295 (1996); Jane J. Mansbridge, BEYOND ADVERSARY DEMOCRACY 237–238 (University of Chicago Press 1983). I dealt with some of these issues in Robert Bennett, *Allocation of Child Medical Care Decisionmaking Authority: A Suggested Interest Analysis,* 62 VIRGINIA LAW REVIEW 285, 307–317 (1976). In Parham v. J. R., 442 U.S. 584, 602 (1979), the Supreme Court said:

> The law's concept of the family rests on a presumption that parents possess what a child lacks in maturity, experience, and capacity for judgment required for making life's difficult decisions. More important, historically it has recognized that natural bonds of affection lead parents to act in the best interests of their children.

See Troxel v. Granville, 530 U.S. 57 (2000).
5. *See, e.g.,* Richard A. Posner, AGING AND OLD AGE 151 (University of Chicago Press 1995); Barnett v. Daley, 32 F.3d 1196, 1200 (7th Cir. 1994) (Posner, C.J.); Dennis L. Murphy, *The Exclusion of Illegal Aliens From the Reapportionment Base: A Question of Representation,* 41 CASE

WESTERN RESERVE LAW REVIEW 969, 991 (1991); Peter Schuck, *Against (And For) Madison: An Essay in Praise of Factions*, 15 YALE LAW AND POLICY REVIEW 553, 575 (1997); *but cf.* Vita Wallace, *Give Children the Vote*, THE NATION, Oct. 14, 1991, 439, at 440 (arguing for the enfranchisement of children and dismissing the objection "that children would vote the way their parents tell them to, which would, in effect, give parents more votes.").

6. Skipping by children altogether, one prominent commentator writes that "even today some citizens (e.g., convicted felons) lack the right to vote." Christopher L. Eisgruber, *Birthright Citizenship and the Constitution*, 72 NEW YORK UNIVERSITY LAW REVIEW 54, 57 (1997). *See* Robert A. Dahl, A PREFACE TO DEMOCRATIC THEORY 49 (University of Chicago Press 1956); Amy Guttman & Dennis Thompson, DEMOCRACY AND DISAGREEMENT 145–152 (Harvard University Press 1996).

I have encountered a handful of published references to the extra votes idea. *See* Posner, *supra* note 5, at 289 (characterizing the idea as "Utopian") (capitalized in original); Rutherford, *supra* note 2; Barnett v. City of Chicago, 141 F.3d 699, 704 (7th Cir. 1998) ("It is not as if the proposal were to give extra votes to families with more than the average number of children, a bizarre suggestion in our political culture but one that could be defended with reference to the concept of virtual representation.") (Posner, C.J.); Sylvia Ann Hewlett & Cornel West, THE WAR AGAINST PARENTS: WHAT WE CAN DO FOR AMERICA'S BELEAGUERED MOMS AND DADS 240–241 (Houghton Mifflin Co. 1998) (" . . . serious consideration should be given to the suggestion that parents be given *the right to vote on behalf of their children.*") (emphasis in original); Alexei Bayer, *Let's Give Parents An Extra Right to Vote*, N.Y. Times, May 4, 1997, at § 3, p. 12. Professor Jost Pietzcker of the law department of Germany's Bonn University suggested to me that the idea has periodically garnered support in Germany over the years. The idea first occurred to me in 1995 or 1996, and my first published reference to it was in Robert W. Bennett, *Democracy As Meaningful Conversation*, 14 CONSTITUTIONAL COMMENTARY 481, 499 n.46, 514 (1997).

7. Wesberry v. Sanders, 376 U.S. 1, 18 (1964); Reynolds v. Sims, 377 U.S. 533, 558 (1964), both quoting Gray v. Sanders, 372 U.S. 368, 381 (1963). All states except Nebraska have bicameral legislatures. The equinumerosity requirement has been extended to local legislatures, as well as many quasilegislative bodies, most of which are unicameral. *See, e.g.,* Abate v. Mundt, 403 U.S. 182 (1971); Board of Estimate v. Morris,

489 U.S. 688 (1989). I am using the words *apportionment* and *districting* interchangeably to mean the allocation of population in the designation of electoral districts, although they might well be given different meanings, the first the allocation of representatives among the states according to population, and the second the intrastate drawing of district lines. *See* Michael R. Lavin, UNDERSTANDING THE CENSUS 393 (Epoch Books 1996).

8. *See* Baker v. Carr, 369 U.S. 186, 192 (1962); *id.* at 253–258 (Clark, J., concurring); Wesberry v. Sanders, 376 U.S. 1, 2, 7–8 (1964); Reynolds v. Sims, 377 U.S. 533, 545–551 (1964).

9. *See* Robert Nozick, *Weighted Voting and "One-Man, One-Vote,"* in NOMOS X, REPRESENTATION 217, 219 (J. Roland Pennock & John W. Chapman eds., Atherton Press 1968); *Note: The Problem of the "Denominator" When Measuring the Value of a Vote,* Paul Brest & Sanford Levinson, PROCESSES OF CONSTITUTIONAL DECISIONMAKING 1087 (Little Brown & Co. 3d ed. 1992); *see also* John E. Nowak & Ronald D. Rotunda, CONSTITUTIONAL LAW 914–915 (West Publishing Co. 5th ed. 1995). There is also ambiguity about what might be meant by the "voting population." In practice the reference is usually to those eligible to vote—whether registered or not—but it might instead refer to those registered to vote, or perhaps even to those who actually did vote in some recent election. In any event, I do not intend to probe that particular ambiguity any further. *See* Gaffney v. Cummings, 412 U.S. 735, 747–748 (1973); Burns v. Richardson, 384 U.S. 73, 92–93 (1966); Nozick, *supra,* at 219 n.4.

10. I use the term "felons" as a catch-all for those who are disqualified on account of criminality, but the definition of disqualifying convictions in fact varies from state to state. *See* Note, *The Disenfranchisement of Ex-Felons: Citizenship, Criminality, and "The Purity of the Ballot Box,"* 102 HARVARD LAW REVIEW 1300 n.1 (1989). Many states do not extend electoral disqualification of convicted criminals after sentences have been served. In states that do prolong disqualification, the definition of disqualifying crimes, the possibilities of reinstatement, and the mechanisms of enforcement vary widely. *See* Note, *Disenfranchisement of Ex-Felons: A Reassessment,* 25 STANFORD LAW REVIEW 845 (1973). There is also great variation among the states with regard to the disqualification of the mentally disabled. *See* Note, *Mental Disability and the Right to Vote,* 88 YALE LAW JOURNAL 1644 (1979). I mean to limit the category of "legal aliens" to those residing indefinitely in the United States. It thus does not typically include students, tourists,

or diplomats. *See* T. Alexander Aleinikoff, *Citizens, Aliens, Membership and the Constitution*, 7 Constitutional Commentary 9, 10 n.3 (1990). In Skafte v. Rorex, 430 U.S. 961 (1973), the Supreme Court dismissed an appeal from a Colorado decision that there was no denial of equal protection in the exclusion of legally resident aliens from the franchise.

11. 376 U.S. at 7–8.
12. 376 U.S. at 18.
13. *See, e.g.*, Wesberry v. Sanders, 376 U.S. 1, 7 ("voters"), 8 ("inhabitants"), 9 ("population"), 11 ("people" and "constituents," favorably quoting James Wilson), 13 ("inhabitants"), 14 ("voters" and "inhabitants"), 17 ("citizens," favorably quoting James Wilson) (1964); Reynolds v. Sims, 377 U.S. 533, 557 ("voters"), 558 ("all who participate in the election," "voter," and "person," favorably quoting Gray v. Sanders, 372 U.S. 368, 379–81 [1963]), 565 ("citizen" and "people"), 567 ("citizen" and "voter"), 577 ("population"), 579 ("population" and "citizen"), 580 ("citizens") (1964). Without displaying any sensitivity to the importance that different definitions of the base might have, the Court in *Reynolds* said: "[w]e realize that it is a practical impossibility to arrange legislative districts so that each one has an identical number of residents, or citizens, or voters." 377 U.S. at 577. *See* Garza v. County of Los Angeles, 918 F.2d 763, 779–781 (9th Cir. 1990), *cert. denied*, 498 U.S. 1028 (1991) (Kozinski, J., concurring and dissenting in part). And note the shifts within a single paragraph of Justice Black's majority opinion in *Wesberry:*

> It would defeat the principle solemnly embodied in the Great Compromise—equal representation in the House for equal numbers of people—for us to hold that, within the States, legislatures may draw the lines of congressional districts in such a way as to give some voters a greater voice in choosing a Congressman than others. The House of Representatives, the Convention agreed, was to represent the people as individuals, and on a basis of complete equality for each voter.

376 U.S., at 14.

The Court is occasionally joined in this casual treatment of the difference among people, citizens, voters, and the like, by the most sophisticated of commentators:

> Apportionment assigns voters to electoral districts. . . . [A] citizen placed in one district is simultaneously excluded from all other districts. Moreover, the Constitution's one-person, one-vote requirement means that including a particular voter within a district demands excluding some other voter in order to equalize the number of persons in each district.

Samuel Issacharoff and Pamela S. Karlan, *Standing and Misunderstanding In Voting Rights Law*, 111 HARVARD LAW REVIEW 2276, 2279 (1998).

14. For obvious reasons, the number of aliens residing illegally in the United States is hard to pin down, although a conservative 1996 estimate put the number at five million, U.S. IMMIGRATION AND NATURALIZATION SERVICE, 1996 STATISTICAL YEARBOOK 197 (Oct. 1997) [hereinafter 1996 STATISTICAL YEARBOOK]. An official 1990 estimate put the entire alien population of the United States at more than ten million. BUREAU OF THE CENSUS, U.S. DEPT OF COMMERCE, 1990 CP-3– 1, 1990 CENSUS OF THE POPULATION: PERSONS OF HISPANIC ORIGIN IN THE UNITED STATES 3–4 (1993). An even softer estimate put the number at thirteen million in 1996. *See* U.S. Bureau of the Census, *Percent of Population Voting by Citizenship Status and Selected Demographic Characteristics: November 1994*, at tbl.3, ⟨http://www.census.gov/ population/socdemo/voting/profile/ptable3.txt⟩ (visited on Sept. 3, 1999) (reporting that as of September 1996, the U.S. adult noncitizen population was 13,007,000). The ineligible population of felons still serving sentences is probably less than one million, but one commentator estimated the total of the disenfranchised felons and ex-felons at about four million in 1991. Andrew L. Shapiro, *Note, Challenging Criminal Disenfranchisement Under the Voting Rights Act: A New Strategy*, 103 YALE LAW JOURNAL 537, 540 n.17 (1993). The number disenfranchised for mental incompetence is also difficult to estimate, although it is not likely very large.

There are also approximately 4.5 million U.S. citizens in the District of Columbia and overseas American territories, *see* Lavin, *supra* note 7, at 367, of whom perhaps three million are potentially eligible voters. Unlike those made ineligible in various states, these citizens in U.S. territories may elect some officials, whereas they have no voting representation in the Congress. There is also a population of perhaps six million American citizens residing more or less permanently in foreign countries who are not typically counted for apportionment purposes but may vote in the states of their most recent residence. Jamin B. Raskin, *Is This America?: The District of Columbia and the Right to Vote*, 34 HARVARD CIVIL RIGHTS–CIVIL LIBERTIES LAW REVIEW 39 (1999).

15. *See* Garza v. County of Los Angeles, 918 F.2d 763, 781, *cert. denied*, 498 U.S. 1028 (1991) (Kozinski, J., dissenting) ("Absent significant demographic variations in the proportion of voting age citizens to total population, apportionment by population will assure equality of voting strength and vice versa."). I say "need not" rather than "will not" be-

cause it is conceivable—albeit, to my mind, barely—that the inclusion decision would have some symbolic significance that would then feed back to the politics of districting.

16. Gaffney v. Cummings, 412 U.S. 735, 746–747 (1973).

17. Gaffney v. Cummings, 412 U.S. 735, 747 (1973); Karcher v. Daggett, 462 U.S. 725, 771–772 (1983) (White, J., dissenting). *See* Garza v. County of Los Angeles, 918 F.2d 763, 774 (9ᵗʰ Cir. 1990), *cert. denied*, 498 U.S. 1028 (1991) ("Basing districts on voters rather than total population results in serious population inequalities across districts."). The interstate variation for children is compiled from STATISTICAL ABSTRACT: 1997, *supra* note 1. With regard to noncitizen population, seven states (California, Texas, New York, Florida, Illinois, New Jersey, and Arizona) apparently accounted for 83 percent of the estimated five million illegal immigrants residing in the United States in 1996. These seven states contained approximately 41 percent of the national population (1996 STATISTICAL YEARBOOK, *supra* note 14). For legally resident aliens, there are likely similar disproportions.

18. The formal ability to influence outcomes at least. In reality, the "ability . . . to influence electoral outcomes," even by voting, depends on a great deal besides the number of other voters in the district. Even apart from the ability of some to influence the information flow that can, in turn, influence voters, the division of sentiment in the district importantly affects the decisional weight of any one voter. In a lopsided district, the voter has less electoral say than he or she has in a closely divided district. *See* the discussion of the "paradox of voting" in chapter eight.

19. Burns v. Richardson, 384 U.S. 73, 92 (1966) (emphasis supplied); *see* Gaffney v. Cummings, 412 U.S. 735, 746–747 (1973). In *Burns*, the Court insisted that *Reynolds* and its companion cases had "carefully left open the question what population was being referred to" (384 U.S. at 91). In WMCA, Inc. v. Lomenzo, 377 U.S. 633 (1964), a companion case to *Reynolds*, the Court had reviewed apportionment of the New York legislature that was based on population counts of U.S. citizens, excluding aliens. Although finding unconstitutional malapportionment, the Court raised no explicit question about this aspect of New York's approach, though through its choice of words ("undervaluation of the weight of the votes of certain of a State's citizens," 377 U.S. at 653), it suggested that the citizen base was permissible.

The problem of racial discrimination in districting has recently given the apportionment base question some incremental visibility. The use of race in the drawing of district lines is not a new phenomenon in

American democracy, but it has taken on new salience since the 1982 amendment of the Voting Rights Act providing that neither race nor color may be used to deprive persons of equal "opportunity . . . to participate in the political process and to elect representatives of their choice" (42 U.S.C. §1973b [1994]). Under this provision, members of a racial minority may assert that district lines have been drawn illegally to their electoral disadvantage—to "dilute" their voting effectiveness. One factor that the courts consider in evaluating such a dilution claim is whether the number of districts where the minority in question is electorally dominant is proportionate to its representation in the population more generally. *See* Johnson v. De Grandy, 512 U.S. 997 (1994). Some minority voting populations have disproportionately large numbers of children or live in proximity to substantial numbers of noncitizens of the same racial or ethnic stock. The courts have generally been clear that electoral dominance is a matter of the *effective* ability to elect a candidate, which means that it is judged by counts of voting population. Johnson v. De Grandy, 512 U.S. 997, 1013 (1994); Beer v. United States, 425 U.S. 130, 141 (1976); Connor v. Finch, 431 U.S. 407, 427 n.2 (1977); City of Rome v. United States, 446 U.S. 156, 186 n.22 (1980); *but see* Daly v. Hunt, 93 F.3d 1212, 1227 (4th Cir. 1996). The other side of the judgment of "proportionality" has been more troublesome. Is the presumptively "fair" number of electoral districts to be proportionate to voting population, or to total population? Or perhaps to voting age population, citizen and noncitizen alike? In Johnson v. De Grandy, 512 U.S. 997, 1014 (1994), the Court upheld districting that provided minority districts proportionate to "voting-age numbers." But it sidestepped an opportunity to decide definitively "which characteristics of minority populations (*e.g.*, age, citizenship) ought to be the touchstone for proving a dilution claim and devising a sound remedy." 512 U.S. at 1008. *See id.* at 1017 n.14, 1021 n.18. And in Shaw v. Reno, 509 U.S. 630 (1993), while allowing a constitutional claim of racial gerrymandering to proceed, the Court raised no question about the state's use of voting-age population in its initial judgment of proportionality (509 U.S. at 634). The difference can be crucial to legislative control in jurisdictions where voting is racially polarized, and this seems as likely an explanation as any of why the question of the political status of children seems recently to have poked its head out into the light of day. *See* Barnett v. Daley, 32 F.3d 1196, 1198 (7th Cir. 1994) (Posner, C.J.).

20. Kirkpatrick v. Preisler, 394 U.S. 526, 530–531 (1969) (emphasis supplied).

21. Karcher v. Daggett, 462 U.S. 725, 732 (1983). "[In] congressional dis-

tricting . . . population equality appears now to be the preeminent, if not the sole, criterion on which to adjudge constitutionality." Chapman v. Meier, 420 U.S. 1, 23 (1975). The evidence in the racial districting case of Bush v. Vera, 517 U.S. 952 (1996) apparently showed that "[e]very one of Texas' 30 congressional districts contains precisely 566,217 persons." 517 U.S. at 1013 n.10 (Stevens, J., dissenting).

22. *See* Abate v. Mundt, 403 U.S. 182 (1971); Mahan v. Howell, 410 U.S. 315 (1973).

23. Gaffney v. Cummings, 412 U.S. 735, 742 (1973); Connor v. Finch, 431 U.S. 407 (1977); *but cf.* Brown v. Thomson, 462 U.S. 835 (1983).

24. The apportionment base question might have been solved by following the lead of the constitutional text. Section 2 of the Fourteenth Amendment provides that the House of Representatives is to be apportioned *among* the various states "according to their respective numbers, counting the whole number of persons in each state, excluding Indians not taxed." This provision is a postemancipation adaptation of the approach to state representation in the House found in Article I section 2, where "respective numbers" was clearly understood to refer to total population, *see* FEDERALIST 54, except as explicitly qualified—by, in addition to the exclusion of Indians "not taxed," the notorious inclusion of slaves at three-fifths of a person each. In the Fourteenth Amendment version, the words *inhabitants* and *citizens* elsewhere appear, reinforcing the conclusion that the different word *persons* refers to all of them. And the consistent practice throughout our constitutional history has been to use total population as calculated by the decennial census for the purpose of congressional apportionment among states (save, of course, for the explicit qualifications). *See generally* Hyman Alterman, COUNTING PEOPLE: THE CENSUS IN HISTORY (Harcourt Brace & World 1969). There is a lively contemporary dispute about whether illegal aliens—a category that was essentially unknown at the time of the Constitution—are to be counted in the decennial census and then in interstate apportionment of the House. For opposed views on this question, *compare* Murphy, *supra* note 5, *with* T. Alexander Aleinikoff, *The Census and Undocumented Aliens: A Constitutional Account,* MICHIGAN LAW QUADRANGLE NOTES (1989).

Still, this interstate apportionment might be viewed as an integral, but not necessarily "principled," part of the bargain necessary to secure agreement at the Constitutional Convention. Garza v. County of Los Angeles, Board of Supervisors, 918 F.2d 763, 784 n. 10 (9th Cir. 1990), *cert. denied,* 498 U.S. 1028 (1991) (Kozinski, J., concurring and dissenting in part); *cf.* Wesberry v. Sanders, 376 U.S. 1, 20 (1964) (Harlan,

J., dissenting). *Compare* Reynolds v. Sims, 397 U.S. 533, 574–575 (1964) (discussing apportionment of the U.S. Senate). That is certainly the reading typically given to the three-fifths provision for the slave population. Frank Easterbrook, *Abstraction and Authority*, 59 UNIVERSITY OF CHICAGO LAW REVIEW 349, 366 (1992); Raymond T. Diamond, *No Call to Glory: Thurgood Marshall's Thesis on the Intent of a Pro-Slavery Constitution*, 42 VANDERBILT LAW REVIEW 93, 108 n.94 (1989). After excising that provision, the Fourteenth Amendment then simply carried over the underlying formulation. If the provision for apportionment of the House among the states is similarly seen as simply part of a compromise, it might not be thought to be especially relevant to the intrastate questions raised by *Wesberry* and *Reynolds. See* U.S. Department of Commerce v. Montana, 503 U.S. 442 (1992). The constitutional formulation for House apportionment among the states continues to hover over our inquiry, but I mostly pursue the problem of children in American politics assuming, as has the Court, that the interstate apportionment question and the intrastate ones are distinct.

25. It was the failure of the Tennessee legislature to live up to such an ideal made express in the Tennessee Constitution that gave rise to the case that began the apportionment revolution of the 1960s. Baker v. Carr, 369 U.S. 186 (1962). *See* Andrew Hacker, CONGRESSIONAL DISTRICTING 4–16 (Brookings Institution 1964). The problem can be traced to colonial times. *See* Max Farrand, THE FRAMING OF THE CONSTITUTION OF THE UNITED STATES 108–109 (Yale University Press 1913).

26. John Adams held, for instance, that propertyless males "have [no] judgment of their own. . . . [They are] to all intents and purposes as much dependent upon others . . . as women are upon their husbands, or children on their parents." Letter from John Adams to James Sullivan, May 26, 1776, *quoted in* Robert J. Steinfeld, *Property and Suffrage in the Early American Republic*, 41 STANFORD LAW REVIEW 335, 341 (1989) (alteration in source). Adams is just one example of important early figures who sounded liberal notes along with republican ones. For other examples, *see* the discussion in chapter two of the hope that American representative government would faithfully replicate what might have been expected from a gigantic meeting of the whole. *See generally* Gordon S. Wood, THE CREATION OF THE AMERICAN REPUBLIC 53–65 (University of North Carolina Press 1969); James Roger Sharp, AMERICAN POLITICS IN THE EARLY REPUBLIC 2 (Yale University Press 1993); Robert A. Dahl, DEMOCRACY AND ITS CRITICS 24–28 (Yale University Press 1989).

27. Alterman, *supra* note 24, at 168–169, 178.
28. Dahl, *supra* note 26, at 289; Wood, *supra* note 26, at 102; Frank I. Michelman, *Foreword: Traces of Self-Government*, 100 HARVARD LAW REVIEW 4, 54 (1986).
29. Edmund Burke, Speech to the Electors at Bristol (Oct. 13, 1774), *quoted in* Wood, *supra* note 26, at 175 (emphasis in original).
30. *Letter from Edmund Burke to Sir Hercules Langriche, in* BURKE'S POLITICS: SELECTED WRITINGS AND SPEECHES ON REFORM, REVOLUTION AND WAR 474, 494 (Ross J.S. Hoffman & Paul Levack eds., A. A. Knopf 1949).
31. *See* Hannah Fenichel Pitkin, THE CONCEPT OF REPRESENTATION 173–174 (University of California Press 1967).
32. On the length of terms, *compare Dissent of the Minority of the Pennsylvania Convention, in* I THE DEBATE 526, 548–549 (Bernard Bailyn ed., The Library of America 1993) (desirability of "short period" of legislative service) *and* "Cato" V, *in* I THE DEBATE, *supra*, at 399, 401 ("safe democratical principles of annual [elections]") *with* "Americanus" V, *in* I THE DEBATE, *supra*, at 487, 490 (longer terms afford "the members more time to acquire a knowledge of public affairs competent to the station they fill") *and* "A Citizen of America," *in* I THE DEBATE, *supra*, at 129, 140 (longer terms of senators allow them "gradually [to] lose their partiality, [and] generalize their views, and consider themselves as acting for the whole"). On the contrast between the House and the Senate, *compare* FEDERALIST 52 (House to have "an immediate dependence on, and an intimate sympathy with, the people") *with* FEDERALIST 63 (a "well-constructed Senate. . . . may be sometimes necessary as a defense to the people against their own temporary errors and delusions."). The Constitution also provides that members of the House of Representatives must be twenty-five years of age (and seven years U.S. citizens), whereas senators are required to be thirty (and citizens for nine years) (U.S. Const., Art. I, § 1, cl. 2; § 3, cl. 3). These differences can also readily be related to the different conceptions of their roles.
33. Wood, *supra* note 26, at 188.
34. U.S. Const., Art. II, § 1, cl. 2; § 2, cl. 2; Am. XVII. Although not required to employ popular election for the choice of its electors for the presidential selection process, all states now do so. *See* Lawrence D. Longley & Neal R. Peirce, THE ELECTORAL COLLEGE PRIMER 2000 25 (Yale University Press 1999).
35. *See, e.g.,* Judith N. Shklar, AMERICAN CITIZENSHIP: THE QUEST FOR INCLUSION 2 (Harvard University Press 1991).

36. *Cf.* Jane J. Mansbridge, Beyond Adversary Democracy 18 (University of Chicago Press 1983).

37. Federalist 10. The real-world effect of expansion of the electorate may often be the attenuation of ties between legislators and the average voter, but the ideology that leads to expansion surely often assumes that the ties are real and important.

38. 377 U.S. at 565.

39. *See* Stuart M. Brown Jr., *Black on Representation: A Question, in* Nomos X, *supra* note 9, at 144, 148; Frank I. Michelman, *Conceptions of Democracy in American Constitutional Argument: Voting Rights,* 41 Florida Law Review 443, 472 (1989). Professor Michelman strives mightily in this article to find republican themes in a second generation of Supreme Court apportionment decisions, where the Court grappled with questions of the franchise in selection of representatives for local governmental units that deal with a limited range of subjects. *Id.* at 458–485. But even in that relatively congenial context, republican themes are not easy to find in what the Court had to say. In the end, Michelman concedes that "[i]t is a *hypothesis* I offer rather than a claim." *Id.* at 486 (emphasis in original). *Cf.* Gerald L. Neuman, *"We Are the People": Alien Suffrage In German and American Perspective,* 13 Michigan Journal of International Law 259, 321–322 (1992).

40. *See, e.g.,* Michelman, *supra* note 39; Cass R. Sunstein, *Beyond the Republican Revival,* 97 Yale Law Journal 1539 (1988); Michael J. Sandel, Democracy's Discontent: America in Search of a Public Policy (Harvard University Press 1996).

41. One prominent commentator, for instance, identifies citizenship with those "who should share in the benefits of a common social, political, and economic enterprise." Eisgruber, *supra* note 6, at 65.

42. *See* Pitkin, *supra* note 31, at 162.

43. Certain legally resident aliens were allowed to vote in a number of states until the early part of the twentieth century. *See* Paul Kleppner, Who Voted? The Dynamics of Electoral Turnout, 1870–1980 8 (Praeger Publishers 1982).

44. *See* Gaffney v. Cummings, 412 U.S. 735, 746 (1973) ("The United States census is more of an event than a process."). Nor is the census count all that precise to begin with. *See* Department of Commerce v. United States House of Representatives, 525 U.S. 316 (1999); Marie Cocco, *Now that I'm in GOP-Land, I'm Sure to Count,* Newsday, Sept. 3, 1998, at A55.

45. *See* note 24, *supra.*

46. Unless perhaps the base were registered voters, as in Burns v. Richard-

son, 384 U.S. 73 (1966), for which fairly precise numbers should be available.

47. Thus I am puzzled by Chief Judge Posner's choice of words in discussing "virtual representation" of children in Barnett v. City of Chicago, 141 F.3d 699 (7th Cir. 1998). After characterizing the extra votes possibility as "a bizarre suggestion in our political culture," he says that giving extra votes to a racial or ethnic group "which happens to have a higher than average number of children. . . . is not a ridiculous idea." *Id.* at 704.

48. I would not think it necessary for "liberal" sensibilities to allow parents to split their votes among candidates, but even that should be manageable if it were thought desirable.

49. U.S. Const., Am. XIV, § 1 ("All persons born . . . in the United States and subject to the jurisdiction thereof, are citizens of the United States").

50. *See, e.g.,* 20 Ill. Comp. Stat 505/5 (West 1998). If it was impossible to muster the political will for surrogate voting in these cases, however, the present allocation of the voting power to the district voting population as a whole would be an obvious fallback position—but for those children alone. There would be a similar problem with assigning votes to state officials on behalf of incompetents who are wards of the state. *See, e.g.,* 405 Ill. Comp. Stat. 5/111 (West 1998).

51. I should perhaps mention that the apportionment decisions suggest the possibility that extra votes for parents would be found unconstitutional. Parents would, after all, have more than "one vote." Such an argument would, however, seem rather perverse. We have seen that "extra" voting power is already being exercised, so that the sense of the "one-person one-vote" requirement in this context is far from clear. Even if this objection were credited, amendment is always possible, which is how the vote was extended to the emancipated slaves, to women, and to eighteen-year-olds (U.S. Const., Ams. XV, XIX, XXVI). *See also* Am. XXIV, abolishing the poll tax. In any event, the mere fact of doubt cast on an idea by a Supreme Court decision (or even a flat-out holding of unconstitutionality) is no impediment to popular expression of dissatisfaction.

52. There may be untoward conversational consequences of that practice, since candidates may not know how to reach out to those voters. There would be no such problem with exclusion from the apportionment base of eligible voters who live and vote in a single location so that candidates know where to direct their conversation.

53. Baker v. Carr, 369 U.S. 186, 258–259 (1962) (Clark, J., concurring).

54. 377 U.S. 533, 543 (1964).

55. *Cf.* Garza v. County of Los Angeles, 918 F.2d 763 (9ᵗʰ Cir. 1990), *cert. denied,* 498 U.S. 1028 (1991).

56. This helps explain why "incumbent senators are far more likely than incumbent representatives to be defeated when they run for reelection." Jonathan S. Krasno, CHALLENGERS, COMPETITION, AND REELECTION 1 (Yale University Press 1994). Krasno provides a somewhat different explanation, but it is hard to believe that the stability of district lines does not contribute to senatorial vulnerability. *See* Daniel D. Polsby & Robert D. Popper, *Ugly: An Inquiry Into the Problem of Racial Gerrymandering Under the Voting Rights Act,* 92 MICHIGAN LAW REVIEW 652 (1993); Karcher v. Daggett, 462 U.S. 725, 777 (1983) ("patina of respectability for the equipopulous gerrymander") (White, J., dissenting).

57. Some support for the amendment came from people who hoped it would help "defuse youthful alienation and unrest." *See* American Bar Association, JUVENILE JUSTICE STANDARDS PROJECT, STANDARDS RELATING TO RIGHTS OF MINORS, §1.1, Commentary, p. 17 (1977).

58. I have been unable to locate data on parent voter turnout.

Chapter 7. Judicial Review and the Sense of Difficulty

1. Marbury v. Madison, 5 U.S. (1 Cranch) 137 (1803); *see* U.S. Const., Art. VI, cl. 2.

2. Alexander M. Bickel, THE LEAST DANGEROUS BRANCH 16–18 (Bobbs-Merrill Co. 1962).

3. An entirely typical invocation of Bickel's terminology is Michael C. Dorf, *Integrating Normative and Descriptive Constitutional Theory: The Case of Original Meaning,* 85 GEORGETOWN LAW JOURNAL 1765, 1771 (1997), treating the countermajoritarian difficulty as simply a fact of life in American politics around which the discussion of other things is to be organized. *See* Stephen M. Griffin, AMERICAN CONSTITUTIONALISM 107 (Princeton University Press 1996) ("Bickel's argument over the 'counter-majoritarian difficulty' . . . set the terms of the contemporary debate over the justification of judicial review, a debate that tended to remain static in the ensuing years."); Erwin Chemerinsky, *Foreword: The Vanishing Constitution,* 103 HARVARD LAW REVIEW 43, 64 (1989); Rebecca L. Brown, *Accountability, Liberty, and the Constitution,* 98 COLUMBIA LAW REVIEW 531 (1998). Writing in a collection of essays on constitutional amendment, David Dow observes that the

"so-called 'countermajoritarian difficulty'. . . . is . . . what drives efforts [of four other contributors] . . . to justify extra-Article V theories of amendment." David R. Dow, *The Plain Meaning of Article V, in* RE-SPONDING TO IMPERFECTION 117, 118 (Sanford Levinson ed., Princeton University Press 1995). A recent article on the nondelegation doctrine (which looks with some disfavor on the delegation of legislative authority to unaccountable administrative agencies), associates the numerous supporters of that doctrine with a "*counter-majoritarian framework*," the "current dominance" of which "can be traced back to . . . Bickel's . . . *The Least Dangerous Branch*. . . ." George I. Lovell, *That Sick Chicken Won't Hunt: The Limits of a Judicially Enforced Non-Delegation Doctrine*, 17 CONSTITUTIONAL COMMENTARY 79, 84 (2000) (emphasis in original). For some examples of nonlawyers concerned about judicial overreaching, *see, e.g.,* William Kristol, *Crowning the Imperial Judiciary*, N.Y. Times, Nov. 28, 2000, at A31; Pat Buchanan, *Better to Shear Shannon—Or the Judges?*, Detroit News, Aug. 18, 1994, at A11. For a selection of criticisms of Bickel's conceptualization, *see* Frank Michelman, *Foreword: Traces of Self-Government*, 100 HARVARD LAW REVIEW 4, 75 (1986); Barry Friedman, *Dialogue and Judicial Review*, 91 MICHIGAN LAW REVIEW 577 (1993) [hereinafter Friedman, Dialogue]; Barry Friedman, *The History of the Countermajoritarian Difficulty, Part One: The Road to Judicial Supremacy*, 73 NEW YORK UNIVERSITY LAW REVIEW 333, 334–343 (1998); Brown, *supra;* Robert C. Post, CONSTITUTIONAL DOMAINS 191 (Harvard University Press 1995); Chemerinsky, *supra,* at 77–83; Griffin, *supra,* at 109; Henry Paul Monaghan, *We The People[s], Original Understanding, and Constitutional Amendment*, 96 COLUMBIA LAW REVIEW 121 (1996); Julian N. Eule, *Judicial Review of Direct Democracy*, 99 YALE LAW JOURNAL 1503, 1531–1533 (1990); Robert W. Bennett, *Democracy as Meaningful Conversation*, 14 CONSTITUTIONAL COMMENTARY 481, 493–500 (1997).

As mentioned earlier (*see* chapter two, note 1, *supra*), Bickel said he was heavily influenced by James Bradley Thayer's classic article urging that judicial review be used sparingly. But Mark Tushnet argues that Thayer may have appreciated that conservative "decidedly nonmajoritarian" forces were quite powerful in American democracy. By Tushnet's account, judicial review represented to Thayer a threat to those conservative forces. *See* Mark Tushnet, *Thayer's Target: Judicial Review or Democracy?*, 88 NORTHWESTERN UNIVERSITY LAW REVIEW 9 (1993). If Tushnet is right, then Bickel must accept an even larger measure of the blame for misdirecting us about the "difficulty" posed by judicial review.

4. Trial courts "make law" in this sense, but judicial lawmaking and policy choices are the focus of concern for appellate courts. Unless the context indicates otherwise, I focus on the appellate level.

5. Herbert Wechsler, *Toward Neutral Principles of Constitutional Law,* 73 HARVARD LAW REVIEW 1, 15 (1959).

6. Many judges at the state level must stand for election and even occasionally face the possibility of direct challenge for reelection. This does mean that electoral—and derivative conversational—incentives will occasionally operate, *see* William Glaberson, *A Spirited Campaign for Ohio Court Puts Judges on New Terrain,* N.Y. Times, July 7, 2000, at A11, albeit typically in much more concentrated form at election time than in the legislative and executive contexts. Even in an electoral setting, however, courts share the dispute-resolving self-conception, by the lights of which it would be quite improper for judges to convene a community meeting to explain a problem that has arisen in an adjudication and to solicit advice on the policy that should be brought to bear in solving that problem. In the oral argument on appeal in the U.S. government's antitrust action against Microsoft, for instance, virtually the entire Court of Appeals for the District of Columbia Circuit was critical of the fact that the trial judge had seen fit to grant media interviews during and after the trial of the case. Stephen Labaton, *Judges Voice Doubt on Order Last Year to Split Microsoft,* N.Y. Times, Feb. 28, 2001, at A1. The dispute resolving self-conception is nicely captured by a letter from a lawyer to the editor of the *New York Times,* objecting to the *Times'* position in favor of television coverage of U.S. Supreme Court proceedings:

> It's not that the public is incapable of understanding the work of the court; it's that oral argument is not a public display and discussion of the issues so much as an inquiry into the legal precedents and their application to the facts as found in the courts below.

Oyez! Oyez! TV in the Court!, N.Y. Times, April 13, 2000, at A26. Further reflecting this self-conception, professional norms operate powerfully to stifle any urge toward broad public conversation. *See* Republican Party of Minnesota v. Kelly, 220 F.3d 882 (8th Cir. 2001); James J. Alfini & Terrence J. Brooks, *Ethical Constraints on Judicial Election Campaigns: A Review and Critique of Canon 7,* 77 KENTUCKY LAW JOURNAL 671 (1988–1989); Steven P. Croley, *The Majoritarian Difficulty: Elective Judiciaries and the Rule of Law,* 62 UNIVERSITY OF CHICAGO LAW REVIEW 689, 731 (1995); Hans S. Linde, *Elective Judges: Some Comparative Comments,* 61 SOUTHERN CALIFORNIA LAW REVIEW 1995, 2001 (1988); Abner J. Mikva, *The Judges v. The People: Judicial Independence and Democratic Ideals,* 19 CARDOZO LAW REVIEW 1771, 1776 (1998);

William Glaberson, *States Rein In Truth-Bending In Court Races*, N.Y. Times, Aug. 23, 2000, at A1. For these reasons, the conversational behavior of elected courts seems to be quite similar to that of appointed ones. *But see* Steve France, *Courting the Voters*, Dec. 2000 AMERICAN BAR ASSOCIATION JOURNAL 34.

I should also mention a few complications that I otherwise ignore for ease of presentation. I do not dwell on the very real differences among clients (and probably also lawyers) in the nature and extent of the discussions between lawyer and client. Those differences may well affect the sense of involvement that clients feel when lawyers do the talking for them in court. Representation by "agents" is, of course, often found in the political arena as well on those occasions when citizens take an "active" conversational role. I also put to the side devices such as intervention and the use of class actions, which may somewhat expand participation—and hence conversational involvement—at the trial level, and then derivatively at the appellate level on occasion. Those complications do not alter in any important way the picture painted in the text of the narrow conversational reach of appellate courts.

7. *See* Joseph D. Kearney & Thomas W. Merrill, *The Influence of Amicus Curiae Briefs on the Supreme Court*, 148 UNIVERSITY OF PENNSYLVANIA LAW REVIEW 743, 757, 764 (2000). The study by Kearney and Merrill found that in the decade from 1986 to 1995 at least one *amicus* brief was submitted in fully 85 percent of the Court's cases (*Id.* at 753). There were 4,907 *amicus* briefs filed in 982 of the cases heard by the Court over that period (out of a total caseload of 1,154), although these data surely exaggerate the democratic conversational reality somewhat, for *amicus* briefs of the Solicitor General of the United States account for a good deal of the volume (*Id.* at 752, 753, 761). On the neutrality question, *see* Samuel Krislov, *The Amicus Curiae Brief: From Friendship to Advocacy*, 72 YALE LAW JOURNAL 694, 703 (1963) ("The amicus is no longer a neutral, amorphous embodiment of justice, but an active participant in the interest group struggle"). A 1997 amendment of the Supreme Court rules for the first time requires disclosure in *amicus* briefs of monetary assistance and of assistance received from parties to the litigation (Kearney & Merrill, *supra*, at 762, n. 54).

8. In Marshall's first four years on the Court, there were no dissents and only one concurring opinion, with Marshall himself writing well over half the opinions. Percival E. Jackson, DISSENT ON THE SUPREME COURT 21 (University of Oklahoma Press 1969). An "explosion" of separate opinions can be traced to the accession of Harlan Fiske Stone to the Chief Justiceship in 1941. The rate of dissonant opinions climbed

steeply until 1948 and has remained high since that time. *See* John P. Kelsh, *The Opinion Delivery Practices of the United States Supreme Court 1790–1945*, 77 Washington University Law Quarterly 137, 138, 175–177 (1999). The annual Supreme Court issue of the *Harvard Law Review* reported that in the 1999 term there were sixty-seven dissents to seventy-seven opinions of the Court. There were in addition fifty separate concurring opinions that term. *The Statistics*, Table I, 112 Harvard Law Review 390 (2000). For an example of the lionization of dissenters, *see* David M. O'Brien, Storm Center: The Supreme Court in American Politics 141 (W. W. Norton & Co. 4th ed. 1996), where a picture of Justices Holmes and Brandeis appears under a caption describing them as "two of the Court's 'great dissenters.'"

There is a growing trend toward "non-publication" of opinions for decisions rendered by the U.S. Courts of Appeals, *see generally* Patricia M. Wald, *The Rhetoric of Results and the Results of Rhetoric: Judicial Writings*, 62 University of Chicago Law Review 1371 (1995), to the point that opinions are now disseminated broadly through standard publication channels in only a little over twenty percent of the dispositions throughout the system. *See* Statistics Division, Administrative Office of the United States Courts, Judicial Business of the United States Courts: 1999 Annual Report of the Director Table S-3 (9000). Although not broadly available, these "unpublished" opinions are not secret. They are made available to the parties and can be privately copied and disseminated. They cannot, however, be cited as precedent. In theory at least, this "non-publication" is reserved for matters without much general interest, *see* Administrative Office of the United States Courts, [1964] Annual Report, so that the conversational implications of the practice are likely much less substantial than the bare percentage figure might suggest.

9. A large percentage of the *amicus* briefs submitted by nongovernmental agencies are filed on behalf of established "interest groups." This is hardly surprising, since spontaneous decision by an individual, or formation of a group to file a brief, is unlikely. After noting the various organizations that had filed *amicus* briefs all on only one side of a case, Justice Scalia noted cynically that this "is no surprise. There is no self-interested organization out there devoted to pursuit of the truth in the federal courts." Jaffee v. Redmond, 518 U.S. 1, 36 (1996).

10. *See, e.g.,* Ryan v. Commodity Futures Trading Comm'n, 125 F.3d 1062 (7th Cir. 1997) (Posner, C. J.).

11. This is not to say that opinions are never formulated with an eye to public reaction. One commentator concludes, for instance, that "poli-

tics played a large role in both the content and the packaging of *Roe [v. Wade]*." Neal Devins, SHAPING CONSTITUTIONAL VALUES 2 (Johns Hopkins University Press 1996).

12. Chief Justice Hughes described dissent as "an appeal . . . to the intelligence of a future day, when a later decision may possibly correct the error into which the dissenting judge believes the court to have been betrayed." Charles Evans Hughes, THE SUPREME COURT OF THE UNITED STATES 68 (Government Printing Office 1928).

13. *See* John Ferejohn, *Instituting Deliberative Democracy, in* NOMOS XLII, DESIGNING DEMOCRATIC INSTITUTIONS 75, 98 (Ian Shapiro & Stephen Macedo eds., New York University Press 2000).

14. Amy Gutmann & Dennis Thompson, DEMOCRACY AND DISAGREEMENT 46–47 (Harvard University Press 1996), while noting that "[s]ome constitutional democrats portray judges as engaged in a 'dialogue' with society," also recognize the fundamentally different conversational behavior of courts.

15. Walter F. Murphy, *Constitutions, Constitutionalism, and Democracy, in* CONSTITUTIONALISM AND DEMOCRACY, TRANSITIONS IN THE CONTEMPORARY WORLD 3, 6 (Douglas Greenberg, Stanley N. Katz, Melanie Beth Oliviero, & Steven C. Wheatley eds., Oxford University Press 1993).

16. *See, e.g.,* Stephen Holmes, *Precommitment and the Paradox of Democracy, in* CONSTITUTIONALISM AND DEMOCRACY 195, 196 (Jon Elster & Rune Slagstad eds., Cambridge University Press 1988); Gutmann & Thompson, *supra* note 14, at 26–27, 33–39.

17. *See* U.S. Const., Art. V. It is, of course, true that interpretation can sometimes obviate the need for amendment of constitutional language, *see, e.g.,* Home Bldg. & Loan Ass'n v. Blaisdell, 290 U.S. 398 (1934), but for purposes of the present discussion I ignore that complication.

18. *See* Robert Bellah, *Civil Religion in America, reprinted in* AMERICAN CIVIL RELIGION (Russell E. Richey & Donald G. Jones eds., Harper & Row 1974). Some version of this point has been made by a large number of commentators. *See, e.g.,* Max Lerner, *The Court and Constitution as Symbols,* 46 YALE LAW JOURNAL 1290 (1937); Thomas Grey, *The Constitution as Scripture,* 37 STANFORD LAW REVIEW 1 (1984); Sanford Levinson, CONSTITUTIONAL FAITH (Princeton University Press 1988). Writing in 1978, Bickel took note of Supreme Court Justice George Sutherland's belief since childhood that "the Constitution 'was a divinely inspired instrument.'" Alexander M. Bickel, THE SUPREME COURT AND THE IDEA OF PROGRESS 14–15 (Yale University Press 1978).

19. *See* U.S. Const., Art. II, § 1, cl. 1; Am XIV, cl. 1.

20. United States v. Lopez, 514 U.S. 549 (1995); Printz v. United States, 521 U.S. 898 (1997); City of Boerne v. Flores, 521 U.S. 507 (1997); Kimel v. Florida Board of Regents, 528 U.S. 62 (2000). Sometimes a statute is held unconstitutional not as a whole ("on its face") but only as applied to a particular situation. In such a case, there need not have been a legislative majority in favor of the position rejected. Indeed, there may not have been a single legislator who cared one way or the other about the issue that the Court actually decides. Even in such a case, however, there will, of course, have been a disappointed litigant. And if the case was momentous enough to have justified Supreme Court review, there will also likely have been a host of disappointed nonparties as well.

21. U.S. Term Limits Inc. v. Thornton, 514 U.S. 779 (1995).

22. *See* U.S. Const., Art. II, §1, cl. 5; James C. Ho, *Unnatural Born Citizens and Acting Presidents,* 17 Constitutional Commentary 575 (2000). There may be a conversational explanation as well, which I take up briefly in chapter nine.

23. It was so from the start. The *Federalist Papers* appeared in New York newspapers as part of the intense New York debate over ratification of the Constitution, but they only scratch the surface of what was a nationwide conversation about the proposed Constitution as a whole and about many of its particular provisions. The Twenty-Seventh Amendment (forbidding the effectiveness of any legislative change in compensation of Senators and Representatives during the term of the House in which it is enacted) is likely the only exception, having snuck up on us because it was ratified piecemeal over the two centuries since it was first introduced as a part of the package of proposed amendments, ten of which became the Bill of Rights.

24. Bickel, *supra* note 2, at 202.

25. William N. Eskridge Jr., *Overruling Statutory Precedents,* 76 Georgetown Law Review 1361, 1362 (1988); *see* Patterson v. MacLean Credit Union, 491 U.S. 164, 172–173 (1988). Eskridge is one commentator who explicitly treats the difference between the countermajoritarianism of judicial review and that of statutory interpretation as a matter of degree. *See* William N. Eskridge Jr., Dynamic Statutory Interpretation 151 (Harvard University Press 1994).

26. *See, e.g.,* Flood v. Kuhn, 407 U.S. 258, 284 (1972); In re Professional Ins. Management, 130 F.3d 1122, 1128 (3d. Cir. 1997); Main v. Office Depot, Inc., 914 F. Supp. 1413, 1419 (S.D. Miss. 1996); Boutwell v. Sullivan, 469 So. 2d 526, 529 (Miss. 1985). The same is true of decisions in which a statute or practice is upheld against constitutional challenge. Adversely affected nonparties may be disappointed and even frustrated

to learn of a court decision on the constitutional merits of which they had little or no forewarning. But there is no dearth of ongoing conversational outlets in such cases, for the issue remains within the reach of ordinary legislative processes.

27. *See* U.S. Const., Art. V.

28. *See* Abner J. Mikva, *The Judges v. The People: Judicial Independence and Democratic Ideals*, 19 CARDOZO LAW REVIEW 1771, 1772 (1998); Devins, *supra* note 11, at 156–162; Martin H. Redish, *Judicial Review and the "Political Question,"* 79 NORTHWESTERN UNIVERSITY LAW REVIEW 1031, 1045–1046 (1985); Chemerinsky *supra* note 3, at 74 (1989) (associating democracy with the "majoritarian paradigm" and asserting that "the Constitution—the basic charter for government in this country—does not support the priority of democracy"; Chemerinsky does later assert that "no branch of government is truly majoritarian" but that "all [sic] existing institutions further the ends of democracy. . . ." *Id.* at 78). For Chemerinsky, to be sure, the courts sometimes hark too closely to majoritarianism. *Id.* at 96–98.

29. Bickel, *supra* note 2, at 25, 64, 188. Bickel's two desiderata were severely criticized as inconsistent. In Gerald Gunther's words, Bickel advocated "100% insistence on principle, 20% of the time." Gerald Gunther, *The Subtle Vices of the "Passive Virtues"—A Comment on Principle and Expediency in Judicial Review*, 64 COLUMBIA LAW REVIEW 1, 3 (1964).

30. *Compare* John Hart Ely, DEMOCRACY AND DISTRUST 120–125 (Harvard University Press 1980), *with* John Hart Ely, *Foreword: On Discovering Fundamental Values*, 92 HARVARD LAW REVIEW 5 (1978). *See also* Steven G. Calabresi, *Textualism and the Countermajoritarian Difficulty*, 66 GEORGE WASHINGTON LAW REVIEW 1373 (1998). The idea of aligning judicial review with the service of popular control has deep roots in constitutional jurisprudence. *See* McCulloch v. Maryland, 17 U.S. (4 Wheat.) 316 (1819); United States v. Carolene Products, 304 U.S. 144, 153–154 n.4 (1938).

31. Robert H. Bork, THE TEMPTING OF AMERICA 139, 141 (Free Press 1990).

32. I will turn shortly to recognition by Bickel of complications in the majoritarian characterization.

33. *Cf.* Daniel Farber and Suzanna Sherry, DESPERATELY SEEKING CERTAINTY: THE MISGUIDED QUEST FOR CONSTITUTIONAL FOUNDATIONS 4 (characterizing the work of diverse constitutional theorists as attempting to reduce "constitutional law to a reliable formula, eliminating any need for judicial creativity and making all of constitutional law inter-

nally consistent"), 5 (characterizing those efforts as ones to provide "interpretive blueprint[s]") (University of Chicago Press 2002)

34. McCulloch v. Maryland, 17 U.S. (4 Wheat.) 316, 407 (1819); Marbury v. Madison, 5 U.S. (1 Cranch) 137 (1803). Bickel was one of those who recognized the tension between the Marshall of *Marbury* and the Marshall of *McCulloch*. *See* Bickel, *supra* note 2, at 15, 73.

35. *See* U.S. Const., Art. I, § 9, cls. 3, 5; Art. III, § 3, cl. 1; Marbury v. Madison, 5 U.S. (1 Cranch) 137, 179 (1803). At one point, Marshall said that judicial review was necessary to prevent the legislature from doing "what is expressly [constitutionally] forbidden." 5 U.S. (1 Cranch) at 178.

36. On the salutary operation of the "irrepressible impulse to advocacy," *see* Steven Lubet, *Rumpled Truth on Trial*, 94 NORTHWESTERN UNIVERSITY LAW REVIEW 627, 629 (2000); *see also* Robert P. Burns, A THEORY OF THE TRIAL (Princeton University Press 1999).

37. This is certainly the pervasive flavor of Raoul Berger's GOVERNMENT BY JUDICIARY (Harvard University Press 1977). Berger, for instance, quotes Hamilton as insisting that "it is indispensable that [the courts] . . . should be bound down by *strict rules* and precedents, which serve to define and point out their duty in every particular case that comes before them." *Id.* at 365 (emphasis in original). *See* Morton J. Horwitz, *Foreword: The Constitution of Change: Legal Fundamentality without Fundamentalism*, 107 HARVARD LAW REVIEW 30, 116 (1993).

38. Bickel, *supra* note 2, at 17–18. Bickel recognized other difficulties with the majoritarian assumption. There was the separation of powers built into our governmental structure, *id.* at 18, as well as the "more important complicating factor" of the disproportionate political power of interest groups. *Id.* at 18; *see also id.* at 193 (discussing "differently weighted constituenc[ies of American political institutions] . . . with the executive's normally being the most straight-out majoritarian"), 197 (suggesting that "even the Supreme Court may enter the 'political thicket' in states where no branch of government, not even the executive, rests on the majoritarian principle"). Bickel's recognition of complexity does allow Stephen Griffin to assert that his "argument was built on an appeal to democratic principles understood as a complex set, not an assumption that majoritarianism was the supreme principle of American democracy (despite the phrase 'countermajoritarian difficulty')." Griffin, *supra* note 3, at 108; *see also* Eule, *supra* note 3, at 1531–1532. This seems more appropriate as a characterization of the position Bickel would come to in later work, where, without being entirely explicit that he had changed his position, he rather clearly dis-

avowed majoritarianism as either accurately capturing American democracy or as normatively appealing. *See* Bickel, *supra* note 18, at 83 (while "elections do influence, and sometimes they determine, the movement of public policy. . . . elections are [in our 'Madisonian model of a multiplicity of factions'] the tip of the iceberg; the bulk of the political process is below"), 110–117 (disparagingly contrasting "[p]opulist majoritarianism" with "balanced Madisonian adjustment among countervailing groups and factions"), 168 n.* ("majoritarian fixation of the one-man, one-vote rule"); Alexander M. Bickel, THE MORALITY OF CONSENT 6–7, 100 (Yale University Press 1975) ("majorities are in large part fictions"). Barry Friedman reaches basically the same conclusion as I do on Bickel's views in the *Least Dangerous Branch.* Friedman, Dialogue, *supra* note 3, at 587.

39. Robert A. Dahl, DEMOCRACY AND ITS CRITICS 190 (Yale University Press 1989); *see* Robert Dahl, *Decision-Making in a Democracy: The Supreme Court as a National Policy-Maker,* 6 JOURNAL OF PUBLIC LAW 282 (1957). Dahl's phrase "lawmaking majorities" is ambiguous. In an earlier work, he explicitly confined the phrase to the "very restricted sense . . . [of] a majority of the voting members of both houses plus presidential acquiescence." Robert A. Dahl, A PREFACE TO DEMOCRATIC THEORY 108 (University of Chicago Press 1956). He makes no special point of the restriction in the more recent work, though perhaps he meant to track the earlier usage. *Democracy and Its Critics* freely discusses majoritarianism more generally, including its imperfect but approximate embodiment in "polyarchies" like the United States. Thus Arend Lijphardt sees Dahl's "polyarchies" as "democratic regimes . . . characterized not by perfect [vote-centered] responsiveness but by a high degree of it." Arend Lijphardt, DEMOCRACIES 2 (Yale University Press 1984). Recognizing some risk that I am oversimplifying his views, I thus associate Dahl with those who basically accept the characterization of the United States form of democracy as majoritarian.

40. *See* Robert G. McCloskey, THE AMERICAN SUPREME COURT (University of Chicago Press 1960); Richard Funston, *The Supreme Court and Critical Elections,* 69 AMERICAN POLITICAL SCIENCE REVIEW 795 (1975); Martin Shapiro, COURTS: A COMPARATIVE AND POLITICAL ANALYSIS (University of Chicago Press 1981); Gerald N. Rosenberg, THE HOLLOW HOPE: CAN COURTS BRING ABOUT SOCIAL CHANGE? (University of Chicago Press 1991), *cf.* Mark Tushnet, TAKING THE CONSTITUTION AWAY FROM THE COURTS 153 (Princeton University Press 1999) ("judicial review basically amounts to noise around zero").

41. Bruce Ackerman, WE THE PEOPLE: TRANSFORMATIONS 3 (Harvard University Press 1998).

42. *See* Bruce A. Ackerman, *The Storrs Lectures: Discovering the Constitution*, 93 YALE LAW JOURNAL 1013, 1016 (1984).

43. *See, e.g.,* Mitchell v. W. T. Grant Co., 416 U.S. 600, 627–628 (1974) (Powell, J., concurring); Lawrence C. Marshall, *"Let Congress Do It": The Case for An Absolute Rule of Statutory Stare Decisis*, 88 UNIVERSITY OF MICHIGAN LAW REVIEW 177, 180–182 (1989).

44. *See* Devins, *supra* note 11, at 23.

45. The classic example is the Supreme Court's rapid change of heart in the Legal Tender Cases after two new appointments. *See* Devins, *supra* note 11, at 25–26. *See also* Akhil Reed Amar, *Popular Sovereignty and Constitutional Amendment, in* RESPONDING TO IMPERFECTION, *supra* note 3, at 112 ("Conventional wisdom emphasizing 'countermajoritarian' judicial review to protect unpopular rights is . . . shortsighted. Presidents select judges, and presidents are elected by majorities."). An example of a change of heart without a change in personnel is Garcia v. San Antonio Metropolitan Transit Authority, 469 U.S. 528 (1985). On legislative involvement in judicial appointments, *see generally Symposium, Confirmation Controversy: The Selection of a Supreme Court Justice*, 84 NORTHWESTERN UNIVERSITY LAW REVIEW 832 (1990). My focus here is on the federal system of judicial selection. The symposium dealt with the U.S. Supreme Court confirmations, but in recent years, the confirmation process for lower court federal judges has increasingly become an occasion for interest group involvement. *See* Thomas Shakow, *Picking Moderate Judges*, 107 YALE LAW JOURNAL 2333, 2336 (1998).

46. *See* Bruce Fein, *Turn Out Lights on Litmus Tests*, April 2000 AMERICAN BAR ASSOCIATION JOURNAL 120.

47. The professional norms of judging mentioned earlier impinge on the process, with the result that nominees may decline to be pulled into discussions that might be thought to compromise their later ability to judge some issue fairly. This restriction has not generally been interpreted to exclude comment in confirmation hearings on decisionmaking philosophy, and the line between the permitted and the forbidden is pretty hazy. When popular concern is substantial, nominees often find some excuse for engaging an issue.

48. In a most unusual move, Justice Blackmun adverted in a court decision involving abortion to the possibility that the confirmation process for his successor might well "focus on the [abortion] issue before us today." Planned Parenthood of Southeastern Pennsylvania v. Casey, 505

U.S. 833, 922, 943 (1992) (Blackmun, J., concurring in part and dissenting in part). *See* Marshall, *supra* note 43, at 177 n. 2.

49. Roe v. Wade, 410 U.S. 113 (1973).*See* Devins, *supra* note 11, at 63; Friedman, Dialogue, *supra* note 3, at 658–668; *cf.* Mary Ann Glendon, ABORTION AND DIVORCE IN WESTERN LAW 48 (Harvard University Press 1987). Another dramatic example of "chipping away" is the ongoing practical challenge to the Supreme Court's school prayer decisions, Engel v. Vitale, 370 U.S. 421 (1962); School District v. Schempp, 374 U.S. 203 (1963).

The courts are hardly oblivious to conversation about what they have done. In the 1992 decision in *Planned Parenthood v. Casey,* 505 U.S. 833 (1992), the Supreme Court reaffirmed what it called "the essential holding of *Roe,*" 505 U.S. at 846, but in fact substantially enlarged the states' room for maneuvering with regard to many highly charged questions surrounding abortion. Although causal lines are hard to trace, it most certainly did not escape the Court's attention that public conversation about abortion was all about it in the years between *Roe* and *Casey.* (In his concurring opinion in Webster v. Reproductive Health Service, 492 U. S. 490, 532, 535 [1989], for instance, Justice Scalia took note of "carts full of mail from the public, and streets full of demonstrators, urging us—their unelected and life-tenured judges . . . to follow the popular will.") Even if there had been no shift in *Casey,* the possibility of judicial movement was always there and hence always providing a degree of encouragement to conversation.

I will turn in the text shortly to the real possibility that the courts' counterconversationalism is felt most immediately by lawyers and law professors. For the general population, the abortion example suggests that there may be a self-limiting quality to any conversational frustration associated with judicial review. The more deep and broad the concern aroused by a constitutional decision, the more political effort will go into doing something about it. Even if constitutional amendment remains a remote possibility, political routes to change are available. Those avenues will likely be tested, and the more they are pursued by some, the more they act as conversational magnets for still others. I do not pursue this possibility further here, but it may suggest why, for all its "counterconversationalism," judicial review is relatively uncontroversial in the citizenry at large.

At the same time, there may be cases in which the opportunities for "chipping away" are not so apparent. The foreclosure of criminal penalties is one thing that the courts are probably well-suited to enforce even in the face of resistance elsewhere in the system. For some perceived problems—like flag burning, perhaps—it might thus be that few avenues short of amendment are available once the court has cut off the criminality possibility. Texas v. Johnson, 491 U.S. 397 (1989); United States v. Eichman, 496 U.S. 310 (1990).

50. The saga is briefly recounted in Griffin, *supra* note 3, at 88–89. For an account of continuing interactions during the period when President Roosevelt's court-packing plan was under consideration, *see* Gregory A. Caldeira, *Public Opinion and the U.S. Supreme Court: FDR's Court-Packing Plan*, 81 AMERICAN POLITICAL SCIENCE REVIEW 1139 (1987).

51. Cooper v. Aaron, 358 U.S. 1 (1958); *see* Larry Alexander & Frederick Schauer, *On Extrajudicial Constitutional Interpretation*, 110 HARVARD LAW REVIEW 1359 (1997). At least the "seeming finality" of judicial review is emphasized by commentators in the countermajoritarian tradition. Harry H. Wellington, *The Nature of Judicial Review*, 91 YALE LAW JOURNAL 486, 499 (1982).

52. *See* Alexander & Schauer, *supra* note 51, at 1360; Friedman, Dialogue *supra* note 3, at 646–649.

53. *See* Stuart Taylor Jr., *Bork at Yale: Colleagues Recall a Friend but Philosophical Foe*, N. Y. Times, July 27, 1978, at A13.

Chapter 8. Rational Choice Theory and the Paradox of Voting

1. Georg Wilhelm Friedrich Hegel, PHILOSOPHY OF RIGHT 202–203 (T. M. Knox trans., Clarendon Press 1942) (1821).

2. Dennis C. Mueller, PUBLIC CHOICE II 349 (Cambridge University Press 1989).

3. Mancur Olson, THE LOGIC OF COLLECTIVE ACTION (Harvard University Press 1971). Concern with the political action of interest groups has deep roots in American political thought. Madison's contributions to the American constitutional design were importantly concerned with the sway of "factions," an inchoate form of interest group. Recognition of the importance of organization grew, and by 1908 Arthur Bentley could insist that "[t]he balance of . . . group pressures *is* the existing state of society." Arthur F. Bentley, THE PROCESS OF GOVERNMENT 258–259 (Principia Press 1908).

4. William Landes & Richard Posner, *The Independent Judiciary in an Interest-Group Perspective*, 18 JOURNAL OF LAW AND ECONOMICS 875, 877 (1975). The emphasis on the rational pursuit of self-interest in the electoral arena is often traced to Anthony Downs, AN ECONOMIC THEORY OF DEMOCRACY (Harper & Row 1957).

5. Donald P. Green & Ian Shapiro, PATHOLOGIES OF RATIONAL CHOICE THEORY (Yale University Press 1994).

6. A number of the responses are collected in THE RATIONAL CHOICE CONTROVERSY (Jeffrey Friedman ed., Yale University Press 1996). The debate was even given prominent coverage—and a mini-version of it reproduced—in the pages of the *New York Times. See Making Science of Looking Out For No. 1*, N.Y. Times, Feb. 26, 2000, at A15.

7. *See* Daniel A. Farber & Philip P. Frickey, LAW AND PUBLIC CHOICE 29–33 (University of Chicago Press 1991). Downs had acknowledged as much. *See* Downs, *supra* note 4, at 27.

8. Dennis Chong, *Rational Choice Theory's Mysterious Rivals, in* Friedman ed., *supra* note 6, at 37, 46, 49 (emphasis in original). For the more general defense of theorizing, *see id.* at 39 (rational choice theory as an "idealized explanatory model"); Morris P. Fiorina, *Rational Choice, Empirical Contributions, and the Scientific Enterprise, in* Friedman ed., *supra*, at 85. One of the early uses of the assumption that legislators are single-mindedly interested in reelection made quite clear both the oversimplification of the assumption and the explanatory justification for that oversimplification. David R. Mayhew, CONGRESS: THE ELECTORAL CONNECTION 13 (Yale University Press 1974). On the role of entrepreneurs, *see* Green & Shapiro, *supra* note 5, at 88–89 & n.16.

9. *See Measures of Elections Past*, N.Y. Times, Nov. 25, 2000, at A15. Markedly fewer—but still a "paradoxically" large number—vote in nonpresidential elections. *See* Jack C. Doppelt & Ellen Shearer, NONVOTERS 1 (Sage Publications, Inc. 1999).

10. Paul E. Meehl, *The Selfish Voter Paradox and the Thrown-Away Vote Argument*, 71 AMERICAN POLITICAL SCIENCE REVIEW 11 (1977); *see* Downs, *supra* note 4, at 244–247, 267; Mueller, *supra* note 2, at 348–369. Mueller traces the rhetorical use of the automobile accident to B. F. Skinner. *Id.* at 350 n.2.

11. If people fully responded to incentives in the way posited as "rational," the predicted voter turnout would be small but more than zero. For as the expected turnout becomes smaller, the chances of affecting the election outcome, and hence the suggested incentive to vote, increase. At the extreme, if an individual assumed that nobody else would vote, it would often make good sense—in terms of rational self-interest—for him or her to do so.

12. *See, e.g.,* Anna Quindlen, *Democracy to be Celebrated, Not Suffered,* Chicago Sun-Times, May 7, 2000, at 38A; Tamar Lewin, *Crime Costs Many Black Men the Vote, Study Says,* N.Y. Times, Oct. 23, 1998, at A12 (quoting Marc Mauer, assistant director of the Sentencing Project

as saying "[g]iven our low rate of voter participation, we should be looking for ways to encourage people to vote, not locking them out."); Doppelt & Shearer, *supra* note 9, at 4–6.

13. Bruno Frey, *Why Do High Income People Participate More in Politics?* 11 PUBLIC CHOICE 101(1971). For the hypothesis that the low stakes free the voter from the constraints of rationality, *see* John H. Aldrich, *Rational Choice and Turnout,* 37 AMERICAN JOURNAL OF POLITICAL SCIENCE 246, 261 (1993).

14. Mueller, *supra* note 2, at 365. On the correlation between income and voting, *see* Lynne M. Casper and Loretta E. Bass, VOTING AND REGISTRATION IN THE ELECTION OF NOVEMBER 1996 5–7 (United States Census Bureau P20–504 1998); *Campaign Study Group, No-Show '96: Americans Who Don't Vote* 3 (unpublished study for Medill News Service and WTTW Television, on file with author). Green & Shapiro, *supra* note 5, at 51.

15. Mueller, *supra* note 2, at 364, makes this point as well.

16. Green & Shapiro, *supra* note 5, at 52.

17. *Id.*

18. *Cf.* Robert D. Putnam, BOWLING ALONE 35 ("It is sometimes hard to tell whether voting causes community engagement or vice versa"), 447 n.2 ("voting is almost always a socially embedded act . . . turnout and social engagement are highly correlated") (Simon & Schuster 2000).

19. *Cf.* Casper & Bass, *supra* note 14, at 7 ("Education may also influence an individual's interest in and commitment to the political process"). One study that showed a large education effect also found that "[n]onvoters are far less likely than voters to follow politics." Campaign Study Group, *supra* note 14, at 3.

Chapter 9. Evaluating the Power of a Conversational Perspective

1. For a variety of questions about the descriptive accuracy of Ackerman's account, *see* Rogers M. Smith, *Legitimating Reconstruction: The Limits of Legalism,* 108 YALE LAW JOURNAL 2039 (1999); Michael W. McConnell, *The Forgotten Constitutional Moment,* 11 CONSTITUTIONAL COMMENTARY 115 (1994); William Fisher, *The Defects of Dualism,* 59 UNIVERSITY OF CHICAGO LAW REVIEW 955 (1992); Suzanna Sherry, *The Ghost of Liberalism Past,* 105 HARVARD LAW REVIEW 918 (1992); Michael Klarman, *Constitutional Fact/Constitutional Fiction: A Critique of Bruce Ackerman's Theory of Constitutional Moments,* 44 STANFORD LAW REVIEW 759 (1992).

2. Smith, *supra* note 1, at 2056.

3. Daniel A. Farber & Philip P. Frickey, LAW AND PUBLIC CHOICE 5 (University of Chicago Press 1991).

4. Richard J. Bernstein, THE RESTRUCTURING OF SOCIAL AND POLITICAL THEORY 82, 110 (Harcourt Brace Jovanovich 1976); *see* James M. Buchanan, *Richard Musgrave, Public Finance, and Public Choice,* 61 PUBLIC CHOICE 289, 290 (1989).

5. Amy Gutmann & Dennis Thompson, DEMOCRACY AND DISAGREEMENT 6 (Harvard University Press 1996).

6. "['Ideals']. . . . should . . . be relevant to human possibilities." Robert A. Dahl, DEMOCRACY AND ITS CRITICS 284 (Yale University Press 1989); *see* Robert P. Burns, *Rawls and the Principles of Welfare Law,* 83 NORTHWESTERN UNIVERSITY LAW REVIEW 184, 192–193 (1989).

7. Bruce Ackerman, WE THE PEOPLE: FOUNDATIONS 17, 314 (Harvard University Press 1991). For criticisms of the historical accuracy of Ackerman's depiction, *see* the authorities collected in note 1, *supra.*

8. *See, e.g.,* Ely's discussion of Reynolds v. Sims, 377 U.S. 533 (1964). John Hart Ely, DEMOCRACY AND DISTRUST 121–125 (Harvard University Press 1980). A more subtle example is provided by John Rawls' *A Theory of Justice.* Rawls provides an elaborate and avowedly normative depiction of what an ideal political system would be, but that depiction closely resembles modern Western liberal democracies. *See* Robert Paul Wolff, UNDERSTANDING RAWLS 138 (Princeton University Press 1977); Brian M. Barry, THE LIBERAL THEORY OF JUSTICE 140–141 (Clarendon 1973); Burns, *supra* note 6, at 192, 270–272; Allen E. Buchanan, *Assessing the Communitarian Critique of Liberalism,* 99 ETHICS 852, 854 (1989); Samuel Scheffler, *The Appeal of Political Liberalism,* 105 ETHICS 4, 20 (1994).

9. David Held, MODELS OF DEMOCRACY 8 (2d ed., Stanford University Press 1996); *see* Buchanan, *supra* note 4, at 290.

10. Bernstein, *supra* note 4, at 228.

11. William F. Harris II, THE INTERPRETABLE CONSTITUTION ix (Johns Hopkins University Press 1993) (emphasis in original).

12. Susanne Lohmann, *The Poverty of Green and Shapiro, in* THE RATIONAL CHOICE CONTROVERSY 127, 131 (Jeffrey Friedman ed., Yale University Press 1996).

13. Stanley Kelley, Jr., *The Promise and Limitations of Rational Choice Theory, in* Friedman ed., *supra* note 12, at 95, 99; Buchanan, *supra* note 4, at 290.

14. Ronald Coase, *How Should Economists Choose?, in* ESSAYS ON ECONOMICS AND ECONOMISTS 15, 16–17 (University of Chicago Press 1991).

My colleague Steven Lubet quotes Richard Feynman as saying that "'You can't look at everything. When you look at everything, you can't see the pattern.'" *Rumpled Truth on Trial,* 94 Northwestern University Law Review 627, 640 (2000).

15. John Ferejohn & Debra Satz, *Unification, Universalism, and Rational Choice Theory, in* Friedman ed., *supra* note 12, at 71, 72. Another commentator remarks on "the need to simplify, to reduce the world to livable dimensions, to choose out of the plenitude some terrain on which to build our settlement." Roger Shattuck, *Decline and Fall?,* N.Y. Rev. of Books, June 29, 2000, at 55.

16. *See* Farber & Frickey, *supra* note 3, at 15–16 & n.14.

17. Albert Einstein, *On the Generalized Theory of Gravitation,* 182 Scientific American 13 (No. 4) (April 1950).

18. A possible exception is the absence of controversy about the apportionment of the U.S. Senate, which I started thinking about more or less contemporaneously with developing the conversational approach. *See* Robert W. Bennett, *Democracy as Meaningful Conversation,* 14 Constitutional Commentary 481 (1997).

19. Public opinion polling consistently shows such a divide. *See, e.g.,* Times Mirror Center for the People and the Press, *Congressional Opinion Survey,* Nov. 3–5, 1994. Commentators have provided a variety of explanations, but those explanations are most convincing when they contrast the "personal qualities" of representatives with the policy outcomes of the legislative bodies. Bruce Cain, John Ferejohn & Morris Fiorina, The Personal Vote: Constituency Service and Electoral Independence 203 (Harvard University Press 1987); *see* Richard F. Fenno, Jr., *If, As Ralph Nader Says, "Congress is the Broken Branch," How Come We Love Our Congressmen So Much?, in* Congress in Change 277, 278 (Norman Ornstein ed., Praeger Publishers 1975); Glenn R. Parker & Roger H. Davidson, *Why Do Americans Love Their Congressman So Much More than Their Congress?,* 4 Legislative Studies Quarterly 53, 56–58 (1979). Most constituents know little about the "personal qualities" of their representatives, however, save as those are manifested in conversational interactions.

20. The puzzle is widely noted and discussed. *See* Charles Cameron, David Epstein & Sharyn O'Halloran, *Do Majority-Minority Districts Maximize Substantive Representation in Congress?,* 90 American Political Science Review 794 (1996); Melissa L. Saunders, *Reconsidering Shaw: The Miranda of Race-Conscious Districting,* 109 Yale Law Journal 1603, 1605 n.12 (2000). A conversational solution is at least suggested in Jane Mansbridge, *Should Blacks Represent Blacks and*

Women Represent Women? A Contingent "Yes," 61 JOURNAL OF POLITICS 628, 641 (1999).

21. U.S. Const., Art. II, § 1, cl. 5.

22. *See* Terry Smith, *Rediscovering the Sovereignty of the People: The Case of Senate Districts,* 75 NORTH CAROLINA LAW REVIEW 1, 3 (1996). Smith's article is a notable exception to the general silence.

23. *See* Thomas G. Walker, Lee Epstein & William J. Dixon, *On the Mysterious Demise of Consensual Norms in the United States Supreme Court,* 50 JOURNAL OF POLITICS 361, 379–384 (1988); John P. Kelsh, *The Opinion Delivery Practices of the United States Supreme Court 1790–1945,* 77 WASHINGTON UNIVERSITY LAW QUARTERLY 137, 138, 174–177 (1999).

24. And conceivably even greater conversational satisfaction for careful readers of a majority opinion. *See* L. A. Powe Jr., *Guns, Words, and Constitutional Interpretation,* 38 WILLIAM AND MARY LAW REVIEW 1311, 1331 (1997) (unanimous Supreme Court decisions associated with likelihood of less than careful consideration).

25. In explaining his attitude (of disapproval) toward dissents, John Marshall said:

> The course of every tribunal must necessarily be, that the opinion which is to be delivered as the opinion of the court, is previously submitted to the consideration of all the judges; and, if any part of the reasoning be disapproved, it must be so modified as to receive the approbation of all, before it can be delivered as the opinion of all.

Philadelphia Union, April 24, 1819, *quoted by* Donald G. Morgan, JUSTICE WILLIAM JOHNSON: THE FIRST DISSENTER 173 (University of South Carolina Press 1954).

26. United States v. Eichman, 496 U.S. 310, 319 (1990). For a particularly dramatic refusal to adhere to an earlier dissenting position, *see* People v. Lewis, 88 Ill. 2d 129, 165, 430 N.E. 2d 1346, 1363 (1981) (Goldenhersch, C. J., concurring).

27. *See* Robert W. Bennett, *A Dissent on Dissent,* 74 JUDICATURE 255 (1991). A 1996 Yale Law Journal Note I have subsequently discovered does provide a justification for the publication of dissonant opinions grounded in the normative case for "deliberative democracy." Kevin M. Stack, *The Practice of Dissent in the Supreme Court,* 105 YALE LAW JOURNAL 2235 (1996).

28. *See* Ann Althouse, *Electoral College Reform: Déjà Vu,* 95 NORTHWESTERN UNIVERSITY LAW REVIEW 993 (2001).

29. *See* Paul Cohan, *Sixty Years with One Chamber and No Parties,* Stateline Midwest, March 1997 (Midwestern Legislative Conference of The Council of State Governments).

30. *See* Robert A. Dahl, A Preface to Democratic Theory 96–97 (University of Chicago Press 1956).

31. Donald P. Green & Ian Shapiro, Pathologies of Rational Choice Theory 69, 194 (Yale University Press 1994).

32. Dennis Chong, *Rational Choice Theory's Mysterious Rivals, in* Friedman ed., *supra* note 12, at 37, 40; Ferejohn & Satz, *supra* note 15, at 72.

33. Donald P. Green & Ian Shapiro, *Pathologies Revisited: Reflections on Our Critics, in* Friedman ed., *supra* note 12, at 235, 266.

34. *See, e.g.,* Stephen Earl Bennett & David Resnick, *The Implications of Nonvoting for Democracy in the United States,* 34 American Journal of Political Science 771 (1990) (collecting support for the proposition that "[p]olitical participation has been a perennial concern for students of democracy"); Brian C. Mooney, *Voter Apathy Across the State: Dearth of Candidates Sapping Interest,* Boston Globe, Aug. 12, 2000, at B2; Dave Powers, *Why Fewer and Fewer People Vote,* Denver Post, March 9, 2000, at B11; John Nichols, *Apathy, Inc.,* 62 The Progressive 30 (Oct. 1998); Robert Kerstein, *Unlocking the Doors to Democracy: Election Process Reform,* 15 Florida State University Law Review 687, 689 (1987); Robert D. Putnam, Bowling Alone 404 (Simon & Schuster 2000).

35. Morris P. Fiorina, *Rational Choice, Empirical Contributions, and the Scientific Enterprise, in* Friedman ed., *supra* note 12, at 85, 90.

36. Ronald Coase's article quoted earlier, *see* note 14, *supra,* was addressed to Milton Friedman's famous claim that "[t]he ultimate goal of a positive science is the development of a 'theory' or 'hypothesis' that yields valid and meaningful . . . predictions about phenomena not yet observed." Coase, *supra,* at 16, *quoting* Milton Friedman, *The Methodology of Positive Economics, in* Essays in Positive Economics 7 (University of Chicago Press 1953). *See* Jeffrey Friedman, *Introduction: Economic Approaches to Politics, in* Friedman ed., *supra* note 12, at 1, 10.

37. Although experimentation with fruit flies and the like has yielded some confirmatory experimental data, "[m]ajor evolutionary change requires too much time for direct observation on the scale of recorded human history." Stephen Jay Gould, Hen's Teeth and Horse's Toes 257 (W.W. Norton & Co. 1983). A major evolutionary textbook summarizes the evidence for evolution in the following way:

> evolution can be observed directly on a small scale: . . . in nature and in experiments species will evolve into forms highly different from their starting point. It would be impossible, however, to observe in the same direct way the whole evolution of life from its common, single-celled ancestor a few billion years ago. . . . As we extend the argument from small-scale observations . . . to the history of all life we must shift from observation to inference.

Mark Ridley, Evolution 43 (Blackwell Scientific Publications 1993). Jonathan Weiner, The Beak of the Finch (Vintage Books 1995) recounts the very recent efforts at systematic verification of Darwinian theory.

38. About the overuse of antibiotics, for instance, *see* Weiner, *supra* note 37, at 257–261.

39. *See* Ferejohn & Satz, *supra* note 15, at 75; James Bernard Murphy, *Rational Choice Theory as Social Physics, in* Friedman ed., *supra* note 12, at 155, 167–168.

40. Green & Shapiro, *supra* note 33, at 259.

41. *See* Weiner, *supra* note 37.

42. For what strikes me as a strained attempt to account for that "anomaly," *see* David W. E. Smith, *Why Do We Live So Long?*, Center on Aging, vol. 15, No. 4, Winter 1999–2000 (Buehler Center on Aging of the McGaw Medical Center of Northwestern University). It might also be that a theory with a modest degree of explanatory power is valued because its (modest) degree of predictive potential is the best we have available. This seems an appropriate way to think about the frequently assumed relationship between global warming and the burning of fossil fuels. *Cf.* Putnam, *supra* note 34, at 23, 26.

43. The surprisingly mixed evidence on the effect of perceived closeness is summarized in Dennis C. Mueller, Public Choice II 357–361 (Cambridge University Press 1989).

44. Or perhaps worse. It might be thought that more educated people are more likely to know of the literature on the paradox of voting, or at least more likely to understand how "irrational" voting is. By that account, rational choice should teach that the more educated will be less likely to vote, just the opposite of what in fact happens.

Chapter 10. Conversational Explanation and Its Normative Use

1. *See* Akhil Reed Amar, *Choosing Representatives by Lottery Voting*, 93 Yale Law Journal 1283 (1984); Dennis Mueller, Constitutional Democracy 316 (Oxford University Press 1996); *cf.* Morris P. Fiorina, *Flagellating the Federal Bureaucracy*, 1983 Society 66, 72 (March–April); *see also* Hannah Fenichel Pitkin, The Concept of Representation 73–75 (University of California Press 1967) (citing several earlier proponents, including Harold Laski); Samuel Issacharoff, Pamela S. Karlan & Richard H. Pildes, The Law of Democracy 765 (The Foundation Press 1998) ("Many leading political theorists of republican government, in-

cluding Montesquieu, Harrington, Rousseau, and Aristotle, believed the lot was *the* democratic selection device, while elections were intrinsically aristocratic in nature") (emphasis in original).

2. *Cf.* Davis v. Bandemer, 478 U.S. 109, 132 (1986).

3. *See* U.S. Term Limits Inc. v. Thornton, 514 U.S. 779 (1995); Cook v. Gralike, 531 U.S. 510 (2001); Harold A. Hovey, *Congressional Quarterly's State Fact Finder: 1996 Rankings Across America D-8* (Congressional Quarterly 1996).

4. Certainly not always, however, as demonstrated by the performance of New York's term-limited mayor Rudolph Giuliani in the wake of the horror for the city of September 11, 2001. *See* E. J. Dionne, *Giuliani's Staying Power*, Washington Post, Sept. 28, 2001, at A39.

5. *See* U.S. Term Limits Inc. v. Thornton, 514 U.S. 779, 845, 922–923 (1995) (Thomas, J., dissenting). Jonathan S. Krasno, CHALLENGERS, COMPETITION AND REELECTION 164 (Yale University Press 1994), however, questions the common assumption that incumbents enjoy an overwhelming advantage.

6. *See, e.g.,* Williams v. Rhodes, 393 U.S. 23 (1968).

7. *See, e.g.,* Peter Schuck, *The Thickest Thicket: Partisan Gerrymandering and Judicial Regulation of Politics*, 87 COLUMBIA LAW REVIEW 1325, 1363 (1987); *but see* Robert A. Dahl, DEMOCRACY AND ITS CRITICS 159 (Yale University Press 1989) (suggesting that such arguments may be "of doubtful validity").

8. *See* Lawrence H. Tribe, *Taking Text and Structure Seriously: Reflections on Free-Form Method in Constitutional Interpretation*, 108 HARVARD LAW REVIEW 1223 (1995); Bruce Ackerman & David Golove, *Is NAFTA Constitutional?*, 108 HARVARD LAW REVIEW 801 (1995).

9. *See* Clinton v. New York, 524 U.S. 417 (1998).

10. *See* Margaret Graham Tebo, *Power Back to the People*, 86 AMERICAN BAR ASSOCIATION JOURNAL 52 (July 2000).

11. *See, e.g., Centinel [Samuel Bryan] I, in* I THE DEBATE ON THE CONSTITUTION 52, 60 (Bernard Bailyn ed., The Library of America 1993); *Letter from the "Federal Farmer" to "The Republican," in* I THE DEBATE, *supra*, at 245, 269; *"Brutus" III, in* I THE DEBATE, *supra*, at 317, 320, 321, 323; *Richard Henry Lee to Governor Edmund Randolph, in* I THE DEBATE, *supra*, at 465, 467; *Dissent of the Minority of the Pennsylvania Convention, in* I THE DEBATE, *supra*, at 526, 533.

12. Operating from a vote-centered perspective, Robert Dahl seems to acknowledge the point. He associates democracy with "one of the most fundamental of all freedoms, the freedom to participate in the making of the laws that will be binding on oneself and one's community."

Robert A. Dahl, *supra* note 7, at 78. But then, recognizing that the degree of "participation" understood in vote-centered terms must diminish as the size of the electorate increases, he suggests that "the greater scale [found in representative democracies] probably stimulates a concern for rights as alternatives to participation in collective decisions." *Id.* at 220.

13. The point about the scale of a representative democracy should perhaps be qualified by the recognition that smaller districts may yield more engaging conversations, if the smaller size brings homogeneity along racial or other salient dimensions that then allows "deeper" conversation. In that sense, the antifederalist point retains some force. Even in such districts, of course, conversational depth would likely come at the cost of breadth. Large districts, moreover, can be homogeneous, and small districts need not be. Without that homogeneity, any conversational advantage thought to attend smaller district size seems likely to be modest. The conversational perspective might, however, suggest that representative democracy is more "democratic" than direct democracy, even of the town meeting variety. If democratic involvement is achieved more through conversation than through voting, we may well have a greater measure of such involvement with the two-stage ongoing process of representative democracy than we ever might hope for with any but the most intimate examples of direct democracy.

14. Giovanni Sartori, COMPARATIVE CONSTITUTIONAL ENGINEERING: AN INQUIRY INTO STRUCTURES, INCENTIVES AND OUTCOMES 56 (New York University Press 1994).

15. Richard D. Anderson Jr., Valery V. Chervyakov, & Pavel B. Parshin, *Discourse and Democratic Participation: An Investigation in Russia,* http://www.polisci.ucla.edu/faculty/anderson/repart2.htm (last visited 7/8/00).

16. The four puzzles to which I gave extended treatment in chapter five through eight differ greatly in the extent to which they are peculiar to American democracy. In comparative terms, the malapportionment of the Senate is apparently extreme among popularly elected bodies, and hence the dearth of expressed concern about that malapportionment is distinctly American. At the other end of the spectrum, voting in public elections seems equally paradoxical in any large electorate. My impression is that the political invisibility of children characterizes all democracies, but I have given no attention to the extent that other democracies use total population for apportionment purposes, or insist on equally "populated" districts. Similarly, I have not done the work necessary to determine if judicial review is assailed as "countermajori-

tarian" or otherwise undemocratic in other democratic countries that have judicially enforced constitutional constraints on what legislatures can do.

17. The story of the discovery of Neptune is engagingly told in Ivars Peterson, NEWTON'S CLOCK, CHAOS IN THE SOLAR SYSTEM 99–119 (W.H. Freeman & Co. 1993).

Appendix. Originalism and the Enduring Need for Conversation

1. Robert H. Bork, THE TEMPTING OF AMERICA 141 (Free Press 1990).

2. *See* Raoul Berger, GOVERNMENT BY JUDICIARY (Harvard University Press 1977).

3. *Compare* Antonin Scalia, *Common Law Courts in a Civil-Law System: The Role of United States Federal Courts in Interpreting the Constitution and Laws, in* A MATTER OF INTERPRETATION: FEDERAL COURTS AND THE LAW 38 (Amy Gutmann ed., Princeton University Press 1997), *and* Bork, *supra* note 1, at 144 (meaning understood at the time of enactment), *with* Robert H. Bork, *Neutral Principles and Some First Amendment Problems*, 47 INDIANA LAW JOURNAL 1, 17 (1971); Richard S. Kay, *Adherence to the Original Intentions in Constitutional Adjudication: Three Objections and Responses*, 82 NORTHWESTERN UNIVERSITY LAW REVIEW 226, 230 (1988); Raoul Berger, *supra* note 2, at 363; Steven D. Smith, *Law without Mind*, 88 MICHIGAN LAW REVIEW 104, 105 (1989); Lino A Graglia, *"Interpreting" the Constitution: Posner on Bork*, 44 STANFORD LAW REVIEW 1019, 1024 (1992); *and* Edwin Meese, *The Battle for the Constitution: The Attorney General Replies to His Critics*, 19 UNIVERSITY OF CALIFORNIA AT DAVIS LAW REVIEW 22, 26 (1985) (understood by some group of authors or enactors).

4. There are questions the answers to which are clear in originalist terms. Most of them are also made clear by the constitutional language, however, and usually never get to court. There might also be questions not so clearly answered by constitutional language as to which the originalist resolution was nonetheless clear. Before the Seventeenth Amendment, for instance, the Constitution provided that U.S. senators were to be "chosen by . . . [each state's] legislature." U.S. Const., Art. I, § 3, cl. 1. By itself, that language does not seem to me to foreclose an argument that executive concurrence (or override of a veto) is required for the choice, just as it typically is for other action by the "legislature." *See* Smiley v. Holm, 285 U.S. 355 (1932). Despite this possibility, and controversy surrounding other aspects of the selection, the

"universal practice [was] . . . against recognizing any such executive participation." George H. Haynes, THE ELECTION OF SENATORS 20 (Henry Holt & Co. 1906). This does not seem to have been the result of explicit attention paid to the question in the debates surrounding the Constitution, but diligent research might reveal (or at least strongly suggest) that everyone in sight at the time simply assumed that no executive concurrence was required. *Cf.* Smiley v. Holm, *supra*. In such fashion, originalism once embraced might succeed in narrowing the field of litigable constitutional issues. For a variety of reasons, however, most historical inquiries into the meaning of a constitutional provision as applied to some contemporary phenomenon uncover plenty of material that needs to be discussed. The text now turns to the reasons that there is likely to be controversy, but for some contemporary examples of the disputes that can arise, *see* U.S. Term Limits v. Thornton, 514 U.S. 779, 789–793, 846–850 (1995); Lee. v. Weisman, 505 U.S. 577, 612–616, 632–636 (1992).

5. Jack Rakove, ORIGINAL MEANINGS 16 (Alfred A. Knopf 1996). Rakove estimates that "roughly two thousand actors served in the various conventions that framed and ratified the Constitution." *Id.* at 6. It is, of course, no answer to this point to say that the inquiry is an "objective" one into the understanding of a reasonable member of the addressees at the time. Recasting the question as what a "reasonable" person thought makes the inquiry normative or at least fictional—and hence not purely historical.

6. *See* Martin S. Flaherty, *Are We to Be a Nation? Federal Power vs. "States' Rights" in Foreign Affairs,* 70 UNIVERSITY OF COLORADO LAW REVIEW 1277, 1292 n.92 (1999) (characterizing such issues as part of a "greatly undertheorized area").

7. *See* Ronald Dworkin, *The Forum of Principle,* 56 NEW YORK UNIVERSITY LAW REVIEW 469, 488–491 (1981). An example that Dworkin uses and that has become commonplace in the literature are intentions that might have accompanied the Equal Protection Clause to secure equal treatment for fundamental interests regardless of race but not to interfere with racially segregated schools (because schooling was not seen at the time as fundamental).

8. Plato, *Cratylus* 402A, *reprinted in* THE COLLECTED DIALOGUES OF PLATO, INCLUDING THE LETTERS (Edith Hamilton & Huntington Cairns eds., Pantheon Books 1989). A formulation I much prefer, which I found in a lecture by S. Marc Cohen reproduced on the Internet, is: "Upon those who step into the same rivers, different and again different waters flow."

Index

abortion, 97, 103, 156n5, 201n48, 202n49
Ackerman, Bruce, 105, 120
  dualist theory of American constitutionalism, 101–2, 117–18
Adams, John, 15, 158n11, 187n26
agency costs, 23–24, 26, 77
agenda control, 11–12, 20, 21–22
aliens, 181–82n10, 183n14, 184n17
  apportionment base and, 68–69, 78
  votes for children of, 80
amicus curiae submissions, 89, 90, 195n9
apportionment, 181n7, 182n13, 186–87n24
  state legislatures, 16, 28, 46, 50, 67, 70, 75–76, 82
  U.S. House, 27–28, 49, 52, 67–70, 78, 164n30, 173–74n9, 187n24
  See also geographical districting; racial districting; U.S. Senate apportionment
apportionment base, 67–71, 77–79, 80, 81–82
Aristotle, 10
Arrow, Kenneth, 12

Baker v. Carr, 82
ballot access for candidates, 143
behavioral manifestations of conversationalism, 6, 138
Bentley, Arthur, 203n3
Bessette, Joseph M., 15–16
bicameralism, 27–28
  conversationalism and, 3, 36, 123, 130, 138, 145
  majoritarianism and, 27, 31
  political parties and, 58–59
  purposes, 3, 27, 28, 54–55
  See also U.S. Senate
Bickel, Alexander, 198n29, 199n34
  judicial review, 9, 86–87, 91, 96–98, 100, 104–5, 152–53n1, 192n3
  majoritarianism, 5, 9, 31, 44, 100–101, 199–200n38
  statutory interpretation, 95, 101
Black, Hugo L., 182n13
Blackmun, Harry A., 201n48
Black representation, 126–27, 138, 143, 171–72n28
Bork, Robert H., 97, 98, 104
Bowling Alone (Putnam), 7–8

Burke, Edmund, 71, 73
Burns v. Richardson, 69–70, 184n19
Burr, Aaron, 165n35

campaign financing, 143
Carson, Rachel, 168–69n6
child labor, 103–4
children's entitlement to political regard, 76–79
children's political status, 4, 76–79, 140
  age cutoff for voting, 77–78
  apportionment base and, 68–71, 77–79
  as citizens, 77–78
  conversationalism and, 81–84, 138, 139–40
  other ineligibles versus, 79–80
  parents' extra vote solution, 67, 71–72, 76–81, 83, 84, 180n6
  as uncontroversial, 4, 67, 81, 83–84, 140
  vote-centered model and, 66–67, 71, 84, 131
  voting eligibility, 66–67, 77–78, 83
  voting on account of, 70–71
Christiano, Thomas, 159n12
civic duty, 110–12, 113
Civil War, 131
Clark, Tom C., 82
Clinton, William J., 30, 156n5
Coase, Ronald, 122
commerce power, 57, 175n25
communications media
  decisionmaking influence, 25
  democratic conversation and, 35–37, 39, 63–65, 140
Condorcet, Marquis de (Marie-Jean Caritat), 12
Constitution, 67, 85, 91–92, 96
  conversationalism and, 92–94, 98, 125
  judicial review versus, 91–94, 98–99
  majoritarianism and, 92
  ratification of, 53–54
  veneration of, 92, 98
Constitutional Commentary, 1
conversation. *See* democratic conversation

conversational entrepreneurs, 37, 168–69n6
conversationalism, 2–4, 46–47, 135, 141–42
  abortion and, 103
  abstention from voting, 114
  behavioral manifestations of, 6, 138
  bicameralism and, 3, 36, 123, 130, 138, 145
  Black representation and, 126–27, 138
  children's political status and, 81–84, 138, 139–40
  Constitution and, 92–94, 98, 125
  as descriptive and explanatory, 6–8, 39, 42, 117, 124–25, 138
  district population size and, 144
  districting and, 3, 36, 43, 62–63, 123, 138–40, 143, 145, 169n7, 212n13
  elections and, 3, 26, 31, 34–35, 37, 40–41, 53, 143
  electoral college and, 130
  evaluation of, 3–6, 42–48, 123–38, 140–41, 168n3
  executive branch and, 3, 36, 93–94, 123, 126–27, 130, 143
  federalism and, 3, 36, 123, 138, 145
  First Amendment protections and, 3, 36, 40, 44, 123, 145
  institutional manifestations of, 6, 138
  judicial opinions and, 90, 127–30, 195n8
  in judicial process, 88–90
  judicial review and, 87–91, 93, 98–99, 102–4, 125, 140–41
  majoritarianism versus, 42, 44, 116, 131–32, 141, 145–46
  normative lessons, 6, 141–44
  originalist interpretation and, 147–49
  pluralism versus, 44–45, 116
  political competition and, 34–39, 43, 45, 123, 137, 140, 145
  political party discipline and, 3, 36, 44, 123
  president as natural-born citizen and, 93–94, 126–27, 130

rational choice theory versus, 47,
132–38, 141
social capital versus, 7–8
statutory interpretation and, 95–96
substantive outcomes and, 6
term limits and, 142–43
U.S. House and, 62–64
U.S. Senate and, 58, 60, 61–65, 93,
123, 138, 140–41, 168n4
vote-centered model versus, 41, 42,
44, 131–32, 144
voting franchise and, 3, 36, 44, 47,
123
voting paradox and, 112–13, 114,
135, 137–38, 141
counterconversational difficulty, 91,
98, 99
countermajoritarian difficulty, 5, 9, 13,
28, 31, 86–87, 91, 95–97, 102
academic disciplines and, 104–5
cyclical voting, 12, 22

Dahl, Robert A., 32, 131
democracy, 211–12n12
judicial review, 101–2, 104–5, 158–
59n12, 200n39
Democracy and Its Critics (Dahl), 32,
200n39
democratic conversation, 2–4, 34–42,
145
broad but shallow versus narrow but
deep, 45, 64, 126–27
as cohesive, 35, 43–45
communications media and, 35–37,
39, 63–65, 140
content of, 39
elections and, 34–35, 37, 40–41
government structure and, 36, 44
nondemocratic versus, 2, 145
passive participation, 2–3, 8, 39, 144
popular identification and involvement and, 35–36, 40–45, 62–64,
82–83, 91, 113, 124
popular satisfaction and, 44–45, 62,
65, 125–26
primary versus secondary, 35
responsiveness versus, 46–47
stability of government and, 35–36,
40, 124, 131

descriptive or explanatory accounts,
117, 118–23, 133
conversationalism, 6–8, 39, 42, 117,
124–25, 138
dualist theory of American constitutionalism, 117–18
evaluation of, 3–4
majoritarianism, 42
necessary incompleteness, 17, 46
predictive versus, 135–37
prescriptive accounts, influence on,
16, 118, 119–20
prescriptive lessons, 122–23
rational choice theory, 107, 133–35,
138
See also positive accounts
Dewey, John, 41
direct democracy, 10, 13
vote-centered model versus, 14–15,
18–33, 144
dissonant judicial opinions, 89, 90,
127–30, 194–95n8, 208n25
districting. *See* geographical districting; racial districting
dualist theory of American constitutionalism, 101–2, 117–18
Dworkin, Ronald, 148, 214n7

Eighteenth Amendment, 94
Einstein, Albert, 123, 136
elected judges, 193–94n6
elections, 5–6
at-large, 61–63, 176n36
conversationalism and, 3, 26, 31,
34–35, 37, 40–41, 53, 143
majoritarianism and, 22, 28–30
presidential, 3, 26, 29–31, 36, 53, 61,
75, 123, 130, 156n8
U.S. House, 49, 55, 62, 74
U.S. Senate, 28, 30, 40, 49, 52, 58–
61, 74, 75
vote-centered model, 22
See also children's political status;
voting paradox
electoral college, 29–30, 157n8,
165n35, 176n35
conversationalism and, 130
selection of, 29–30, 62, 188n34
winner-take-all rule, 30

electoral status of children. *See* children's political status
Ely, John Hart, 97, 100, 118, 120–21
equal state voting power in U.S. Senate. *See* U.S. Senate apportionment
Eskridge, William N., Jr., 1, 4, 9, 197n25
evolutionary theory, 40, 122, 136–37, 171n25
executive branch
complexity of, 28–29
conversationalism and, 3, 36, 93–94, 123, 126–27, 130, 143
judicial review, leverage over, 102–4
president, as natural-born citizen, 93–94, 126–27, 130
veto, 29
executive branch, election of, 3, 26, 29–31, 40, 53, 61, 75, 130, 156n8
conversationalism and, 3, 36, 123, 130
majoritarianism and, 28–30
See also electoral college
explanatory accounts, 121–23, 133
predictive versus, 135–37
See also descriptive and explanatory accounts

Farber, Daniel A., 1
federal courts and constitutional review. *See* judicial review; U.S. federal courts
federalism, 30–31, 55
contemporary jurisprudence, 93
conversationalism and, 3, 36, 123, 138, 145
majoritarianism and, 31
Federalist Papers, 20, 25, 54–57, 197n23
federalists, 15, 18, 158n11
felons, 181n10
apportionment base and, 69, 183n14
virtual representation of, 79–80
voting franchise and, 68, 180n6, 183n14
First Amendment protections, 3, 131
conversationalism and, 3, 36, 40, 44, 123, 145

Fourteenth Amendment, 67, 186–87n24
"free rider" possibilities 107, 109–10
Friedman, Barry, 151–52n3, 200n38
Friedman, Milton, 209n36

geographical districting, 181n7
apportionment and, 67–71, 77–79
at-large elections versus, 61–63
census and, 78, 80, 82
choosing by lot versus, 139–40
conversationalism and, 3, 36, 43, 62–63, 123, 138–40, 143, 145, 169n7, 212n13
majority voting and, 13, 163n25, 184n18
state legislatures, 16, 28, 46, 50, 67, 70
U.S. House, 27–28, 52, 70, 176n36
U.S. Senate, 61, 161n15
voters' ties and, 75–76
governmental structure, democratic conversation and, 36, 44. *See also* bicameralism; federalism; judicial review; separation of powers; U.S. Senate apportionment
Great Compromise, 54, 182n13
Green, Donald P., 108, 112, 132–33, 134, 136–37
Gunther, Gerald, 198n29

Hamilton, Alexander, 54, 55, 155n2
Hand, Learned, 40–41
Hegel, Georg Wilhelm Friedrich, 106
Heraclitus, 149

incumbent protection
state legislature apportionment, 82–83
term limits and, 142
U.S. House versus U.S. Senate, 83
information flow, 7–8
in conversationalism, 2–3
virtual representation and, 73
in vote-centered model, 14, 23–24
institutional manifestations of conversationalism, 6, 138

intensity-weighted model of political
equality, 11–12, 20–21, 24–25,
161n9
interest groups, 2, 31, 162n20
amicus curiae briefs, 195n9
factions, 55, 162n23, 175n26, 203n3
majoritarianism and, 24–25
pluralism and, 32–33
rational choice theory and, 24, 107–
8, 138
issue definition, 11–12, 21–22

Jay, John, 54
Jefferson, Thomas, 72, 155n2, 157–
58n11, 165n35
judges, elected, 193–94n6
judicial independence, 26
judicial process, 88–90
judicial review, 85–86, 140–41, 153n1
academic disciplines and, 104–5
amicus curiae submissions, 89, 90,
195n9
Constitution versus, 91–94, 98–99
as controversial, 86–87, 140, 202n49
conversationalism and, 87–91, 93,
98, 102–4, 125, 140–41
dissonant opinions, 89, 90, 127–30
dualist theory of American constitutionalism, 101–2, 117–18
elite attitude, 6
interpretational approaches, 96–100,
104–5, 147–49
in larger democratic context, 101–4,
105
legislative and executive leverages
over, 102–4
majoritarianism and, 5, 9, 13–14,
86–87, 96–102, 147–49, 152–
53n1, 192n3
opinion publication, 90–91, 128
as policymaking, 86, 87–88, 93
recourses for disaffected, 92, 94,
102–4
statutory interpretation versus, 94–
96, 101

The Least Dangerous Branch (Bickel),
9, 86, 96, 101
Lee, Frances E., 57, 63, 64

Legal Tender Cases, 201n45
legislative districts. *See* geographical
districting; racial districting
liberal versus republican decisionmaking, 19–20, 21, 23–24, 159–60n3
children's political status and, 76–
81
civic republican literature, 8, 41, 76
interests of others, 77
legislator selection and, 74–75
political equality, 160n6
term length and, 73–74
virtual representation and, 72, 74
voting franchise and, 74–75
Lijphardt, Arend, 200n39
Lincoln, Abraham, 30
Lincoln-Douglas debates, 60, 61
line-item veto, 143
lobbying. *See* interest groups

Madison, James, 54
bicameralism, 27–28, 164n31
factions, 175nn26–27, 203n3
representative versus direct democracy, 20–21, 25–26, 54–55, 75,
161n8, 162–63n23
U.S. Senate, 51, 56
majoritarian ideal in judicial review,
97–98, 100, 118, 120–21
majoritarianism, 4–5, 9–17, 131
agenda control, 11–12, 21–22
bicameralism and, 27, 31
children and, 4, 66–81
concern with outcomes, 42
Constitution and, 92
conversationalism versus, 42, 44,
116, 131–32, 141, 145–46
evaluation of, 5, 18–33
First Amendment protections, 131
interest groups and, 24–25
judicial review and, 5, 9, 13–14, 86–
87, 96–102, 147–49, 152–53n1,
192n3
parents' extra vote possibility and,
67, 76–81
pluralism, 31–33, 116
plurality versus, 12, 13
quorum requirement, 156n4
statutory interpretation and, 95, 101

majoritarianism (*continued*)
  unanimity versus, 12
  U.S. Senate and, 9, 13, 26–28, 31, 50
  U.S. Senate apportionment and, 5, 27, 58, 61
  vote trading, 11–12, 20–21, 24
  voting franchise and, 10, 18
  voting paradox and, 5, 110, 113
  See also vote-centered model
Marbury v. Madison, 85, 89, 98–99, 199n34
Marshall, John, 89, 98–99, 194n8, 199n34, 208n25
mass media
  decisionmaking influence, 25
  democratic conversation and, 35–37, 39, 63–65, 140
McCulloch v. Maryland, 98, 199n34
mentally incompetent citizens, 68, 77, 80, 181n10
minority representatives, 126–27, 138, 143, 184–85n19
Montesquieu, Baron de (Charles-Louis de Secondat), 55

Nader, Ralph, 168n6
noncitizens. *See* aliens
nondemocratic conversation, 2, 145
normative accounts, 117, 118–21
  civic republican literature as, 8, 41
  conversationalism and, 6–8, 39, 42, 141–44
  majoritarian ideal in judicial review and, 118, 120–21
  positive accounts and, 6, 16–17, 33, 42, 116–23, 141–44, 146
  social capital and, 7–8
  vote-centered theory and, 15–17, 146

Olson, Mancur, 107, 134
"one person, one vote" requirement, 16, 27–28, 46, 50, 67–70, 75–76, 190n51
  incumbents and, 82–83
Oppenheimer, Bruce I., 57, 63, 64
optimist pluralism, 32–33, 44–45, 116
originalist interpretation in judicial review, 97, 98, 100, 147–49

paradox of voting. *See* voting paradox
parents' extra vote solution, 67, 71–72, 79, 81, 180n6
  citizen children of alien parents, 80
  conversationalism and, 83–84
  steps in normative case, 76–81
Planned Parenthood v. Casey, 202n49
pluralism
  conversationalism versus, 44–45, 116
  majoritarianism and, 31–33, 116
  optimistic, 32–33, 44–45
plurality versus majoritarianism, 12, 13
policymaking. *See* judicial review
political competition
  conversationalism and, 34–39, 43, 45, 123, 137, 140, 145
  marginal voters, 37, 45
  U.S. House elections, 64
  U.S. Senate elections, 64
  vote-centered model and, 22
political equality, 4, 10–12, 15–17, 19, 21, 39–41, 157n10, 160n6
political party discipline, 52, 53
  conversationalism and, 3, 44, 123
popular identification and involvement with government, 35–36, 40–45, 62–64, 82–83, 91, 113, 124
popular satisfaction with government, 17, 32, 38
  conversationalism and, 44–45, 62, 65, 125–26
  vote-centered model, 125
popular versus elitist attitudes, 6
positive accounts, 117, 118–23, 133
  conversationalism, 6–8, 39, 42, 124–25
  dualist theory of American constitutionalism, 117–18
  incompleteness, 17
  majoritarianism, 42
  normative accounts and, 6, 16–17, 33, 42, 116–23, 141–44, 146
  predictive versus, 135–37
  rational choice theory, 107, 133–35
Post, Robert C., 41
predictive versus explanatory accounts, 135–37

prescriptive accounts. *See* normative accounts
president
  election of, 3, 26, 29–31, 36, 53, 61, 75, 123, 130, 156n8
  as natural-born citizen, 93–94, 126–27, 130
  See also executive branch
presumption of correctness, 95, 102
principle in judicial decisions, 88, 96, 98, 100, 198n29
public duty. *See* civic duty
public ignorance, 162n20
Putnam, Robert D., 7–8, 171n25

racial districting, 126–27, 138, 143, 184–85n19
Rakove, Jack N., 15, 148
rational choice theory, 5, 107–9
  behavioral phenomena, 138
  conversationalism versus, 47, 132–38, 141
  as descriptive and explanatory, 107, 133–35, 138
  entrepreneurs, 108, 134
  evaluation of, 108–9, 111–12, 132–38
  interest groups, 24, 107–8, 138
  vote-centered theory versus, 133–34
  voting paradox, 5, 107, 109–12, 113, 134–35, 138
Rawls, John, 158n12, 206n8
reconciliation. *See* popular satisfaction with government
representation reinforcement theory. *See* majoritarian ideal in judicial review
representative democracy. *See* vote-centered model
republican versus liberal decisionmaking. *See* liberal versus republican decisionmaking
Reynolds v. Sims, 50–51, 75–76, 82, 164n30, 169n7
  apportionment base and, 67–68, 182n13, 184n19
Roe v. Wade, 103, 195–96n11, 202n49

Sartori, Giovanni, 144
Scalia, Antonin, 195n9

Schattschneider, E. E., 33
scientific theories
  discovery of Neptune, 145–46
  evolution, 40, 122, 136–37
separation of powers, 55
September 11, 2001, 36
Seventeenth Amendment, 28, 30, 49, 52, 61
Shapiro, Ian, 108, 112, 132–33, 134, 136–37
Sherry, Suzanna, 1, 4, 9
Sizing Up the Senate (Lee and Oppenheimer), 57
social capital versus conversationalism, 7–8, 171n25
Social Choice and Individual Values (Arrow), 12
Souter, David H., 175n25
stability of government, 17, 32–33, 35–36, 40, 43, 124, 131
stare decisis, 95, 102
state legislature apportionment
  apportionment base, 67–69
  districting, 16, 28, 46, 50, 67, 70
  incumbent protection and, 82
  voters' ties and, 75–76
state power, 30–31
statutory interpretation, 94–96, 101, 125
Stevens, John Paul, 129
Stone, Harlan Fiske, 128, 194n8
surrogate voting. *See* parents' extra vote solution; virtual representation

term limits, 73–74, 93, 142–43
Thayer, James Bradley, 152–53n1, 192n3
theory building
  parsimony versus pretentiousness, 132–35, 137–38
  positive versus normative, 117–21
  prediction in, 109, 135–37
  rational choice controversy, 108–9, 132–38
  scientific, 40, 122, 136–37, 145–46, 171n25
A Theory of Justice (Rawls), 206n8
Thoreau, Henry David, 43–44

Tushnet, Mark, 192n3
Twenty-Sixth Amendment, 84, 178n1

unanimity versus majoritarianism, 12
unicameralism. *See* bicameralism
U.S. democracy
  conversationalism and, 36, 44
  heterogeneity, 35
  interest groups, 31
  judicial review, leverage over, 102–4
  liberal and republican ideals, 71–
    76
  majoritarianism and, 12–17, 25–31,
    192n3
  oppression, curbs on, 25–26, 27, 54–
    55
  popular identification and involve-
    ment with, 35–36, 40–45, 62–64,
    82–83, 91, 113, 124
  popular satisfaction with, 17, 32, 38,
    44–45, 62, 65, 125–26
  representation and growth, 73–76
  scale, 12–13, 35, 143–44
  separation of powers, 26, 31, 55
  stability, 17, 32–33, 35–36, 40, 43,
    124, 131
  state power, 30–31
  vote-centered model, 14–17
U.S. federal courts
  dispute resolution, 87–88
  majoritarianism and, 5, 9, 14, 28
  political levers, 102–4
  selection of judges, 75, 103
  See also judicial review; U.S.
    Supreme Court
U.S. House of Representatives
  constituent attitudes, 62, 125–26
  conversationalism and, 62–64
  election of, 49, 55, 62, 74
  functions, 29, 30
  judicial review, leverage over, 102–4
  majoritarianism and, 13, 26–28
  powers, 49–50, 172n2
  presidential elections and, 29
  relative prestige, 56–57, 64, 65
  as representing the people, 51
  as representing states, 52, 53
  revenue measures, 49
  term of office, 28

U.S. Senate versus, 56–57, 63–65,
    177n42, 188n32, 191n56
U.S. House of Representatives appor-
    tionment
  among states, 27–28, 52, 173–74n9,
    187n24
  apportionment base, 68–70
  by population, 27–28, 49, 67, 78,
    164n30
U.S. Senate
  constituent attitudes, 62, 125–26
  conversationalism and, 58, 60, 61–
    65, 93, 123, 138, 140–41, 168n4
  election of, 28, 30, 40, 49, 52, 58–61,
    74, 75
  functions, 27, 55–58, 103, 164n31
  judicial review, leverage over, 102–4
  majoritarianism and, 9, 13, 26–28,
    31, 50
  political parties and, 59
  powers, 49–50, 172n2, 174n13
  relative prestige, 56–57, 64, 65
  as representing the people, 52
  as representing states, 51–53, 54,
    57
  revenue measures, 49
  selection by state legislatures, 58–
    61, 74, 75
  term of office, staggered, 28, 56,
    161n15
  U.S. House versus, 56–57, 63–65,
    177n42, 188n32, 191n56
U.S. Senate apportionment, 1, 4, 31,
    50–65, 140, 173n4
  conversationalism and, 58, 60, 61–
    65, 93, 138
  district lines and, 63
  explanations for, 31, 51–58
  majoritarianism and, 5, 27, 58, 61
  state population and, 65
  as uncontroversial, 1, 4, 51, 58, 61,
    65, 140
  See also Seventeenth Amendment
U.S. Supreme Court
  abortion and, 97, 103, 201n48,
    202n49
  amicus curiae submissions, 89, 90,
    195n9
  apportionment base and, 69–70

child labor and, 103–4
Constitution and, 85
dissonant opinions, 89, 127
judicial review, 93, 103
majoritarianism and, 5, 9, 13–14
opinion publication, 90–91, 128
selection of, 201n.45
state legislative apportionment and,
  16, 28, 46, 50, 67–70, 75–76, 82–
  83
term limits and, 142
U.S. House and, 52

Virginia plan, 51
virtual representation, 73, 74, 79–80
vote-centered model
  abstention from voting, 110
  agenda control, 21–22
  Black representatives and, 126–27
  children's political status, 66–67,
    71, 84, 131
  close elections, 22
  conversationalism versus, 41, 42, 44,
    131–32, 144
  direct democracy versus, 14–15, 18–
    33, 144
  district population and, 144
  evaluation of, 130–32
  information flow in, 14, 23–24
  interest groups and, 24–25
  judicial review and, 100
  liberal versus republican decision-
    making, 19–20, 21, 23–24
  pluralism, 31–33
  popular satisfaction and, 125
  as prescriptive, 34, 146
  public policy outcomes and, 131

rational choice theory versus, 133–34
re-presentation in, 14–17
as straw man, 106
vote trading, 20–21, 24–25
voting age and, 66–67
voting paradox and, 5, 110, 113
See also majoritarianism
vote trading, 11–12, 20–21, 24–25,
  161n9
voting franchise, 3, 18, 40, 72–75
  apportionment base and, 68–71, 77,
    78, 80, 81–82
  conversationalism and, 3, 36, 44, 47,
    123
  excluded categories, 66–67, 68–69,
    72, 77–78, 84
  liberal versus republican decision-
    making, 72–76
  majoritarianism and, 10, 18
  modern democracy and, 34
  purposes, 3
  voting age, 66–67, 84
  See also children's political status
voting paradox, 5, 106–7, 109–15, 133,
  141
  civic duty, 110–12, 113
  conversationalism, 112–11, 135,
    137–38, 141
  majoritarianism and, 5, 110, 113
  rational choice theory and, 5, 107,
    109–12, 113, 134–35, 138
voting requirement, 111, 155n4

War of Independence, 54
Wesberry v. Sanders, 67–68, 163n29,
  169n7, 177n42, 182n13
Wood, Gordon S., 74, 75